Live to the Truth

The Life and Times of Cyrus Peirce:

Crusader for American Public Education

Founder of the First Public Teacher Training School in the Nation

Barbara Ann White

Also by Barbara Ann White

*A Line in the Sand: The Battle to Integrate Nantucket Public
Schools, 1825-1847*

Book Design by Mark F. White

Jacket Design by Jay Avila

Stained glass window photo by Peter John Roberts

ISBN: 978-0-9905874-0-8

DEDICATION

For Mark, Nicholas, Jessica, David, Willy, Cole, Otis, Henry and Sage

To the millions of hard working educators who deserve our support and gratitude

Yours truly,
C. Peirce

CYRUS PEIRCE

Nantucket Historical Association

The art of teaching must be made the great, the paramount, the only concern.

Cyrus Peirce

Education should be a teaching of the truth; for the want of this nothing can compensate, neither strength of argument, nor beauty of composition, nor elegance of language, nor ingenuity of theory, nor any other thing....Yes, all that is really worth anything is the truth.

Cyrus Peirce

Table of Contents

Acknowledgments

This book has been a long time in the making and, like most endeavors, I have a lot of people to thank who have assisted me along the way.

First and foremost, I have to thank my husband, Mark White, who read the book countless times. Mark took charge of the photos and all the technical issues involved with self publishing. He drove miles to help hunt down pieces of this story, including patiently digging in the National Archives in Washington, D.C. seeking an unfiled, unregistered petition. Miraculously, it was Mark who found a segment with Peirce's name on it.

Two patient and skillful readers shepherded the book in its many permutations over several years. Both improved the book immeasurably. Judith Powers, retired librarian and historian, contributed her vast knowledge of education and history. Frank Morral, retired English professor from Carleton College, combed through the manuscript carefully, suggesting language to made the writing clearer. They are, however, absolved of errors that may remain.

Archivists and librarians throughout New England have been of great assistance. The Nantucket Historical Association's Research Library is unparalleled. The team of Elizabeth Oldham, Marie Henke and Betsy Tyler provided photos, suggestions and moral support. Nantucket Historical Association Research Fellow, and good friend, Frances Kartunnen, was ready with encouragement; she sets a high standard of research to which I aspire. Lincoln Thurber at the Atheneum library on Nantucket tracked down books from far and wide. Marianne Stanton at *Nantucket Today Magazine* gave my work on Peirce a welcome forum.

Colleen Previte at Framingham State University's research library dug out journals from normal school students, some which I read on site, and some that she sent digitally; she also sent digital copies of photos. Colby College sent me a copy of Cyrus Peirce's 1824 sermon, only two of which are in existence, saving us a road trip.

Gayle Smalley at the Unitarian Church in Newton opened her home and the church to us. She sent a digital copy of church records proving Peirce's and Mann's pivotal roles in its founding. She let us photograph the stained glass window dedicated to both men and she gave us lunch! The history museum in West Newton was also helpful in providing resources about Peirce's time there and the historical society in Waltham sent us a digital map.

Scott Sanders, archivist at Antioch College, generously sent photocopies of some of the school's archives on Horace Mann which gave me the first glimpse of the attack by Matthew Hale Smith.

The Congregational Church Archives in Boston pulled out original copies of *The Christian Register* for us to photograph.

Christine Small, an alumna of the Washington Academy in East Machias, Maine, sat us at her kitchen table, pulling out personal records to help us to figure out what Cyrus Peirce was doing so far from home after his retirement from the normal schools.

Willy Hutcheson, our son-in-law, came to our rescue when we were struggling with technical issues over formatting.

Jay Avila graciously designed the cover

Introduction

Cyrus Peirce has been largely forgotten in the history of American public schools. Yet, together with Horace Mann, Peirce battled for the advancement of public education, and singlehandedly created the first normal school for teacher training in the nation in 1839. He advocated for better schools and better teachers. Peirce worked to elevate the status of public schoolteachers and fought for equal pay for women teachers. He fought to establish requirements for becoming a teacher and he fought for student rights. He worked to reform the public school curriculum, and to increase the time students spent in the classroom. He worked tirelessly to humanize teaching. He fought against corporal punishment in the classrooms, liberally used in American classrooms of his era. Furthermore, Peirce was the first to require that prospective teachers spend time as student teachers under the observation of a supervisor. Together with Mann, Peirce created the first state college system in the United States, which evolved as the University of Massachusetts. Peirce paid a high personal toll for his commitment to public education. Powerful forces attempted to ruin his reputation, but Peirce persevered, sacrificing his health in the process. Within decades of the opening of the doors of the Lexington Normal School, dozens of normal schools had been established modeled on the curriculum he created. Inexplicably, Cyrus Peirce and the vital role he played in the development of American education have been overlooked.

Chapter 1: Roots for a Moral Compass

Cyrus Peirce, born in 1790, believed that the fragile experiment that was the American system of government was at risk because of the perilous state of public education. Only one generation removed from that of the Founding Fathers, Peirce worried that the democracy they had created would not succeed if the nation failed to create excellent public schools. He dedicated his life to that cause.

Peirce's passion to professionalize teaching eventually led to his vilification as a radical who threatened the moral fabric of American society. His opponents regarded him as an incarnation of the Devil, and portrayed him as licentious and depraved. Their attacks on his reputation led the state legislature to investigate the quiet and upright Peirce, an unlikely candidate for attacks on morality. Understanding how he became headline news in the 1840s reveals deep schisms in the early days of the American republic as it struggled to create and sustain itself.

During the period following the American Revolution, education was haphazard, inadequate and dull; there was little support for the notion of public education. Education is not mentioned in the body of the U.S. Constitution, nor is the right to education included in the Bill of Rights. Individual states and local communities were left to devise educational standards for their children, and the result was fragmented at best. Male members of the upper class benefited from a system of private schools and tutors, who were also male. A rudimentary education was deemed sufficient for the bulk of the American people, especially women. It was considered enough for most people to be able to read at a basic level and understand simple mathematics. Tradesmen and craftsmen had on-the-job training to teach them the specific skills required in their work. Most Americans were illiterate or barely literate.

It is not surprising that the battle in support of public education started in Massachusetts. From early in its history, Massachusetts was noted for educational leadership. In 1636, the Great and General Court of the Massachusetts Bay Colony voted to establish the first university in North America when it created Harvard. Eleven years later, in 1647, Massachusetts became the first colony to establish universal public schools. Communities with more than fifty families were required to hire a schoolteacher to teach reading, writing and religion. However, enforcement was lax and many communities did not fully comply with the law. In 1789, shortly after the Revolutionary War, Massachusetts passed a law that required all towns to provide free public elementary and grammar schools. Again, enforcement was weak, and exactly what public education was supposed to entail, was not specified. However, the law was on the books waiting for a time when there would be leaders prepared to enforce it; Cyrus Peirce became one of them.

There was little in Peirce's childhood to indicate he would grow up to be one of the most important educational leaders in the

Peirce family farm Waltham, MA

Framingham State University Archive

United States, a person who would transform public schools and turn teaching into a profession. Peirce had a typical upbringing for boys born into middle-class farming families in New England.

He was brought up, as were the vast majority of the residents of Massachusetts, in the Congregational Church.

From the founding of the colony inherent tensions arose between an authoritarian theocracy, and the notion of democracy and exercise of freedom of expression. Massachusetts had been a theocracy since the colony's founding by English Puritans. During the colonial era, the government was firmly controlled by the church that became known as Congregational. The Puritan view of moral behavior was strictly enforced by civil law.

Massachusetts was still a theocracy after the American

Revolution. In fact, it remained a theocracy until 1834 when Peirce was in his forties, despite the adoption of the Bill of Rights with the First Amendment's guarantee of freedom of religion and expression. The conflict between those who favored retaining theocracy, and those who favored nonsectarianism, threatened the movement to establish public schools.

The Puritans were patriarchal. Children were regarded as the property of their parents with many of the same rules applied to them as to other kinds of property. Since women were seen as potential instruments of the Devil because of the temptation they posed to men, colonial constables enforced strict rules for women's dress, hair, and behavior.

Multiple rules governed the observance of the Sabbath in the Massachusetts Bay Colony. Those who did not attend church services were fined, jailed, or punished in other ways, such as being put in public stocks. People who were absent from church services could be dragged into church by the local authorities, and people who fell asleep during a church service were punishable by public whipping. Some towns closed their gates to prevent anyone leaving town on the Sabbath.[1]

Public monies supported the church and paid for the education of ministers, giving them lucrative salaries. Ministers were among the most influential and respected people of every community. Every household had a Bible and those too poor to afford one, could obtain one free from the state.

By the time of independence, the power of the clergy had

diminished and, while Massachusetts was still officially a

Peirce family home top left

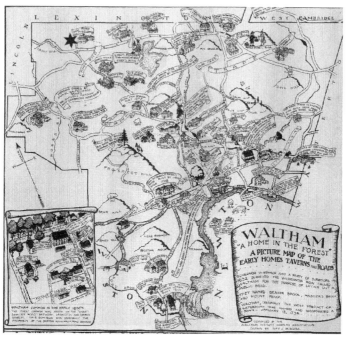

Waltham Historical Society

theocracy, it was considerably weakened. Nevertheless, remnants of the Puritan traditions, habits, and moral codes were still very much in evidence during Peirce's lifetime and would come into conflict with his educational reforms.

The Peirce family traced its heritage to the early days of the colony. They were proud of their service to the new country and young Cyrus was raised on stories of their heroism. Several Peirces had fought in the Revolutionary War, including his grandfather, Lieutenant Isaac Peirce. His great uncle, Abraham Peirce, was a hometown hero, having been the captain of a company in the Battle of Lexington. Both brothers, Isaac and Abraham, fought at the Battle of Bunker Hill.[2]

When Peirce was born in Waltham, Massachusetts in 1790, the ink was barely dry on the Constitution, ratified only a year before. The Bill of Rights was not added until he was a year old. The future of the United States was uncertain.

Like their neighbors, the Peirces were members of the local Congregational Church and several served the church in various capacities. One ancestor, Benjamin Peirce, was a deacon in the church as far back as 1703. Both Peirce's grandfather and father were deacons in the First Church of Waltham, his grandfather serving in that capacity for over twenty years.[3]

Cyrus Peirce, however, eventually split with the church and became a leading member of the radical wing of Congregationalism, which eventually evolved into Unitarianism. Understanding Unitarian philosophy is key to understanding Peirce's eventual approach to children and to education, as well as his political stances on the issues of his day, such as the abolition of slavery, woman's suffrage, temperance, and the peace movement.

Peirce was youngest of twelve children on a farm in Waltham, a community of scattered farms with no distinct center about eleven miles west of Boston. When Peirce was born, the village had 882 inhabitants. Almost everyone in the village - millers, blacksmiths, weavers, even the minister - owned a farm, even if they had another profession. With four older brothers and six older sisters at home, young Cyrus was not needed to work on the farm.

It was eventually evident to his parents that their youngest child was more interested in academic pursuits than in working with his brothers in the fields, although he did his fair share of farm chores. According to his first biographer and close friend, Samuel J. May, Peirce "enjoyed the good influences of a well-ordered family, and of a steady, judicious parental discipline."[4]

At the age of six Peirce was sent to the local public school where he "went through the dull routine then usually pursued with little children." Even at that tender age, Peirce complained about the inadequacy of the school to his parents, reporting that his teacher was not teaching him all that she could. "He intimated that, at some future time, if he should himself keep school, he would show how it ought to be done."[5]

The public school Peirce attended was typical for the time. Most schools were closed for nine months a year, meeting for just a few weeks in winter and summer terms. The length of the school year was not uniform from community to community. Nothing existed that resembled a professional teaching corps and there were no qualifications for prospective teachers. A job applicant merely had to convince the local authorities that he or she could read, write, and maintain order. Nathaniel Allen, who taught under Cyrus Peirce years later, recalled that he obtained his first teaching job mostly due to his ability to make a quill pen! Teachers were required to prepare their students' pens, and Allen reported that he cheated to get the job, passing off a pen that had been carved by someone else.[6]

The schools themselves were uninviting and uncomfortable. Most were one-room affairs with hard benches attached to the floor in neat rows. Teachers sat on raised platforms, symbolically conveying their authority over the children. Student desks were not built for comfort, but designed to be uncomfortable in the way church pews were constructed, the intent being to keep students upright and alert.

Classroom walls were kept bare to minimize distraction and daydreaming. Most school buildings had poor ventilation and few windows; they were stiflingly hot in summer and hand-numbingly cold in winter. Students had the task of keeping the stove fires going in the winter terms. Coping with such discomfort was considered fundamental to building character.

One-room schools accommodated children of all ages, from as young as four up to age sixteen or seventeen. The teachers had no control over the number or ages of the students they would instruct. One teacher reported that he had a twenty-three-year-old in his classroom who had spent time in prison. Teachers were responsible for creating lessons suitable for their diverse students with little or no resources. Few textbooks were available even if a community wanted to purchase them. The Bible was the text of choice and rote memorization the most common method of instruction.[7]

Providing room and board as partial remuneration meant that teachers had little choice of accommodations. The practice was more common in small towns and villages than in cities, and much of such housing was no larger or better equipped than an unheated shed. One teacher wrote that he had only a six-foot-square room with a window that would not close. Women teachers, who were usually hired locally, usually did not require room and board, but if they did, they were usually boarded in a private home.[8]

Maintaining discipline was problematic due to the mix of ages, scanty resources and dull, meaningless lessons. Beatings, also considered character building, were administered freely to miscreants. Male teachers were deemed preferable to female teachers for disciplinary reasons, particularly in the instruction of older children because of a man's perceived strength and ability to physically take on classroom bullies.

In summer terms, young women from the community, most ill prepared for the job, were hired as teachers because men could find more lucrative work during the summers, usually on farms. Some women teachers were as young as sixteen, their training limited to their own attendance at a school. Too often bullied by their students and unable to establish control over them, many quit before summer was over. If no replacement was found, students were dismissed for the remainder of the term.

Some women, however, were successful teachers and some communities were fortunate to have capable women who provided educational stability. Once a woman married, however, she was forced to give up her position, depriving students of a pool of experienced teachers.

Disparity was common in the pay of men and women teachers.

Even after six years as the Secretary of Education, Horace Mann reported inequity, even after he lobbied against it, calling the salary disparity "indefensible on any principle of justice or policy." In 1842, he reported that male teachers earned more than double that of their female counterparts. Men were paid an average of $32.22 per month, compared to only $12.78 for women.[9]

Young men sometimes taught the winter terms while they were on vacation from their colleges, especially in Massachusetts, and in general were from less prosperous families and needed the money for their tuition. The vast majority of them did not take up teaching after graduation and never looked on it as a serious profession, viewing it simply as a temporary source of income. In 1837, a report to the state legislature pointed out that many of these young men were "exceedingly incompetent in many respects, teaching from necessity and often with a strong dislike for the pursuit." As a result, the report concluded, winter terms were often a waste of time. "Time, capacities, and opportunities of thousands of the children are now sacrificed."[10]

Teachers were poorly paid, and a man would have been hard pressed to support a family on a public schoolteacher's salary, even though he was paid more than women teachers. Although there were undoubtedly some good male schoolteachers at the time, the job became associated with men of low character who had difficulty holding jobs due to drunkenness or incompetence. Some of these became itinerants who wandered from town to town accepting teaching positions for a year or two and moving on.

It was a dismal situation that did little to properly educate the young people of a young country. During Peirce's teaching career, he would address all of the issues plaguing the public schools and attempt to rectify them.

With public education so inadequate, many parents opted to send their children to the many private schools established in most communities, particularly if they had an eye to sending their sons to a university. This was the case with Peirce, whose parents were convinced that their youngest son should be prepared to go to Harvard College. They were prosperous enough to remove him from the inadequate local public school and send him to board at a private school. At some indeterminate time, they sent him to live at Framingham Academy, thirteen miles away. Unfortunately, no records survive from the time period he was there.

Another option for parents to educate their children was to engage a private tutor, many of whom were ministers supplementing their income. Peirce attended Framingham Academy until he was fifteen, when his parents arranged for him to study with Dr. Charles Stearns, a Congregational minister in the nearby town of Lincoln. A Harvard graduate of the class of 1773, he was distantly related to Peirce through his maternal grandmother. Stearns had operated his own private school in Lincoln, called the Liberal School, for ten years, beginning in 1793. After it closed, he offered private tutoring, and it was then that Peirce studied with him for a term just prior to taking the entrance examination for Harvard.

Stearns was an orthodox Congregational minister, but he influenced Peirce in another way. Stearns was renowned for writing short plays for schoolchildren, creating what is now recognized as "the first substantial body of plays for young people written by an American." His plays are short with moral plots drawn from life in agrarian New England communities. He believed that theater "could show moral dilemmas in action." Although Peirce did not attend the Liberal School, Stearns' belief in drama as a teaching strategy made an impression on Peirce, who later used theater in his own classrooms - a practice that caused controversy among those who considered the theater scandalous and especially unsuitable for young ladies.[11]

Stearns prepared Peirce for Harvard's rigorous examination, which began at 6 a.m. on a day in July 1806. College president Samuel Webber, along with several professors, administered the daylong examination. The process was designed to probe a student's knowledge in ten different subjects, including Greek, Latin, grammar, and mathematics. Some tests required written answers, but most of the examination was oral. The time allotted for each subject was limited to an hour, so that students could finish by nightfall. Peirce passed the examination and entered Harvard that year with approximately sixty other students.

As he set off to study at Harvard, there was little in Peirce's early years to suggest he would do battle with the Congregational establishment of his youth, but there were some hints. For one, Peirce grew up in the formative years of the American Revolution, only five miles from Lexington and eleven miles from Bunker Hill. Virtually every adult in his life had played a role in the Revolutionary War and was committed to the ideals of democracy. The men revered in his own family were those who had sacrificed personal safety for the principles of the Revolution.

Yeoman farmers like Peirce's father, Isaac, were familiar with the ideas of the Enlightenment, with the writings of John Locke, Thomas Jefferson, Benjamin Franklin, and Thomas Paine. They read and debated the Declaration of Independence with its list of grievances against the British government and its assertion that people had certain "inalienable rights." They were familiar with Paine's pamphlet, *The American Crisis,* which was read to the troops of the Continental Army encouraging them to continue their fight against tyranny. His parents' generation had lived for several years under the ineffective Articles of Confederation, and they followed the debates that led to the writing of the Constitution and the arguments for and against its ratification.

These were men unafraid to stand up for their beliefs, and they were dedicated citizens. The Peirce family had a long history of public service, many members of his extended family having served as selectmen and other town officials throughout New England. Given his heritage, it is not surprising that Peirce made the sacrifices he did during his lifetime for the causes he believed in, dedicating himself to the good of the nation, as he saw it.

People like the Peirces paid attention to the political shifts, debates, and controversies of the new nation. One of those shifts concerned a growing rift in the Congregational church. The year before Peirce enrolled at Harvard, Samuel Ripley was ordained at the Peirce's home church. Ripley was said to be "the first Unitarian minister" in the United States. That Isaac Peirce remained a deacon under Minister Ripley suggests that Peirce's father supported the new liberal thinking of the Unitarians.[12]

In addition, the influential and controversial Unitarian writer, Joseph Stevens Buckminster, settled in Waltham in 1808 as a tutor. There is no evidence that Buckminster tutored Peirce, but their paths surely crossed in the village of less than nine hundred inhabitants, particularly as the Peirces were influential members of the church Buckminster attended. Buckminster belonged to the group of the most radical religious thinkers of the time, those who regarded the New Testament as inspired by man and not the word of God. Furthermore, Buckminster was not interested in the Old Testament at all. This rejection of the entire Bible as God's word put him among the most extreme theologians of the early nineteenth century.

In sending their son to Harvard, Peirce's parents knew he would be attending the most liberal institution in the United States. Shortly before their son left to study in Cambridge, the leadership of the college had become firmly lodged in the hands of the liberal wing of the Congregationalists.

Thus, the young Cyrus Peirce set off to study at Harvard, having been exposed to the ideals of the American Revolution, to the liberal ideas of the Enlightenment, and to the new philosophy that would become American Unitarianism. Peirce was an idealistic young man who wanted to follow in his family's tradition of service to his country.

Chapter 2 Harvard

Cyrus Peirce was only sixteen when he matriculated at Harvard in 1806, the most prestigious institution of higher learning in the United States. Harvard had undergone a radical transformation just before Peirce's arrival. The college had broken away from orthodox Congregationalism and aligned itself with the liberal wing of the church later known as Unitarianism. Peirce's exposure to the latest liberal theology had a lasting impression that shaped his philosophical outlook about the nature of people and the nature of God.

Whatever their vocational interest, students at Harvard studied a similar and traditional course of study intended to prepare them to be well educated gentlemen suited for the law, medicine or the ministry. While the leadership of the college had changed, the curriculum remained essentially the same. Students were expected to study astronomy, grammar, moral philosophy, ethics, mathematics, rhetoric, Latin, and Greek. Hebrew was offered to those who were interested. It was in the tutorial sessions that the burning theological debates took place with an increasing number of teachers and tutors from the ranks of the liberals.

Peirce's transformation into a radical Unitarian went almost hand-in-hand with the development of the Unitarian church itself. He had been introduced to some liberal thought in his childhood, but as an undergraduate at Harvard, he was exposed to the most liberal Unitarian philosophers of his era. It would take Peirce more than a dozen years to completely abandon Congregationalism and embrace Unitarianism. Similarly, the Unitarian transition from a wing of the established Congregational church into a separate institution was not formalized until 1825.

Harvard had trained Congregational ministers for generations. When proponents of the Unitarian wing came to dominate the school's leadership, it shook the venerable institution to its core. Harvard was still recovering from its epic struggle during Peirce's undergraduate years, and every student on the campus was affected by its aftermath.

Harvard had been the foremost institution of the Congregational Church in the theocracy of Massachusetts. Designed to educate ministers, the college had been supported by the state since the days of the Puritans. From the beginning, however, there were internal and external challenges to church doctrine within Massachusetts, not surprising in a colony founded upon the ideal of religious freedom, or at least freedom for the Puritan dissenters who had fled English persecution.

During the Great Awakening of the 1740's, two groups of dissenters sought to reform Christianity in the American colony. Both groups questioned who had the authority to interpret Scripture, and both took the interpretation of the Bible out of the hands of ministers and into the hands of individuals. The evangelical dissenters preached an immediate, personal, and emotional spiritualism. They threatened the established church with their belief in the possibility of individuals being able to sustain a personal and direct relationship to God. This view eliminated the need for intervention by ministers, a clear threat to the authority and the livelihood of ministers. The second group, the rationalists, took an opposite approach, equally troubling to the Congregational establishment. The rationalists applied reason to Christianity, undermining the blind faith then preached from the pulpit. Similarly, this view threatened the role of ministers. The Congregational leadership struggled to quell both of these challenges to their core beliefs.

Jonathan Mayhew, minister at the West Church in Boston during the mid-1700s, belonged to the rational school of thought. Mayhew was an outspoken critic of the concept of the Trinity. He did not believe that God could rationally consist of a father, a son, and a holy spirit. He preached the idea of a single, monolithic, or unitarian god, and was shunned by the orthodox clergy who refused to exchange pulpits with him. Some consider Mayhew's West Church to be the first Unitarian church in America, although the label "Unitarian" had not yet come into use.

Challenges to mainstream religions multiplied in the post-Revolutionary War era as public discourse became more open. Ordinary people wrestled with philosophical questions concerning liberty, equality and self-governance as the nation struggled to write its constitution. These questions permeated every aspect of the life of the new country, including questioning the role of religion in the new society.

By the time the Constitution was written, New England had absorbed Methodists, Quakers, and other mostly Protestant faiths to its religious mixture. These new religions presented more challenges to the theocracy of Massachusetts. Besides the differences between the new religious groups and Congregationalism, schisms emerged within the various religions, further complicating matters.

The established church in Massachusetts continued to be the Congregational church, but a gulf between liberal and conservative factions within the church widened by the turn of the nineteenth century. Besides questioning the notion of God and the Trinity, liberals called Arminians, challenged the concept of original sin and the idea that all people are born with its stain on their souls. In their doubting of eternal damnation, they were skeptical that God would condemn people to everlasting Hell based on their earthly conduct. As to whether God was benevolent or punitive, they believed Him benevolent. Just as the American Constitution heralded individual freedoms and rights, liberals emphasized an individualism that saw "every man [as] free to accept or to reject religious truth." An even more radical group questioned the divinity of Jesus Christ, speculating that Jesus was a mortal man, not a deity. This belief especially was considered a serious heresy, as it doubted the literal truth of the New Testament upon which Christianity was based.[1]

The liberalization of New England's churches was gradual, "almost insensible" at first. Individual preachers were free to choose not to follow doctrines with which they had difficulty. "They simply ceased to emphasize those doctrines" from their pulpits.[2]

But by 1800, these rifts could not be ignored and began to divide Congregational communities. Of the two hundred Congregational churches east of Worcester County in Massachusetts, 125 "were liberal in their theology." And, eight of the nine churches in Boston were "considered unsound on the Trinity." Harvard, which had trained generations of Congregational ministers, was thought to be an increasing "hot bed of heresy" by the Congregational establishment.[3]

The conservatives fought off ever-mounting challenges, but had few tools to use against their liberal brethren because of the structure of their organization. The Congregational church has no central authority or governing board. Thus, there was no way to issue decrees mandating which beliefs were acceptable and which were heretical. Their bottom-up organization invited freethinking, if their dogma did not.

For example, individual congregations appointed their own ministers. Ministers, in turn, were free to choose which doctrines to emphasize, and which to ignore, in their sermons and homilies. Such free license meant that congregations were easily divided, depending upon whom they had hired as their ministers. It became increasingly common for congregations to dismiss their ministers based on whether they preached in a liberal or conservative vein. As even the most controversial of ministers had a core of supporters, firing them divided many congregations in the early 1800s when ministers were hired and fired with regularity. The remnants of these splits are reflected in towns across New England with their many First and Second Congregational churches. The large majority of Second Congregational churches represent the liberals who left the more orthodox congregations.

As the religious division of the Congregationalists became more entrenched, both sides resorted to the press to push their agendas and to malign the opposition. Liberals and conservatives published their own newspapers and journals, and it became apparent that the views of each faction within the Congregational church were increasingly irreconcilable.

It did not take long before Harvard became a battleground. Shortly before Peirce enrolled, Reverend Jedediah Morse of Cambridge, a conservative, sought to eliminate liberals from Harvard's administration. When David Tappan, a moderate who held the Hollis Professorship of Divinity at Harvard, died in 1803, choosing his successor was so contentious that it took over a year to resolve. The divisions between both camps were insuperable and compromise looked impossible. Debate over who would head Harvard's Divinity department brought the stark differences between the camps into the headlines.

The crisis escalated when Harvard's president, Joseph Willard, died the next year, in 1804. Willard's death created another important vacancy and the factions jockeyed to put one of their own in both positions. Deals were made and broken behind closed doors as the process dragged on for months. For a short time it appeared that a liberal candidate would assume one post and a conservative the other, but the sides were too polarized to consider giving either to an opponent seen as heretical.

Eventually Professor Henry Ware, a liberal minister from Hingham, was put forth by the Harvard nominating committee to assume the Hollis Professorship as head of the Divinity department. The oldest endowed chair in the United States, the Hollis professorship was considered too important for the conservatives to lose. At an explosive meeting of the sixty-four members of Harvard's Board of Overseers, the conservatives tried desperately to prevent Ware's appointment with Morse leading their effort. After lengthy and acrimonious debate, Ware was appointed by a margin of ten votes, prompting Morse's resignation from the Board in protest. He subsequently published a pamphlet setting forth his specific objections to both Ware and the method by which he was elected titled, *The True Reasons on Which the Election of a Hollis Professor of Divinity in Harvard College was Opposed at the Board of Overseers.*

The following year, conservatives were again defeated when Samuel Webber, another liberal, was appointed president of Harvard. With this second appointment, the conservatives considered Harvard hopelessly lost to the heretics and they abandoned it. They founded the Andover Theological Seminary in 1808 to educate ministers in traditional Congregational doctrine. As far as they were concerned, Harvard had succumbed to heresy.

Morse continued his crusade against the liberals, who by this time were sometimes labeled as Unitarians. Morse made it his mission to find, identify, and expose Unitarian-leaning ministers in Congregational churches across New England, no easy task, as most ministers did not fit neatly into one camp or the other.

From colonial times onward, it was customary for Congregational churches to routinely exchange ministers for short periods of time, often just for one Sunday. It was a way for ministers to take holidays and to visit other communities. But as the religious climate became increasingly polarized, some Congregational churches, in an attempt to prevent Unitarian thought from spreading, began to deny their pulpits to those suspected of Unitarian thinking. Refusing to share pulpits with fellow ministers was almost unheard of in New England before this time, but the practice grew in the early years of the nineteenth century due to the growing list of those not acceptable to orthodoxy.

Despite the efforts of the Congregationalists, Unitarianism gained ground steadily in New England during the early nineteenth century, even though most people remained officially within the Congregational fold. In addition, because the Unitarians represented a disproportionate number of intellectuals, writers and politicians, their influence grew. The leaders of the reform movements that proliferated after the American Revolution were disproportionately of a Unitarian leaning.

When Peirce arrived on the Cambridge campus in August 1806, Harvard, under the leadership of President Webber, was firmly in the hands of Unitarian faculty. Given this environment,

Peirce had maximum exposure to the emerging Unitarian system of belief.

Peirce was a good student, though not considered a brilliant one. One classmate remembered him as "faithful," and "persevering," words used to describe Peirce throughout his life. The same classmate recalled that Peirce was known to investigate topics "thoroughly," unwilling to give up until he was satisfied that he had complete understanding. Peirce rarely left his room, making it clear he was at the college to study. He and his parents had sacrificed in order to send him to the school and he was determined not to disappoint them or waste their hard-earned money.[4]

Professors lived in their own houses around Cambridge, but lower level tutors lived in Harvard Yard and ate with the students. Tutors were usually recent graduates; they had little authority over the students and were frequently the butt of student jokes and pranks. Students often regarded the tutors as their enemies, and tutoring at Harvard was not an appealing job. John Quincy Adams, a freshman at Harvard in 1786, wrote that tutors were "much too young" and often ill prepared. Of one tutor he wrote, "he is hated; he is reputed to be very ill natured and severe in his punishments." According to Samuel Eliot Morison, students who regarded a tutor as a friend were looked down upon and derided as "fishermen." Tutors were low in status and made little money. In addition, they were forbidden to marry. Not surprisingly, the average tutor remained for only three years.[5]

The school year was divided into two terms, one beginning in

August and the other in February. There was a winter vacation of five weeks and a summer vacation of six weeks. Each school day began at 6 a.m. with morning prayers, usually led by the president, and followed by breakfast. Lectures and lessons lasted until a noon lunch break and recommenced at 2 p.m. Students were required to study after dinner under the eyes of the tutors. Students were promoted to the next year on the basis of reports by the tutors and professors.

Twice a year, selected juniors and seniors were chosen to give public exhibitions that included debates and dialogues. Professors judged the exhibitions and prizes were awarded. As early as 1758, students put on theatrical performances.

Harvard students formed several societies, some quite secret. The most prestigious and aristocratic club when Peirce was a student was the Porcellian Club. Hefty dues precluded membership to the less affluent in the student body, such as Peirce. The famous Hasty Pudding Club was also in existence during Peirce's years at the school. His name does not appear in the lists of any of Harvard's clubs or societies, probably due to his economic circumstances, as well as to his focus on his studies.

Harvard students had a reputation for being the best and the brightest of their generation, but they also had a well-documented history of wild behavior involving alcohol and pulling pranks. In fact, during Peirce's second year, twenty-six of his fellow students were expelled for inappropriate behavior. Expulsion was the most serious punishment in the college's hands, reserved for the most flagrant misbehavior. Expelled students were brought before the entire student body where their crimes were pronounced aloud. The names of expelled students were literally cut out of the official wooden board of student names. When the twenty-six students were expelled in 1807, President Webber wrote to the president of Brown University warning him that some of "these inconsiderate young men" hoped to be admitted to Brown. Webber wrote, hoping that his colleague would act with "good understanding and harmony" and refuse to admit them.[6]

Lesser punishments than expulsion were also meted out. "Rustication" was reserved for serious infractions, considered not quite bad enough to warrant expulsion. Rustication meant that a student was temporarily expelled, usually to spend a term or more at a quiet country parsonage under the attentive eye of a minister.

For less serious infractions, students were fined. Once a student had missed one lesson, he was fined for subsequent absences. After missing two public lectures in a term, more fines were levied. In addition, students were required to attend the prayers that started and ended the school day, prayers usually conducted by President Webber. Students who were absent were fined, although seniors were allowed to miss prayers twice a week without being penalized. Freshmen were only excused three times in two weeks.

Regardless of Peirce's determination to be a serious student, there were unavoidable customs and unwritten rules that affected his daily life. The student hierarchy was based on year level with freshmen at the bottom. Within days of arrival on campus, freshmen were escorted into a chamber over the library, read the "College Customs," and warned of penalties in store for those who disobeyed them. One rule, for example, forbade the wearing of hats within Harvard Yard. If a freshman encountered an upperclassman outside the Yard, he was required to doff his hat. Freshmen were not allowed to throw balls in the Yard. More annoyingly, they had to run errands for upperclassmen. Juniors could take freshmen away from sophomores, and seniors could take them away from juniors. Typical errands involved menial tasks such as taking clothes to be washed and pressed and taking notes from one upperclassman to another. They were also ordered to local taverns to fetch food and drink.

There were also many official rules that applied to all students. A strict dress code was enforced, for example. All students had to wear blue-grey coats and academic gowns to classes during Peirce's time at the school. Special black gowns were required for particular occasions, such as commencement. No one was permitted to wear silk because it would magnify class distinctions within the student body.

While many of Harvard's students were from wealthy families, the school admitted students like Peirce from the middle class. Harvard provided financial aid to qualified young men who did not have the means to attend the school otherwise. Tuition fees were expensive for the time, about $20 per year at a time when the average income in the United States was only $100 per year.

Peirce is not listed as being a scholarship student indicating that his family could afford his tuition and other fees, but it stretched their resources.

Students had to pay for their meals, which were provided by stewards. The year before Peirce enrolled, Harvard students participated in what was called the "Bread and Butter Rebellion." They staged a walk-out to protest the poor quality of their food. The college suspended half of the students involved. It was such a large number that the Board of Overseers appointed a committee to investigate the rebellion. The committee recommended re-admitting the suspended students, but the Board chose to disregard the report and chose to uphold the suspensions.

Buildings at Harvard were built to the highest standards, containing every comfort of the time, under the assumption that students would "live like gentlemen." The college charged rent, with freshmen and sophomores paying $1.00 less than upperclassmen who paid $5.50 per term. Once students were sophomores, they could rent separate study spaces for a nominal fee called "study rent." Other fees included $.50 to $1.00 per term for library use. Wealthier students paid to board their horses nearby and horse races amongst those students, while frowned upon, were commonplace.[7]

The less affluent students often taught school between terms, especially during the winter break. In 1807, Peirce accepted a teaching position in nearby Newton during his winter term. With a population of less than two thousand, Newton was connected to

Boston by stagecoach. Peirce moved to the village, as the distance was too far to commute from the family farm in Waltham. He taught in Newton for parts of two years to subsidize his education. No records exist to confirm whether he taught in a private academy or in a public school.

During his senior year, Peirce was singled out to study with Henry Ware. Ware was the Hollis Professor whose selection had caused the rift in the school with the conservative Congregationalists in 1804. In 1810, Professor Ware invited a group of students to begin a course of divinity studies with him. Only fourteen students were selected by Ware, so it was a great honor for Peirce to have been included to study with one of the world's leading Unitarian thinkers. One of Peirce's fellow students in the course, Joseph Allen, became a lifelong friend.[8] (Note)

Seniors took examinations in all their subjects in June. Any professor could drop in to ask them questions, and degrees were granted on the basis of the recommendation of the faculty. In July, seniors held a Class Day to celebrate their years at the school. On Class Day, the faculty and public were guests of the class. Valedictory speeches were given and a class poem was delivered.

Commencement was a formal affair on the last Wednesday in August. Every senior had to give an oral disputation in Latin, usually practiced for months in advance. After the ceremony, graduates were invited to the president's house for refreshments.[9]

Peirce's class of 1810 was one of the college's largest to date with sixty-three graduates. Peirce's former tutor, Charles Stearns, was granted an honorary doctorate degree at the same ceremony. Unfortunately, the fifty-one-year-old President Webber died suddenly, a month prior to graduation. Henry Ware delivered Webber's eulogy, noting how saddened the students were at the death of their beloved mentor, calling Webber a kindly surrogate father. Ware observed that the student body had been struck by other tragedies during their time at Harvard, including the death of Webber's eldest son, a young man one year behind Peirce at the school. In addition, two others members of the school died just before commencement, one from a fever and one from drowning. These deaths cast a pall over the commencement exercises of the Class of 1810.[10]

Peirce's years at Harvard had exposed him to the best classical education to be had in the United States, as well as to the most modern thinking of the day. Under the educational leadership of the Unitarians at Harvard, he was led to think deeply about the nature of God, man, nature and society. He joined the most elite group in his country, the well-educated graduates of Harvard, men who were expected to lead the United States in the future. Peirce would eventually fulfill that expectation by becoming a visionary teacher who changed the face of American public schools.

At the time of his graduation, however, he had just turned twenty and he was ready to take a break from academic studies. He wanted to have a paying job as well as an adventure before embarking on his eventual profession, which he thought would be in the ministry.

Peirce had enjoyed the winter terms he had spent teaching in Newton, and when he was offered a teaching position at a private boys' school on Nantucket Island, it seemed a good choice. The job would allow him to save for possible further study in the ministry, give him time to ponder life's choices and have an adventure at the same time. It may be that Seth Swift, whose years at Harvard overlapped those of Peirce, recruited him. Swift had graduated and gone to teach at a private school on Nantucket. The next year, at age twenty-one, Swift was ordained as the first minister of the Second Congregational Church on the island.

So, Cyrus Peirce sailed to the island of Nantucket, thirty miles off the coast of Cape Cod for his first real job.

Note: Allen later married Henry Ware's daughter, Lucy.

Chapter 3: The Reverend Cyrus Peirce

Cyrus Peirce did not intend to teach for the rest of his life when he took the job on Nantucket. It was a time for him to take a break from academia and earn some money to return to Harvard to study for the ministry. Thus, after just two years of teaching on the island, Peirce returned to Harvard in 1812 and enrolled in the Divinity department.

Peirce had continued to develop his liberal religious views while living on the island, joining the Second Congregational Church in 1810, the year after it was founded. The church with its liberal leaning congregation had split amicably from the more conservative First, or North, Congregational Church. So friendly was the split, the minister of the First Congregational Church gave the dedicatory prayer at the dedication of the Second Congregational Church. The Second Congregational, or South Church, officially became a Unitarian church in the late 1830s. Reverend Seth Swift had been Peirce's contemporary at Harvard, and both men were in their early twenties. When Peirce left the island to return to Harvard two years later, the church council recommended him to the Church of Christ in Cambridge, a liberal leaning church was closely allied with Harvard.[1]

John Thornton Kirkland was Harvard's president when Peirce returned to Cambridge. Kirkland's tenure from 1810 until 1828 is considered "one of the great eras" of Harvard. Even though Peirce had only been gone for two years, the school's environment had changed for the better. Building projects were underway and Harvard Yard cleaned up, its many latrines removed and the brewery that had existed there for years dismantled. New pathways were laid out and trees planted.[2]

When Peirce returned to pursue the ministry, Harvard did not yet have a separate Divinity school. Divinity was still a department within the college. However, the department had grown under Henry Ware and it is not surprising that Peirce was among the first to enroll in the new graduate course in divinity, having been part of a select group of Ware's as an undergraduate.[3]

While the department claimed to be nonsectarian, it was totally under the control of Unitarians, although the Unitarians had not officially split from the Congregational establishment and not everyone assumed the label Unitarian. There was, however, no doubt which people belonged to each camp and no non-Unitarian faculty members were employed at Harvard Divinity School until 1870.

Arguments over what to accept or reject of mainstream Congregational doctrine had accelerated, and the beliefs of the Unitarians and the Congregationalists had become irreconcilable. Divinity students under the guidance of Ware wrestled with theology and examined the core principles of Congregationalism and Christianity. The Bible was front and center of their debate, subjected to scrutiny and interpretation. Ware's courses included *Evidences, Doctrines and Ethics of Religion* and *Biblical History and Criticism.* In the process of debate and examination, the students helped build the beliefs of Unitarianism.[4]

Peirce struggled to articulate and organize his beliefs. He threw himself into his studies, "often sleeping only four hours a night." A perfectionist, Peirce "studied until he was satisfied that he had arrived at the truth." He sought what he considered rational reasons to substantiate his beliefs, and if he could not find a reason for something, he rejected it, even if it was "the faith of his childhood." [5]

After three years of intense study and introspection, Peirce left the divinity department. He and his fellow students never officially graduated because separate degrees in divinity were not recorded until two years after they left the school. (Note)

Harriet Coffin Peirce

Nantucket Historical Association

Once again, Peirce needed a job. Whether by choice or not being offered a job in the ministry, he returned to Nantucket. His former school, unable to find a satisfactory replacement for him, lobbied the twenty-five-year-old to return. The school had grown and now included girls. Peirce accepted the offer probably because he had fallen in love with Harriet Coffin, a "most distinguished" young woman whom he had met when boarding with her family during his first island stay. They married during his second year back on the

island. Shortly before their marriage, she was baptized in the
Second Congregational Church and became a life-long Unitarian.
She was twenty-two and he was twenty-six.[6]

Peirce taught on the island from 1815 to 1818. He enjoyed the
inclusion of girls in the classroom and was impressed by their
abilities to learn alongside boys. His intelligent young wife
undoubtedly influenced his belief and he would forever after be an
advocate of equal education for women.

The North Church

Reading historical Society

Despite his growing ties to the island, Cyrus and Harriet Peirce packed their bags at the end of 1818 and moved off island when he was offered the opportunity to become a minister, still his
profession of choice. The North Church in North Reading,
Massachusetts, invited Peirce to "settle with us and assist Eliab
Stone, an elderly minister who had been at the church since the
colonial era. The committee offered Peirce an excellent salary-
$640 per year, plus $300 for moving expenses. The Peirces were
also given half an acre of parish land upon which to build a house.
It seemed likely they would settle down in the town for the rest of
their lives and that Peirce's dream was about to be realized.[7]

Several months later, the church council voted money earmarked for Peirce's ordination ceremony on May 19, 1819. Peirce's Nantucket church was asked to assist in the ceremony and sent three members, including Reverend Swift. Church records in North Reading note that Harriet Peirce was admitted to their congregation the year her husband was ordained.

It is unclear why Peirce accepted this particular job. The Second or North Parish Church in Reading was not in the liberal faction of the Congregational church. Yet, Peirce served there for nine years, first as an assistant, and later as the sole minister. His initial answers on church doctrine must have satisfied the church council, despite his membership in the liberal Second Congregational Church on Nantucket and his years at Harvard under the well-known liberal Henry Ware. Perhaps some members of the church council were looking for a younger, more liberal minister to replace the elderly Stone when he died, as there were those in the congregation who wanted a more liberal minister. Undoubtedly, the opportunity to move closer to his hometown of Waltham played a part in Peirce's decision. In addition, he knew he was intended to become the sole minister after Stone's death, a prestigious appointment. He must have been optimistic he would fit into the community as easily as he assimilated on Nantucket.

Eliab Stone had been minister of the North Reading church since 1760. Something of a town hero, he had fought with the Minutemen at the Battles of Lexington and Bunker Hill, and then served two years in the Continental Army. Three years after

Peirce's arrival, Stone died at the age of eighty-six. After six decades with the same minister, the congregation understandably found it hard to accept their new young minister, only in his early thirties, even if he had assisted the much-loved Stone for several years. It did not take long before dissension within the congregation developed in response to Peirce's liberal theological views.

With Stone gone, preaching was now Peirce's responsibility. His sermons increasingly expressed liberal views, leading to tension between the more liberal parishioners and those who favored established Congregational doctrine. The *Proceedings of the 250th Anniversary* of the town notes that Peirce "was a man who frankly admitted before his ordination not knowing where in the scale of being to place the Lord Jesus," an indication of his uncertainty of the Trinitarian view of Jesus, which suggests skepticism about the divinity of Christ, a heretical notion to the orthodox.[8]

By the early 1820s, it is estimated that about one-third of the Congregational churches in Massachusetts had become Unitarian. While Peirce was serving as the minister in Reading, the break was formalized when a constitution for the American Unitarian Association was adopted on May 26, 1825 by a group of Unitarian churches. The two other Congregational churches in Reading were firmly in the hands of conservatives and, despite a minority who supported a more liberal approach, the majority of Peirce's parishioners wanted their church to remain Congregational and did not want a liberal pastor.

But Peirce was a liberal pastor, and unhampered by the oversight of Reverend Stone, Peirce declared himself a Unitarian from the pulpit. While only one of his sermons has survived, it has enough evidence to pinpoint Peirce's unequivocal allegiance to the most radical of Unitarian thinking.

Given on Christmas Day 1824, the sermon was published at "the request of the hearers," the liberal minority within his congregation. To the conservative majority, however, the sermon was a radical manifesto. Peirce freely quoted the radical religious philosopher Joseph Buckminster who had challenged the religious establishment during his short life. (Buckminster died in 1812 at the age of twenty-eight.) Peirce's sermon expressed views about God, salvation, and the nature of man that put him at odds with the majority of his congregation.

In his sermon, Peirce emphasized God's mercy and kindness. There is no trace of an angry, vengeful God. His description of God is unambiguously Unitarian, portraying God as a father who cares for "his creatures especially his rational offspring." Describing humans as "rational" was a keystone of Unitarianism with its emphasis on the role of reason applied to religion. It left no doubt that Peirce was a Unitarian.[9]

Peirce's sermon took issue with the orthodox view that Heaven is reserved for a chosen few. He told his congregation to rejoice on Christmas morning in the knowledge that the blessings of the Gospel, "the good news of salvation," are *without end and* for *all people*."

Peirce also declared his support for three radical reforms in his sermon, reforms that would not become part of mainstream discourse for at least another decade. While he told the congregation that he believed Christianity was responsible for mankind's "gradual advance," he urged them to strive for more justice.

In this connection, Peirce first called for the "improved condition of the female sex," noting that although women are "one half of the human race," they were not valued as much as men. He claimed that the condition of women had gradually improved in Christian nations in contrast to their treatment in non-Christian areas where polygamy and ownership of women were accepted. "In Christian countries only, is woman the companion and partner of man." Despite that progress, Peirce lectured that women needed to be more than "pure maidens and faithful wives," but also "thinkers and students."

Secondly, Peirce called for an end to slavery, almost a full decade before the creation of the Anti-Slavery Society. He told his parishioners that he hoped that they would see slavery "entirely removed" in their lifetime.

Finally, Peirce called for an end to warfare, urging swords to be turned into ploughshares and spears into pruning hooks. His pacifist views reflect those of the Massachusetts Peace Society then in its infancy and led by the Unitarian Noah Worcester. Peirce's views on women, slavery and nonresistance put him in a distinct minority and at odds with the majority of his congregation in North Reading.[10]

As a consequence, attendance at Peirce's church suffered. During the final two years of his ministry in 1826 and 1827, not a single new person joined his church. To his great disappointment, his North Reading Church did not join the Unitarians when it formally split from the Congregational Church.[11]

Peirce was elected to the Reading School Committee in 1847. His election was not unusual; ministers were frequently elected to school committees in New England. Many, in fact, were Unitarians who had a strong belief in the importance of education. It is not surprising that Peirce was interested in serving on the school committee. He was an ideal candidate as a minister who had also been a schoolteacher. Unfortunately, no records of his year on the school committee survive.

Many of Peirce's parishioners were unhappy with his liberal outlook and pressure was put on him to resign. On May 19, 1827, the eighth anniversary of his ordination, Peirce tendered his resignation as minister of the North Church, a resignation unanimously accepted by the church council.[12] (Note)

The forced resignation was a turning point for Peirce. He emerged from it a bolder, more outspoken political activist bolstered by a fully committed Unitarian conscience. As the Unitarians had themselves officially split from the Congregationalists, Peirce followed the same arc. He was an outspoken Unitarian for the rest of his life, and although he continued to be referred to as "Reverend Peirce," he decided that the ministry was not the proper place for his talents, philosophy, or energy.

By this point, Peirce fully rejected the traditional Calvinistic view regarding the depravity of man. He rejected the Calvinist belief that God predetermines those who will be "elected" for salvation, instead embracing an optimistic view of mankind, and of a benevolent God. In fact, his optimistic view that society would improve became a trademark.

Peirce believed the best way to build a moral and ethical society was through the education of children. He concluded that he could do the most good in reforming society by working in the classroom. He never wavered from that view despite numerous setbacks.

Leaving the church in North Reading was liberating for Peirce. It freed him from satisfying a church council and a congregation. He was able to fully and publically participate in the radical movements that he supported. For example, Peirce became a zealous advocate of the most extreme form of temperance, complete abstinence from alcohol, denying even its accepted 'medicinal' use, which was supported by moderate temperance organizations. Peirce also supported the most extreme form of nonresistance, rejecting violence even in self-defense. He joined the ranks of the most radical abolitionists, those who advocated immediate abolition, as opposed to the more mainstream abolitionists of the 1820s who supported the gradual removal of slavery.

Peirce never returned to the ministry, although he remained active in the Unitarian church to the end of his life. His commitment to Unitarianism was more important than compromising his principles to suit parishioners. Those principles guided him for the rest of his life. Whatever uncertainty he might have felt earlier in his life about Unitarian beliefs was gone. He emerged from his experience in North Reading more resolved than before, although, having lost home and job, he and Harriet faced a precarious financial future.

Note: It was not until 1819, after Peirce had left, that Harvard Theological School, as it was first called, was officially created with its own president and faculty. It took several more years to build a separate facility for the school, Divinity Hall.

Note: Peirce's resignation did not heal the rift in the North Reading church, which remained divided after his departure. Several years later, North Church divided preaching responsibilities based on the split within the congregation. Thirty Sundays were reserved for conservative Congregational preachers and twhenty-two for liberal Unitarian preachers. In 1833, the congregation divided in half for good.

Chapter 4: Teaching: The Formative Years

A teaching career had been a possibility for Cyrus Peirce from his early days at Harvard, although his original dream had been to become a minister. Like his fellow university graduates, he regarded teaching as a temporary occupation. However, he found it had an appeal that he could not ignore.

Peirce never wrote about his first teaching job in Newton when he was in college, but his battle to ensure teachers were adequately trained before entering a classroom lends credence to the notion that he believed he was less prepared than he should have been. His return to teaching for his first job after graduation, however, also indicates that the experience was not so horrific that he rejected teaching as a possible career.

Thus it was that Peirce accepted his first permanent teaching job when he moved to Nantucket in 1810, at the age of twenty, although he regarded the job as temporary, expecting to return to Harvard later to study divinity. He quickly gained a reputation as a good teacher who set high standards for his pupils, although there is no evidence that he was anything more than a slightly above average schoolteacher. Like the vast majority of teachers, he believed students needed to be conquered and tamed in order to learn. Corporal punishment was expected and Peirce did not hesitate to use it.

Peirce moved to the island at a time when Nantucket was suffering from American foreign policy decisions. The purpose of the Embargo Act, passed at the end of 1807, was to hurt England

and France economically by cutting off trade with the United States. Unintentionally, the law was disastrous to Nantucket's economy with its dependence on whale oil trade with both countries. By 1811, most of the island's whale ships and whale men were idle.

The economy, however, did not play a role in Peirce's decision to leave the island. His heart was set on becoming a minister. Having saved enough money by teaching, he left Nantucket to study divinity at Harvard for three more years.[1]

After completing his divinity studies, Peirce returned to the island and to teaching, probably motivated by his desire to woo Harriet Coffin.

During the time he had been gone, Nantucket had changed. The island had recovered quickly from the effects of the War of 1812 when the island lost most of its whaling fleet. When peace was declared early in 1815, it ushered in Nantucket's golden age. By the end of 1815, twenty-five whaling ships had sailed in search of what whalemen called "greasy luck." Peirce was returning to a prosperous community.

Socially, the island was also changing, becoming more diverse. Quaker influence was in decline and the religious composition of the island included not only the two Congregational churches, but a Methodist church as well. The racial composition of the island was also more diverse with an increasing number of black people, most involved in the whaling industry where a man's pay was determined by his work, not his color.[2]

When he returned to Nantucket, a revolution was also appening in the world of education, much of it attributable to Unitarian thinking. "Unitarians were remarkable even among Yankees for their devotion to education. It is no exaggeration to say that such Unitarian religious leaders considered the school as sacred an institution as the church."[3]

Unitarian church

Nantucket Historical Association

Unitarians were among the most convinced believers in progress the world has known. Unitarian reformers led movements for the humane treatment of prisoners, the insane, and the disabled. They worked to clean up slums. They were leaders in the temperance and peace movements. They were also leaders in the crusade to abolish slavery.

Underlying all these movements was the belief that all reform would come about through proper education. Unitarians like Peirce were optimistic about the possibility of positive change. They believed that information and understanding would lead to social justice. Simply put, informed citizens would reform society. The future of America depended on it. Thus, public education was of paramount importance.

The Unitarian view of human possibilities and of human nature led to new methods of teaching. Reformers pinned their beliefs to new theories about learning, some based on new discoveries in the sciences, rather than on the Bible, again bringing them into conflict with traditional Congregational thinking.

Reform-minded educators like Peirce were also influenced by two European educators: Joseph Lancaster in England, and Johann H. Pestalozzi in Switzerland. Lancasterian teachers rejected rote memorization in favor of a hands-on approach to learning, involving as many senses as possible. This was a methodology Peirce embraced throughout his long career. "The Lancasterian system became the successful educational reform in the Western world during the first thirty years of the nineteenth century," according to educational historian Carl Kaestle.[4]

Anna Gardner, an early pupil of Peirce's on Nantucket, wrote that Peirce's "central educational achievement was the replacement of rote memorization with the Socratic method." Gardner, who became an important teacher of freedmen in the South during Reconstruction, was heavily influenced by Peirce and also applied Lancasterian principles in classrooms throughout her life.[5]

Another key component to Lancasterian reform was the "monitorial system." Monitorial schools addressed the difficulties of teaching multi-level students in one-room schoolhouses by using older students to teach small groups of younger students.

Most teachers will verify that a good way to learn something is to teach it. The monitorial system eliminated undue idle time, a problem in early one-room classrooms, as teachers focused on one group at a time. "Due to the use of student monitors, children could be almost continually engaged in active, competitive groups." This led to classifying students into what is now recognized as grade levels. Towns steadily abandoned one-room schoolhouses in favor of introductory, primary, grammar, and high schools.[6]

Competition between students was embedded in the Lancasterian approach. It was a concept that early American reformers like Peirce initially favored because they believed healthy competition in the classroom would negate the need for corporal punishment. The belief was that students would be so focused on advancement over others, motivated by a system of prizes, that awards would replace punishment. Peirce and others later rejected the competitive practices of Lancasterianism when they observe its negative effect on children, finding that competition actually led to discord as students vied with each other for prizes or to sit in the front. Seating by class rank was popular for a time, but Peirce and others found the practice counter productive.

The ideas of the Swiss educator Johann Pestalozzi also had a major impact on American educational reform. Pestalozzi advocated child-centered classrooms in opposition to the teacher-centered classrooms of the era. He "urged his teachers to view their pupils, not as miniature adults, but as children whose mental, moral, and physical development must be nurtured with tender care." This view of children coincided nicely with Unitarian beliefs. Pestalozzi rejected the use of corporal punishment in favor of praise and self-discipline. Reformers believed in teaching children to monitor their own behaviors and to think for themselves, again an idea compatible with Unitarianism.[7]

Another new teaching technique put forth by Pestalozzi was 'object' teaching. This technique had a major impact on progressive educators like Peirce who practiced 'object' teaching in their classrooms. Pestalozzi believed the most effective lessons were active, not passive in nature, through the use of what were

Peirce's globes

Framingham State University Archive

termed 'objects.' Knowledge was to be learned by seeing and doing, not merely listening and accepting. Pestalozzians believed each child was born with individual innate capabilities and that it was the teacher's job to find and to cultivate those capabilities, "to nurture and excite children's curiosity, allowing these natural tendencies to unfold." As such, children needed to get out of their seats and into their communities to experience as much as possible first hand.

The arts were considered as important as the standard academic subjects of reading, writing and arithmetic to the Pestalozzians. Music and drawing were added to the curriculum of progressive schools. Whenever possible, students were involved in their own learning. Subjects were integrated with each other whenever possible. Vocabulary words, therefore, were chosen from reading lessons drawn from science, history or geography lessons. Classrooms became exciting and enriching, the bare walls of the average classroom no longer sufficient. They were decorated with objects such as maps, charts, globes and clocks. Blackboards were introduced as effective teaching aids.

Teaching materials had to be adjusted to fit the needs of Lancasterian and Pestalozzian approaches. William McGuffey created a famous series of readers used by generations of American schoolchildren. The purpose of his six-level series was to "provide a comprehensive system of reading instruction." Charts, spellers and other materials that were compatible with the philosophy of 'object teaching' supplemented the McGuffey series.[8]

Pestalozzian pedagogy turned every-day teaching upside down. To help teachers adapt to this new approach, Pestalozzians were among the earliest to advocate for specialized teacher training, and the movement to require teacher training took much from the Pestalozzians.

Pestalozzi, who died in 1827, never visited the United States. His impact during his lifetime was mainly in Europe and, in particular in Prussia, which incorporated Pestalozzian practices in its school systems and required specific training for teachers. Progressive American educators read about the Prussian model. Some, such as Horace Mann and Edmund Dwight, visited Prussia to observe the approach firsthand.

One of the unintended consequences of the reform movements was their negative impact on women teachers, particularly those who taught the upper levels. As grammar and high schools developed, they required a more complete grasp of individual subjects by teachers, bolstering a belief in the necessity of teacher training. Because colleges and universities were all male, however, it was assumed that only men were sufficiently prepared to teach higher-level classes. This led to the practice of hiring men to teach at the grammar and high schools, and women to teach at the primary and elementary schools, a gender differentiation still seen today. Furthermore, it was assumed that men were better able to discipline older boys. These factors led to increasing pay disparity between men and women teachers and an increase in the number of male teachers. During most of Peirce's professional lifetime, about sixty percent of public school teachers were female, but by 1860, women made up less than thirty percent of the teaching force. It was a trend in teaching that Peirce resisted. He believed that properly trained women were as able as men to teach upper level subjects and keep well-disciplined classrooms.[9] (Note)

Educational reform played a part in the growing schism between the Congregationalists and the Unitarians. Educational philosophy and practice became divided between traditional educators who were considered "hard-line" educators, and those called "soft-line educators," who supported the reforms of Lancaster and Pestalozzi.

Soft-line educators, while believing in the importance of moral suasion and example in the classroom, supported separation of church and state. They rejected sectarian education, which brought them into conflict with orthodox Congregationalists. This does not, however, mean they were nonsectarian in modern terms. Even soft-line educators believed in putting Protestant values at the core of the curriculum. Reformers took for granted that the Bible would continue to be part of every day instruction, and memorization of the Scriptures would continue to be a daily practice. Nevertheless, secularism alarmed the hard-liners who regarded the reformers as dangerous radicals intent on undermining traditional Congregational doctrine and substituting Unitarianism in its place.

Influenced by his divinity studies and his evolving Unitarian beliefs, Peirce's educational philosophy had changed significantly during his three-year break from teaching. Unitarian theology rejected the Calvinist view of the depravity of man subject to the "hands of an angry God," as Jonathan Edwards described in his famous sermon in 1741. Edwards told his congregation, "the bigger part of men that have died heretofore have gone to Hell."

Those who followed strict orthodoxy preached fear of hell and the prospect of eternal damnation. "If you cry to God to pity you, he will be so far from pitying you....he will only tread you under foot." Children were born with the stain of sin and not excused from the vision that "the pit is prepared, the fire is made ready." Corporal punishment of children was, therefore, necessary and desirable. Classrooms under the sway of a strict Congregationalist were based on rote memorization, authoritarianism, order and fear.[10]

Unitarians like Peirce believed in a kinder, gentler God, with an emphasis on eternal salvation over eternal damnation. They rejected the basic depravity of man and the notion of original sin. Unitarians believed children were innocent at birth and believed in the possibility of eternal salvation based on individual deeds. They did not consider corporal punishment desirable, although they did not rule out its occasional use. Classrooms under the sway of Unitarians like Peirce were based on individualism, gentleness, and inquiry.

Peirce continued to demand excellence from his students, but tempered those demands with more gentleness and persuasion than he had before. He resorted to corporal punishment less and less frequently because he approached his students as rational human beings, demonstrating his care for their learning and wellbeing. This approach led to his students developing a sense of devotion and loyalty to him, evident throughout the remainder of his lengthy teaching career. One of his first female students recalled her time in his classroom as "the best and happiest" period of her life, going on to describe him as her "spiritual guide and leader." Such accolades occur often and are well documented over the course of his life.[11]

During his three-year stay on Nantucket, from 1815 -1818, Peirce became involved in island life in a way he had not during his first visit. For one, he had married into a large island family that traced its ancestry to the arrival of the English. Harriet's sister, Martha was married to the influential Samuel H. Jenks, editor of the *Inquirer*, Nantucket's main newspaper. Jenks was the tireless and foremost advocate who pushed the town to establish a publicly funded school system. On this topic he found an ally in his new brother-in-law.

Despite growing ties to the island, however, Cyrus and Harriet Peirce packed their bags at the end of 1818 and moved off island when Peirce accepted the preaching job in North Reading. After his forced resignation from the ministry there, people on Nantucket tried to convince him to return to Nantucket, but the couple decided to remain off island.

Peirce was, instead, "induced" to go to North Andover in 1828 to teach with a distant relative, Simeon Putnam, at the Franklin Academy. The private academy, built in 1799, was incorporated by the state in 1801 as the North Parish Free School, the first incorporated academy in Massachusetts to admit girls. It comprised two rooms, one for girls and one for boys. In 1803, the name was changed to the Franklin Academy.[12]

On the surface, Franklin Academy seemed a perfect fit for

Peirce with his strong belief in equal education of girls. Indeed, under Samuel L. Knapp, one of the previous principals, the school had acquired the reputation of being a liberal institution with a relaxed atmosphere. For example, young men and women were allowed to host dances, something no conservative institution would have permitted. By the time the Peirces moved to North Andover, however, the school was no longer the liberal institution of its reputation.

Simeon Putnam and Cyrus Peirce were only a year or two apart in age. They had attended Harvard within a year of each other, and it appeared they had much in common. The more they worked together, however, the more apparent it became that their approach to teaching was diametrically opposite. Stern "Old Put," as he was called behind his back, could not have been more different from the gentle Peirce with his belief in the benevolent Unitarian view of mankind and in the innocence of children.

Putnam governed Franklin Academy with rigid discipline. In fact, the trustees of the academy had dismissed him in 1825 for just that reason. In response, Putnam built his own school nearby which quickly filled with students, in turn emptying the Franklin Academy. Two years later, with Franklin Academy on the verge of collapse, the trustees were forced to ask Putnam to return. Putnam then leased the building he had recently built to the Franklin Academy to be used as the girls' department.

It was at this juncture that the victorious Putnam hired Peirce to assist him, putting him in charge of the girls. Despite their different approaches, the reputation of Franklin Academy flourished under their joint leadership. According to *Historical Sketches of Andover,* the school was "inferior to none." Putnam's reputation for harshness, however, continued to grow. He was "often unjust, always harsh, and sometimes cruel." In addition, Putnam's health was in decline, which did not improve his cantankerous disposition. In spite of Putnam's famous ill temper, the school remained fully enrolled, even with competition from Phillips Academy only two miles away.[13] (Note)

It is not surprising that Peirce tendered his resignation after almost four years of working with the authoritarian Putnam. The "discordance was embarrassing" to both men, and Putnam's harsh disciplinary practices had a lifelong impact on Peirce. "Old Put" did not believe in sparing the rod, even as Peirce was increasingly opposed to corporal punishment. He was growing more and more convinced that authoritarian methods hindered children's learning and moral development and that teachers like Simeon Putnam were unfit.[14]

The Peirces returned to Nantucket in 1831. Family and friends welcomed them back after their eleven-year absence. One Nantucketer said to Peirce, "There has been no period since you left the island when you could not have had a school here, of any number of pupils that you would have undertaken to teach, and at any price that you would have thought it fair to charge."[15]

The years off island had been difficult. Peirce had been forced to resign from the church in North Reading due to his Unitarian principles. He had also resigned from teaching in North Andover because of those principles. It would not be the last time his Unitarian values would get him into trouble, but the two experiences also solidified his philosophy and his belief that the educational system in the United States had to change.

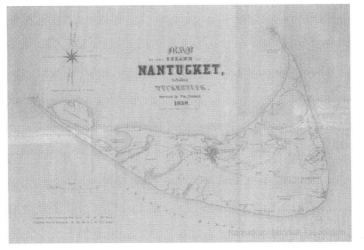

Nantucket Historical Association

Note: Introductory schools were similar to what are now pre-schools. Primary schools were for ages 5-10. Grammar schools were for students 10-14 and high schools admitted 14-18 year olds who passed the entrance requirement.

Note: Simeon Putnam died in 1833.

Chapter 5: Influential Citizen of Nantucket

Nantucket

Nantucket Historical Association

Harriet and Cyrus Peirce moved back to Nantucket in 1831 at an exciting time in Nantucket history. Nantucket ships roamed the globe and brought back news and goods from exotic cultures. The island's chief export, whale oil, was in demand, lighting the streets of American and European cities. Candles made from spermaceti burned long and bright, and candle factories abounded on the island. Everyone on Nantucket - from bankers to shopkeepers - benefited from the effects of the whaling economy. The whaling industry spawned many jobs, as it required coopers, blacksmiths, sail makers, rope makers and ship builders. Consequently, the island population had swelled to over seven thousand.

The Nantucket community became more diverse as whale ships picked up crewmembers from around the world. When ships returned home, some of those men chose to settle down on the island. These newcomers were from Asia, Africa, the Caribbean, and the far Pacific islands. In addition, the island had a growing population of black people, some escapees from southern slavery, others descendants of northern slaves, and a few from Africa itself. People of color generally settled in the New Guinea neighborhood just south of town, a place where foreigners were accepted. Not everyone was comfortable with the newcomers. It was a time of change not only on the island, but also in the nation, which had survived past the generation of its founding, leading to the commonly accepted assumption that the American experiment was on firm footing. A new generation had taken the place of the founding fathers and optimism was in the air.

The country was in period of growth, fueled by westward expansion, slave labor in the South, the beginnings of the industrial era, the growth of markets at home and abroad, and immigrants from unfamiliar places. The changes, however, did not affect every segment of the country uniformly. Turmoil accompanied the economic growth as former sources of prosperity and power were displaced by the new. Portions of society were left behind, unwilling or unable to adapt.

Social changes during the post Revolutionary War period ushered in what some people consider to be the largest reforming spirit the country has ever seen. America became what has been called "a nation of joiners," particularly in Massachusetts where organized groups abounded, especially those dedicated to reform. These groups enabled "people from all backgrounds to organize so as to pressure neighbors and leaders on issues as diverse as whether to prohibit the sale of liquor, limit the number of hours in a working day, abolish slavery, or promote education and the arts."[1]

Newspapers and journals proliferated, giving voice to the many social movements that developed around those who wished to cling to the past, and those who looked to the future. Americans who shared the Jeffersonian ideal of a society based on yeoman farmers, were alarmed by the rapid growth of American cities, increasingly peopled by immigrants who brought in new cultural practices and religions. Poor conditions in those cities gave rise to reform movements aimed at improving urban life. Slums, populated by immigrants and the displaced, were segregated from mainstream Americans by culture and language. Democratic ideals were strained as Americans pondered who among the newcomers, and those already in the country, including women and blacks, deserved to fully participate in the nation's life. More women took their places in the work force as industrialization expanded. Women joined reform movements demanding to add their voices to public discourse. The free black community also pressed for rights, demanding to be heard and advocating for their enslaved brethren.

Scientific knowledge was also growing exponentially. Some scientific discoveries directly challenged traditional religious thinking about the nature of the universe, giving rise to frequent, often-bitter debates about the merits of faith versus reason. An example would be what fossils revealed about the age of the earth as compared to the age of the earth as determined in the Bible.

Depending on a person's point of view and condition in life, it could be an exciting time to be alive. New horizons opened, both geographically and intellectually, offering many choices. Harriet and Cyrus Peirce embraced many issues of their day and were generally optimistic about the future of the country. To the Peirces and their fellow Unitarians, the future of the country depended upon the quality of education available to the upcoming generation, and how it would determine the nation's ability to make correct choices. They devoted their lives to the notion that it was the education of a society's children that would shape the future.

The Peirces established a private school on Nantucket, open to both boys and girls where they taught side by side. For the first time in his career, Cyrus Peirce had no supervisors to whom to answer and he was free to implement his evolving educational philosophy without interference. The couple quickly became active in the community. Given the school's success, the Peirces soon needed an assistant. They were fortunate to hire the sixteen-year-old Maria Mitchell, who would later be acclaimed as the first American woman astronomer. She became their lifelong friend.

The Peirces moved both their residence and their school several times. They bought a home at 15 Orange Street in 1832 and lived upstairs, keeping the school on the ground floor. An advertisement in the local paper promoted the school's expertise in

Orange Street

Nantucket Historical Association

the teaching of French and Spanish. By 1834, the school had done well enough for them to live separately from their work, and they moved the school to 24 Orange Street and their residence just down the street to 19 Orange Street. In 1837, an advertisement indicated that they moved the school yet again, this time to space rented at the Masonic Hall on Main Street.[2]

The hard-working Peirce offered private lessons in the evenings after his regular school day. He advertised his availability for penmanship lessons, as well as "Algebra, Elements of Surveying and Navigation, Latin, Greek and Spanish" during the evening hours.

Harriet and Cyrus Peirce threw themselves into the life of Nantucket becoming members of many groups and societies. Both gave time and leadership to reform movements on the island, and were active in the Unitarian church where Seth Swift was still the minister.

Harriet Peirce joined abolition and temperance societies and she became the secretary of the Fragment Society, a women's charitable group dedicated to aiding the poor. In 1834, the society reported it had assisted twenty-eight island families that year.[3]

In 1834, the Nantucket Atheneum was incorporated "to promote the cultivation of Literature, the Sciences and the Arts, and thereby advance the best interests of our native town." Part library and part museum, the Atheneum became a leading intellectual force in the community and important to the lives of the Peirces.[4]

The Atheneum's first librarian was Maria Mitchell who left her teaching job at the Peirce's school to assume the post. Mitchell stayed at the library for twenty years, spending her evenings studying the night skies. In 1847, she became the first person ever to discover a comet using a telescope. This discovery earned her a gold medal from the king of Denmark. One year later, Mitchell became the first woman elected to the American Academy of Arts and Sciences. In 1865, Mitchell became the professor of astronomy at Vassar College, a position she held until her retirement in 1888.

The Atheneum quickly became an important part of Nantucket's intellectual life. The trustees embraced the Lyceum movement that began in England. Lyceums were educational institutions founded to foster knowledge, and they did much to educate Americans before the Civil War through lectures, debates, classes, and dramatic performances often given by roving presenters. Many lectures, by both local and off-island thinkers, were hosted at the Atheneum. Luminaries such as Henry David Thoreau, Ralph Waldo Emerson, and John James Audubon journeyed to the island to speak. More frequently, local authors, thinkers, and reformers were invited to lecture. (Note)

Cyrus Peirce lectured often at the Atheneum on a wide range of topics reflecting the scope of his intellect. Many of his talks were scientific in nature, including presentations on pneumatics and hydrostatics. Peirce, however, was more frequently called upon to talk about the many social causes of the day, especially temperance, a cause Peirce advocated his entire life.

Shortly after returning to the island, Peirce was invited to speak at the Methodist church about alcohol abuse. Almost one thousand islanders attended, an astonishingly large number that filled the church past its capacity. Peirce's lecture "dwelt particularly on the necessity of total abstinence." A newspaper account described his manner of speaking as "energetic and graphic." In his lecture, he asked the audience to envision two drunken men lying on the floor by his feet. He asked the audience if they could tell which of the men was drunk from wine and which from rum. "This was done with great power," according to the newspaper. When the audience could not distinguish from the two imaginary drunkards, Peirce drove home his point that wine was just as damaging as rum. This "energetic" style was typical of Peirce who came alive in front of an audience. Students in his classroom described his teaching style in a similar fashion – passionate, animated, and involved. Due to Peirce's persuasion, the Nantucket Association for the Promotion of Temperance was formed shortly after his lecture.

Other temperance groups followed, including the Young Men's Total Abstinence Society for younger islanders. For even younger islanders, the Cold Water Army enlisted schoolchildren in the quest to create a non-drinking society. In 1842, more than six hundred pupils marched through town to the annual sheep shearing fair under the banner of the Cold Water Army. Women formed their own temperance society, the Daughters of Temperance. The black citizens of New Guinea also organized chapters of these temperance groups, and cooperated in many activities and events with their white counterparts. Off-island speakers were engaged to lecture on temperance at both black and white organizations.

Peirce's most ardent lectures during the early 1830s concerned the importance of public education and new approaches to teaching. One of his Atheneum lectures, "The Art of Reading with practical illustrations," is a good example of Pestalozzian 'object' teaching. His method rejected starting with the alphabet. Peirce later wrote in the *Common School Journal* that teaching the alphabet was a "miserable waste of time." He favored teaching words in context with reading material. Peirce also lectured frequently about the importance of public education to democracy, a cause he supported vigorously with his influential brother-in-law Jenks.[5]

Both Peirce and his brother-in-law Jenks took Nantucket to task for its neglect of public schools. For years, Nantucket had ignored the 1789 law requiring all towns to provide free public elementary and grammar schools. Many private schools, such as the Peirce's, were available on Nantucket and there was little push for the public to pay for the education of those too poor to afford those schools. In this way, the island succeeded in breaking the law for several decades.

It was not until 1818, almost thirty years after the law was passed, that a school committee was created on the island. The committee was assigned to investigate whether the island had a need to establish schools at public expense. It reported back to the town that the island did, in fact, have about three hundred poor children unable to attend private schools. The committee recommended that it was time for the island to comply with state law. Even then, the island dragged its feet for many more years.

Evasion of the public school mandate was accomplished mainly by under funding, making it appear that the island was in compliance with the law, when, in fact, the public options were inadequate. It took the passion of an off-islander to put the issue of public schools, quite literally, on the front page. Jenks had moved to the island in the early 1820s and became the editor of Nantucket's only newspaper of the time, the *Inquirer*. In his columns he became a forceful advocate for the almost nonexistent public schools. After three years of Jenks's public and insistent politicking, the town finally made a half-hearted start, allocating $1500 to help children of the poor receive some education. The money was mostly used to send these children to the island's private schools. Even then, the committee only spent half the money the town had allocated. However, progress had been made and the notion of public funding was accepted. By the mid 1820s, five small public schools had been established with an enrollment of 180 children. One of those schools, the African School, was in the New Guinea neighborhood.[6]

Led by the newspaper, proponents of public education kept up their pressure. Jenks castigated the Quakers in particular for opposing public funding of education, accusing them of providing quality schooling for their own children while denying it to others. He blamed the captains of the whaling industry for wanting to maintain an uneducated populace so that a life at sea would be a viable option for Nantucket youngsters. Jenks wrote that the whaling industry feared that young men would become "full-grown physicians and lawyers" and turn away from the harsh life onboard whale ships.

It was not until 1827, almost forty years after the state mandated public schools that Nantucket truly complied with the law. Interestingly, it was the same year that another influential private school was begun on Nantucket, the Coffin School, a school based on Lancasterian principles.

Sir Isaac Coffin, an English admiral, created the Coffin School for the Nantucket descendants of his ancestor Tristran Coffin. The progressive school embraced the most modern educational practices of the time. The presence of a Lancasterian school on the island had a major influence on the growing public schools because local teachers were exposed to new teaching techniques. It was not uncommon for teachers to go between the public schools and the Coffin School for teaching positions, and there was a spirit of cooperation between the public schools and the Coffin School.

While the public elementary schools had made strides, the island continued to flaut state law for eleven more years by refusing to establish a public high school. The Coffin School filled part of the gap, taking some pressure off the town, as the Coffin School permitted students not able to prove kinship with the Coffins to attend for a fee. During those eleven years, Jenks relentlessly kept pressure on the town through his columns, despite the fact that his own children, qualified through kinship, attended the Coffin School.[7]

By this point, many reform-minded town fathers had joined Jenks's campaign. A group officially calling itself "the Nantucket County Association for the Promotion of Education and the

Improvement of Schools," more commonly known as the Education Society, was formed. Cyrus Peirce, newly arrived back on the island, quickly became involved and was elected its secretary. The primary goal of the Education Society was to establish a high school at public expense.

Meanwhile, Horace Mann had just been appointed as the first state Secretary of Education in the country, making Massachusetts, in 1837, the first state to create a board in charge of public education. Pressure to create a department to oversee the state's instruction came from educators around the state. Support came from the American Institute of Instruction, established in 1830. It was "the most influential association of teachers in New England."[8]

Eight members were appointed to the first board of education with the governor acting as its chairman *ex officio.* Unitarians, enthusiastic supporters of public education, outnumbered the other denominations on the board. One, James G. Carter, was especially linked to teacher education, having championed the cause over a decade before it became popular. In 1825, Carter had written a pamphlet describing the curriculum of a teacher-training academy, and in 1827, he submitted a proposal to the state Senate to establish teacher training schools. In addition, Carter was a founding member of the American Institute of Education and was the chair of the legislature's committee on education.

The board appointed Horace Mann as their secretary. Mann had been elected to the Massachusetts House of Representatives in 1827 where he served until his election to the Massachusetts

Senate in 1834. In 1836, Mann was elected the president of the Senate until he was asked to become the first state Secretary of Education in the nation. Charged with overseeing the state's schools, Mann became the most famous of the educational reformers.

On a trip to observe some of the state's schools, Mann visited Nantucket. He delivered a lecture about the importance of public education at the Methodist Church in October 1837. Although only

Horace Mann

Framingham State University Archive

a small group was in attendance that day, Mann's talk was so well received by those present that he was asked to repeat his lecture the following day, when the audience was much larger. It was during this visit that Mann met Peirce for the first time, initiating a friendship that lasted throughout their lives. They shared a passionate belief in the importance of public schools.

Mann contacted Peirce shortly after his island visit asking him to serve on a state-wide committee to examine school libraries, as well as to consider apparatus that would be useful in the state's classrooms, another example of Pestalozzian 'object' teaching. Peirce accepted the invitation and traveled to Worcester for the first committee meeting. Serving with him was James G. Carter, a member of the new board of education. It was Peirce's first involvement with educational reform at the state level, and he immediately began to make a name for himself as an important contributor to the discourse on public education.

Nantucket's Education Society invited Mann to return to the island later that year while the secretary was on his first inspection tour of the state's schools. On this occasion, Mann's address was delivered at the Unitarian church where Reverend James Edes, an 1828 graduate of Harvard Divinity School, was then its pastor. The *Inquirer* reported that Mann spoke to "as large an assembly as could possibly be contained within the walls of that edifice," which must have been several hundred.

While visiting the island, Mann met privately with Peirce and took the opportunity to observe him in his private school. Mann had high praise for the progress Nantucket's schools had made in one year, much based on new philosophies and techniques. He praised the island for its "competent teachers, suitable school-books, libraries, and good apparatus." He noted that every schoolhouse had "new and comfortable seats," as well as good ventilation. "The organization," he declared, "is now perfect."[9]

In 1838, not long after Mann's visit, Peirce and three members of the Education Society wrote a twenty-four-page booklet, *Address to the Inhabitants of Nantucket on Education and Free Schools.* Peirce's co-authors were his brother-in-law William Coffin, Henry F. Mitchell (Maria's brother) and Reverend Edes. The four men wrote passionately about their certainty that public education was indispensable for the survival of America's democracy. "Every patriot, every friend of virtue and well regulated society, must therefore, be the friend of education, and of the system of free schools." They argued that schools needed to be supported by property taxes and that all children should be required to attend school, even if their parents were illiterate and saw no need to send their children to school. They encouraged every citizen to visit the town's public schools to see firsthand the high quality of education offered there. They urged the public to support teachers and to teach their children to respect them. The men drew a link between crime and lack of education, a theme Peirce would return to later. They also linked human happiness with education, contending that those with higher education were happier people. Finally, they argued for the establishment of a public high school on Nantucket.[10]

1838 was a banner year for Nantucket reformers. The *Address to the Inhabitants of Nantucket* had its desired effect. After almost fifty years of agitation and delay, the town voted, on January 6 at the annual town meeting, to create its first high school. A committee that included two of Peirce's brothers-in-law, Jenks and William Coffin, was created to report on how much a high school would cost the town, and in February, the town voted to fund the high school. The vote was a major victory for those who had lobbied for a public high school for many years.

Later in February, the newspaper reported that Peirce had been appointed as the principal of the town's first high school. It reported that the new school would instruct in "the higher branches of English education" and that the curriculum would include the teaching of Greek and Latin. The newspaper praised Peirce's appointment because of his "eminent qualifications and great experience as a teacher of youth." The paper noted that Peirce's private school would stay open for six weeks, as the high school room was made ready in one of the town's public grammar schools. Three days later, the paper reported that Peirce's school would be taken over by his brother-in-law William Coffin, formerly a teacher at the Coffin School. Little did they all know that family unity was about to be shattered as its members lined up on opposite sides of a new and contentious issue that would consume island politics for the next decade.

March 1838 was a busy month for Peirce as he prepared to relinquish his private school to his brother-in-law, and to establish the first public high school on Nantucket. He certainly had enough to do, but his commitment to public education spurred him to do even more, and he opened a tuition-free night school for sailors.

Peirce made a point in his newspaper advertisement that the night

South Grammar School and 1st high school

Nantucket Historical Association

school welcomed both "native Seamen" and "foreigners," noting that such men had "not "enjoyed the advantages of early education" because of "unfavorable circumstances" not of their own making. Peirce's free classroom was open to seamen of "every class," as he sought a diverse group of men, including men of color. It was a foreshadowing of the issue that would divide his island family – the education of African-Americans.

A year later, Peirce served on a committee for the Nantucket's Seaman's Society to establish and supervise a nonalcoholic boarding house for seamen which included a reading room. Besides an indication of Peirce's strong principles, both his after-hours teaching and his work to establish the reading room, are examples of the time and effort Peirce devoted to helping others have access to education.

March 1838 was also an important time for educators at the state level. The board of education convinced the legislature to support the creation of the first teacher-training institutions in the nation. On March 10, Edmund Dwight, board member, Unitarian and wealthy philanthropist, offered to donate $10,000 to a teacher training school if the legislature would match his offer, which they did under the leadership and support of Governor Edward Everett. According to Mann's *First Annual Report to the Board of Education*, without Dwight's donation, "many years must have passed before the state legislature could have been induced to appropriate any money for 'Teachers' Seminaries."[11]

Dwight had visited Prussia and been impressed with their system of teacher training. The Nantucket Education Society sent a letter to the legislature, encouraging acceptance of Dwight's offer. The legislature approved the appropriation on April 19, 1838, the anniversary of the Battle of Lexington. The date's significance was not lost on the reformers who believed that their battle to create a professional teaching corps was as vital to the maintenance of American democracy as had been the battle of Lexington. Governor Edward Everett signed the bill. The state of Massachusetts had approved the creation of the country's first teacher training schools.

Thus, both Peirce and the state were making history. Peirce prepared to assume his role as the island's first high school principal, and the state began to prepare to establish the first teacher training school. Mann began to compile a list of possible directors for that first school. Peirce was unaware that his name was about to go on that list and that he would only be the principal of the island's high school for one year.

A letter to the editor, written five years after Peirce's death, remembered the first day of the new high school, taught in one room on the second floor of North Grammar School. The writer

Nantucket Historical Association

recalled feeling "awe and wonder" being in the first class, especially as the youngest one admitted. The author recalled "Father Peirce as clearly as if I had parted with him an hour ago." Peirce was praised for his "kindly manner" and "patient drilling" but also noted that "his standard was high." While he was known later as "Father of the Normal Schools in America," the writer reminded Nantucketers that he was also the "Father of the Nantucket High School as well!" [12]

Note: The Atheneum still functions in that capacity today, serving as the island's library and continuing to sponsor intellectual and cultural events in the heart of downtown Nantucket. The lower portion of the converted Universalist church, which the Atheneum trustees purchased, was converted to a lecture hall, which could seat up to 450 people. The early records of the Atheneum were lost in the Great Fire of 1846, but it is assumed that original membership cost $10.00 with yearly dues of $2.00. These fees were used to buy books, maintain the building and hire a librarian. These were steep fees then and would have precluded membership by the working class. However, for $3.00 a year, non-members could take out books and for $.15, they could visit the museum. Shares were sold to proprietors who oversaw the private institution. For a full history of the Atheneum, see Betsy Tyler's, *The Nantucket Atheneum: A History.*

Chapter 6: Nantucket Refuses to Integrate its High School

With the cause of public education seemingly settled in Nantucket, Harriet and Cyrus Peirce devoted more of their reforming zeal to the abolitionist crusade. Both were already founding members of the Nantucket Anti-Slavery Society formed at the end of 1837. The abolition movement increasingly demanded both Peirce's time and attention at a time when race was on the verge of dividing the island community. The issue became so inflammatory that families were split and violence resulted.

As debate on abolition became increasingly divisive, several meeting halls in Nantucket were closed to abolition meetings. In 1838, even the Atheneum closed its doors to the abolitionists. A slew of letters to the newspaper debated the wisdom of the ban. Shortly thereafter, the Atheneum went even further, barring black people from the building altogether, even from taking books out. This prompted a two-year boycott of the institution by some abolitionists, including Nathaniel Barney, a leading citizen and one of the Atheneum's trustees. His brother, Obed Barney, opened a free anti-slavery reading room over his store on Main Street where black and white citizens could take out books and gather to read up-to-date publications.

The abolition movement itself divided over both tactics and organization as the nation lurched toward civil war. William Lloyd Garrison, the fiery publisher of the *Liberator*, led the radical wing. The Garrisonians believed in immediate emancipation of slaves with no compensation given to slaveholders. Less radical abolitionists argued for gradual emancipation of slaves with the possibility of compensation for their owners. The abolitionist groups also differed in tactics. The

Garrisonians increasingly opposed using the political process. Believing that the political system was corrupted beyond repair, Garrison stopped voting in elections.

The role of organized religion in the movement also divided abolitionists. Many early leaders were clergymen from various denominations. These churches were under increasing attack from the Garrisonian wing, however, because of their affiliation with their fellow churches in the South whose members were slaveholders. Many Unitarians like the Peirces supported the radical wing.

The role of women in the abolition movement was another source of contention. The Garrisonians favored full and equal participation of women, while more conservative abolitionists favored women being relegated to a separate group as was common in other societies, temperance among them.

Until 1839, the abolitionists managed to cooperate with each other. That year, however, a group of ministers walked out of the annual meeting of the Massachusetts Anti-Slavery Society to form a rival organization to the Garrisonians. The new group condemned the Garrisonians as "a women's rights, no-government" organization because of the Garrisonians inclusion of women as equal members and their rejection of the ballot box as a means to end slavery.[1]

From Massachusetts, the schism spread to the national level. At the annual meeting of the American Anti-Slavery Society in New York City in 1839, those opposed to the Garrisonians tried to amend the annual report to read that abolitionists had a civic duty to vote. The Garrisonians objected, believing that a voting boycott sent a clear message that the United States was not a democracy as long as it allowed slavery to exist. When the amendment failed, conservative abolitionists launched their next attack on the issue of women's equal participation in the organization.

Women had come to the New York convention anticipating full participation for the first time. One of the Massachusetts delegates was Nantucketer Eliza Starbuck Barney, Nathaniel's wife. She spoke at the convention in favor of equal participation of women. After two days of intense debate over the words "men" or "persons," the Garrisonian faction was victorious and female delegates were seated as equal members. The admission of women resulted in the withdrawal of many conservative abolitionists. After the schism, it was the Garrisonian faction that gained strength nationwide, becoming the predominant abolitionist organization. Women, as well as blacks, found themselves welcome.[2]

The Nantucket abolitionists, including Harriet and Cyrus Peirce, sided with the Garrison wing and reorganized their local chapter shortly after the New York convention. On the first page of the record book of the Nantucket County Anti-Slavery Society, it says the new society "shall embrace men and women on terms of perfect equality in accordance with the spirit and sentiments of the American Anti-Slavery Society." A month later, the Women's Anti-Slavery Society on the island, of which both Harriet Peirce and Eliza Barney were members, officially joined their ranks.[3]

Garrison himself may have disparaged political participation, but he did not impose his philosophy on his followers. Local groups were active politically in most places, including on Nantucket. Abolitionists ran for political office on the island, especially for seats on the board of selectmen and the school committee. Many of these men refused to vote, however, in national elections. Nathaniel Barney, who held many local offices, proudly wrote, "I have not cast a vote for a national or State officer since 1824." [4]

Nantucket Quakers had been early opponents of slavery, but the issue of abolition divided them in the nineteenth century. Members of the Society of Friends found themselves in turmoil over Quaker doctrine and the extent to which members should become involved in secular affairs. Splinter movements arose, the largest a group of separatists who followed Elias Hicks. The Hicksites spoke forcefully and publicly against slavery and were expelled, or "disowned" by the orthodox Quakers. The most famous of the Hicksite abolitionists were Lucretia and James Mott of Philadelphia. Lucretia Mott was an islander by birth and kept close ties with the island. She lectured in Nantucket on numerous occasions. One such occasion was to the island's black community. In 1842, the newspaper reported that at a lengthy meeting where she spoke, "more than 100 neatly-clad people of color were present and were orderly, quiet and apparently deeply attentive".

Local abolitionists were disowned from the Nantucket Meeting of the Society of Friends. The husband-and-wife team of Eliza and Nathaniel Barney, and a local schoolteacher and friend of the Peirce's, Anna Gardner, were all disowned, as were Maria Mitchell and her father. Being disowned had serious consequences because Quakers were forbidden to associate with those who had been disowned. Disownment split families, neighbors, and business associates. In the Mitchell family, for example, Maria's brother, William Foster Mitchell, continued to be a lifelong Quaker, even while others in the family were disowned. The Quakers, however, were in decline, and the effect of disownment was less disruptive than it had been in previous decades.[5]

The abolitionist issue became more immediate in 1839 when a

young black teenager, Eunice Ross, qualified for entrance to Nantucket High School. Ross was a fifteen-year-old student at the African School located in the heart of the New Guinea neighborhood and the daughter of James Ross, one of the few Nantucket black citizens to have been born in Africa. (Note)

Few descriptions of New Guinea exist, but a real estate advertisement from the mid-1830's described the neighborhood as "a delightful spot composed of persons of correct habits, living by their own industry, and in perfect harmony." By this point, the black community numbered about five hundred. The neighborhood included a sizeable middle class where people owned their own businesses such as grocery stores and boarding houses. Nantucket had two known black whaling captains, Absalom Boston and Edward J. Pompey. Boston became the wealthiest man in the New Guinea community. In 1822, his whale ship, *Industry*, had sailed with one of the first all-black crews in American history. He invested his money well, particularly in real estate. Pompey was the captain of the whaler *Rising States* that sailed from New Bedford. Like Boston, he invested well and became a merchant on the island, as well as the local agent for the *Liberator* and an original member of the integrated Nantucket Anti-Slavery Society.[6]

Absalom Boston

Nantucket Historical Association

Nantucket was mainly segregated in practice, although whites and blacks spent their money in stores all over town. Whites patronized businesses owned by the citizens of New Guinea, some of which were outside New Guinea. For example, at least two barbershops in downtown Nantucket were owned and operated by black men. The island had a separate burial ground for people of color in use as far back as 1798. In 1807, the cemetery was described as "The Burying Ground That Belongs to the Black People or the People of Colour." Eventually, there were two churches in New Guinea - one a Baptist church, also known as the African Meeting House, and one an African Methodist Episcopal church, commonly called Zion's church. Until the establishment of the two churches, blacks attended other local churches. The Second Congregational Church recorded most of the black marriages, including the marriage of Absalom Boston to Phebe Spriggins in 1814, ten years before the New Guinea community established a separate church.[7]

African Meeting House

Nantucket Historical Association

The African Meeting House at the corner of York and Pleasant

Streets was built around 1824. The Meeting House was owned and built by and for the black community. It served many purposes over the years. It was a lecture hall and meetinghouse for temperance and abolitionist meetings. Vaccinations against smallpox were administered there. Picnics took place on the lawn. Simply put, the Meeting House was the heart of the black community. Its primary function, however, was that of a church, but from the beginning it was also used as a school. In fact, when African-American Jeffrey Summons sold the land to the trustees of the Meeting House, he stipulated that a schoolhouse would be built and maintained there. The earliest public reference to the building was on January 3, 1825 when the newspaper wrote that a building "for the purpose of accommodating the coloured population, will be consecrated as a house of worship, tomorrow afternoon at 2 o'clock."

While the white community of Nantucket had been squabbling about the necessity of providing tax-supported public schools, the black community had not waited, opening their school in 1825, a year in advance of the town establishing public schools. In 1826, the African School was incorporated into the public school system and received public funding. The school was a typical one-room schoolhouse of the era. Children of all ages attended the school, with older students assigned to teach younger ones, as the African School adopted the new system of classifying students by ability levels.

As schools on the island proliferated and began to divide into primary, intermediate and grammar schools, however, black children could only attend the crowded one-room African School, which was forced to accommodate all three levels of schooling, whereas white children could attend the town's primary, intermediate and grammar schools.

In 1838, Anna Gardner, the secretary of the local Anti-Slavery Society, became the African School's teacher. She was a member of one of the oldest island families, and a close friend of Harriet Peirce. Her parents, Oliver G. Gardner and Hannah Macy Gardner, had earned their abolitionist credentials when they harbored a runaway slave family in their Vestal Street house in 1822, when Anna was only six years old. That year, several lawmen arrived on Nantucket with slave catcher Camillus Griffiths, who had been hired by Cooper's ex-owner in Virginia to capture Cooper and his family. When the bounty hunters arrived at the Cooper house in the early morning, the black community alerted several white abolitionists including Anna's father, Oliver. These men successfully delayed the slave catchers and the Coopers escaped to hide at the Gardner house. Anna later wrote,

> I stood (I was then six years old) upon our back-
> stairs, when a man, black as midnight, with lips so
> paled with fright that they were as white as snow,
> came up the back steps, and stood in the doorway.
> The striking contrast of white lips and black face
> was shocking. Such a sight was too indelibly
> impressed upon the mind of a child ever to be
> forgotten. He and his family were concealed for
> weeks in our attic and cellar. I remember that
> it was with fear and trembling that any of the
> children dared to put their heads out of the cellar
> door.[8]

Gardner taught at the African School for four years. It was during her tenure that the controversy about Eunice Ross began. This was no coincidence. In 1838, in their annual report, the school committee based on visits to the school, praised Gardner's teaching as "zealous and faithful." One of the star students Gardner presented to the committee was undoubtedly Eunice Ross. The committee would later regret the zeal with which Gardner pursued the quest to get Eunice Ross into the new high school.[9]

Eunice Ross, at age fifteen, had reached the limits of the one-room schoolhouse. She was ready for a high school education and took the entrance examination in 1839 with seventeen other pupils. She passed, evidently with flying colors, but the school committee turned her down. Her qualification and her goal to enter the high school were to change history, on Nantucket, in the state, and later, the nation.

Being against slavery in the far away South was not the same as allowing local black children to sit side by side with the white children of Nantucket. With the school committee's refusal to admit Eunice Ross to the high school, the trustees of the African Meeting House retaliated by refusing to allow their building to be used as a segregated schoolhouse. The closure created a problem for the school committee. Not wanting to place the students of the African School in their existing schools, the school committee quickly built a new schoolhouse in New Guinea, specifically to educate the black students. Anna Gardner quit her job in protest, refusing to oversee her pupils' removal to a segregated building, or to cooperate with the school committee in keeping black children segregated. It was at this time that Gardner was disowned by the Society of Friends.

In the spring of 1839, the Education Society, with Cyrus Peirce as its secretary, debated whether "the present public provision for popular Education be enlarged as to furnish what is commonly called 'liberal education' to all qualified applicants." Reading between the lines, this debate was about whether Eunice Ross should be admitted to the high school as one of those "qualified applicants."[10]

The debate over whether to admit Ross to the high school set off a bitter controversy that engulfed island politics for eight tense years. Like

a stone thrown into a pond, its ripples spread beyond the case of young
Eunice Ross and spread beyond the shores of the island, helped by the
off-island abolitionist press, particularly the *Liberator.*

Nantucket town meetings from 1840-1847 were dominated by
rancor over school integration. Arguments that developed over a single
motion could extend for days of debate. Page after page in Nantucket's
town records are devoted to the meetings, as both sides offered
convoluted and increasingly desperate parliamentary procedures to score
points for their sides.

Abolitionists entered the political fray with zeal and focus. The fight
had shifted from a far-off ideal to one in their backyard. There was no
question of sitting this one out. The abolitionists entered candidates for
both the board of selectmen and the school committee during the years of
the controversy. In 1839, as the issue was heating up, thirty people ran to
be on the five-member board of selectmen. One was Absalom Boston,
who also ran unsuccessfully for the school committee several times
during the period of controversy.[11] It was in the midst of the controversy
about Eunice Ross that Cyrus and Harriet Peirce left the island once
again. The Nantucket abolitionists lamented the departure of the Peirces
who left the island just as the group was reorganizing to join the
Garrisonian abolitionists. In their first meeting in June 1839, Eliza
Barney moved that the group:

> deeply regret the loss which the Anti Slavery
> cause in this place has sustained by the removal
> of those faithful and persevering friends of the
> oppressed, Cyrus and Harriet Pierce and that we
> console ourselves for the loss to our ranks by the
> assurance that their labors will be as unremitting
> in that section to which they have transferred
> their residence, as they have been while among
> us."[12]

Peirce had fought long and hard for the establishment of the island high school and had been its principal for just one year. At forty nine, he was in the prime of his teaching career. Both he and his wife were immersed in the life of Nantucket. Despite being an off-islander, Peirce had risen to be one of the town's most respected leaders. Losing the principal of the high school, a man who could have been counted on to advocate for the admission of Eunice Ross to that very school, was a huge loss to the abolitionists. Only something enormously important could have enticed him to move off island at such a critical time, committed as he was to her admission.

Peirce had been offered a job he could not refuse. He had been asked by Horace Mann to take charge of the first teacher training institution in the United States. It was an exciting and challenging project Peirce could not turn down with his strong belief in the need for teacher training. It was also an honor that reflects the respect Mann had for Peirce's abilities as a teacher and a leader. Although the decision to leave Nantucket was difficult to make, Peirce could not turn away from the opportunity to influence the next generation of public school teachers. Mann recalled later that Peirce had been "most reluctant" to take on the job. "A humble person, unassuming, and troubled by self-doubts, Peirce was also judged one of the finest teachers in the Commonwealth." Peirce asked Mann: "Is it true that in old enlightened Massachusetts, you can find nothing better?"[13]

On June 11, 1839, Mann took the steamer from New Bedford to ask Peirce in person to take the job, and within two days Peirce officially accepted. While on Nantucket, Mann spoke to the school committee. He wrote in his journal that he "obtained the consent of the School

Committee for [Peirce's] discharge from his engagements to them," the committee accepting Peirce's resignation "with the greatest reluctance." In accepting Peirce's resignation, the committee referred to the "long and arduous" workload Peirce had maintained during his year as principal and their hope that "the change may improve your health." Given his tendency to work to exhaustion, both Peirces might have speculated that the move to Lexington would prove less stressful than the job in Nantucket. If so, they were mistaken.[14]

Mann, convinced he had found the right man, was pleased with the results of his trip, although he returned from Nantucket "worn down with fatigue. I believe we have a competent principal for one of our Normal schools; and this is a subject for unbounded rejoicing."[15]

Cyrus and Harriet Peirce had been living on Nantucket for the previous

Nantucket Historical Association

eight years and were respected and involved members of the island community. Their years on Nantucket had been a contrast to the years in Reading and Andover when Peirce had been dismissed from his church and had quit his teaching job. Harriet Peirce had been glad to return to her hometown and her large extended family. She had, however, suffered four losses in her immediate family. Her father died in 1835 and her mother in 1837. Two siblings shortly thereafter: her beloved only brother William in 1838, and her sister Winnifred in February 1839. In view of these losses, it may have come as somewhat of a relief to leave the island.

It was also clear that Peirce was heading directly into the controversy about Eunice Ross's application. Although not a man to run from controversy, particularly one with high moral overtones, this one would have squared Peirce off directly against his brother-in-law Jenks. Peirce would not have left the battle, however, if he was not convinced that he was being called for an even higher purpose. (Note)

In Peirce's estimation, the answer to every social ill, from abolition to temperance, was to be found in a well-educated populace. While it was important to fight for the admission of Eunice Ross to the high school on Nantucket, he also believed that an educated populace would have admitted her without hesitation. It was a question a choice between working to change an individual situation or an entire society. Leaving his beloved island students was not easy, and Peirce wrote to them shortly after he left, saying that he had separated from them with great reluctance. "There is nothing of which I now think with more interest and more frequency than my former pupils…" He told them that he would "like much to look in upon you and see your pleasant and thoughtful countenances." He implored them to write back to him, either individually or as a class. He suggested they ask their teacher to allow them to write to him as a substitute for a composition assignment. "Much or little will be acceptable." He said that he was working hard "trying to make what I trust you will all become – good scholars, and what some of you, I hope are destined to be, good teachers." He described Lexington as a "pleasant country town," and that he was very close to the former battlefield "which was first moistened by blood spilled in the opening of the Great Dreams which led to our glorious independence." He admitted his pacifist beliefs. "To be candid, I think our forefathers ought not to have resisted into blood."[16]

Note: It is not clear how James Ross came to Nantucket.

Note: Harriet Coffin's sister, Eliza, who had been married to Samuel H. Jenks died in 1822. Jenks remarked, so he was technically a former brother-in-law of the Peirce's by the time of the controversy.

Chapter 7: Creating a School from Scratch: The Lexington Normal School

Cyrus Peirce was about to make history as director of the first teacher training institution in the United States. The term 'normal school' was derived from *écoles normales*, teacher training schools in France. The word 'normales' was derived from the Latin word meaning "square," an instrument used by carpenters. As applied to education, it meant "a rule, a pattern, a model; or, more generally and modestly, an

Sketch by Electa Lincoln

Framingham State University Archive

aid or agency to teach teachers how to teach."[1]

Lexington, Massachusetts, site of the Revolutionary War battle was chosen for the school. The association of Lexington with the Revolutionary War was not lost on the reformers who believed the normal school movement was as important for America as the Revolutionary War had been. The school was located on the village green in the center of town; the building in which it began still stands, now owned by the Simon W. Robinson Masonic Lodge.

Mann seems to have had Peirce in mind as a possible director for the normal school early in the process. In his first observation of Peirce, Mann wrote in his journal that he was "charmed" by the way Peirce ran his school in Nantucket. James G. Carter, a member of the Board of Education, supported Peirce's appointment. Carter had become acquainted with Peirce when they served together on the committee for libraries and apparatus in the state's schools.[2]

Mann was as passionate about the importance of teacher training as Peirce. Without excellent teachers, he wrote, "public schools" would become "pauper schools." In turn, these "pauper schools" would produce "pauper souls" and ignorant voters. Ignorant voters would become "venal voters," resulting in the probability that "profligate men" would be elected to govern the nation. No less than the future of the nation, he concluded, rode on the success of the normal schools and the creation of a professional cadre of public school teachers. Seen through that lens, properly educating the nation's youth was a heavy responsibility.[3]

Not everyone agreed with Mann's viewpoint, and from the start, there was stiff opposition. Mann recognized what he was up against, writing in his journal that "ignorance, bigotry and economy" were lined up against the normal school experiment.[4]

Leaving Nantucket to accept the new post was a life-altering decision for the Peirces. Lexington was well known to Cyrus; Waltham was nearby, and he had lived in several of the surrounding communities. He had close relatives in the village, including four first cousins. One,

Loring Peirce, held several town offices during the time Peirce directed the normal school. Some of his cousins' children and grandchildren lived in Lexington, including Ebenezer and Nathaniel Peirce, who were close in age to Cyrus.[5]

Mann may have felt "unbounded rejoicing," and Peirce excitement about his appointment, but neither had time to bask in the glow, as the enormity of their endeavor set in. Little did they know they would engage in their own fierce battles in historic Lexington; the opposition to their mission was larger and stronger than they imagined. To those who favored normal schools, it was obvious the tree of liberty needed to be nourished by a well-educated citizenry. It was clear to them that a good public education system was essential. Having fought for over ten years to get this far, they were not naïve to the opposition, but they did not foresee just how determined their opponents were to see them fail. The stakes were high.

Lexington Normal School

Framingham State University Archive

First, the school had to be organized from scratch. There were no schools in the United States to copy and there was no time to reflect or to consult others. Peirce accepted the position on June 13, 1839 and the school was slated to open only three weeks later. It was a daunting task.

Every aspect of preparing the school was left solely to Peirce. He had no assistants and there was little money. There was no curriculum and there were no books. Mann sold his private library to pay for some books and both men contributed $1300 to the project. The majority of the prospective students, all female, would board at the school. Thus, Peirce was also responsible for the well-being of the teenaged girls who would live there, including providing for their meals. None of the classrooms or dormitories was furnished when he and Harriet arrived in Lexington.

To add to the difficulties, Mann and Peirce believed the Lexington Normal School needed to offer immediate opportunities for the fledgling teachers to practice on real children. On top of creating the normal school, they felt it necessary to establish what they called a "model school," a town school where student teachers would hone their teaching techniques. Both felt it imperative for the model school to be up and running almost simultaneously with the opening of the normal school. Peirce had to use all his powers of persuasion to convince the Lexington school committee to entrust some of the town's children to the normal school experiment in the hope that the teachers-in-training would be up to the task. Permission to open a model school was granted in the fall of 1839.

Three weeks of frenetic activity got the normal school ready. The two-story school building, fifty feet long by forty feet wide, had a kitchen, dining room, washroom and storerooms in the basement. On the ground floor were a parlor and steward's bedroom, a sitting room for the girls, and one schoolroom. Describing that schoolroom fifteen years later, graduate Lydia Drew Morton recalled "that old room, with its green topped desks, and its formidable blackboard." She remembered being afraid when called to the front of the classroom to demonstrate knowledge on that blackboard.

On the second floor were five dormitory rooms and another schoolroom. Four more dormitory rooms were squeezed into the attic. There were two stoves for heating, two maps, two globes, and a library of about one hundred books.

The school could accommodate twenty boarders and each schoolroom seated up to eighty students at full capacity. Normal school students were charged $2.00 per week for room and board, but paid no tuition. Money from room and board paid for a steward charged with providing meals and maintaining the building and its furnishings. In return, the steward lived in the schoolhouse free of charge.[6]

Finding and keeping the right steward to supervise the girls' dormitory proved problematic from the start. In October 1839, Lydia Stow (Adams) wrote in her journal that she found a note in the girls' sitting room from the steward, name unknown, saying that the "inmates of the Normal House seem to have forgotten the hour for retiring." He continued, "if they do not like the rules they had better seek a home elsewhere." The next month, the steward complained to Peirce that the girls were "too noisy," especially when dancing. Peirce met with a committee of the girls to hear their side of the story. Peirce laid down a rule of conduct: "Whatever would be proper for you to do in a well regulated family that you may do in this establishment." He wrote to the complaining steward to that effect and the steward was "much disturbed and angry" at his letter, and threatened to "go away." Peirce met with him to remind him "of some defects about his establishment." The steward was instructed to feed the girls better food, especially better bread, and to keep "a good fire" because the building was too chilly. There may have been some improvement over the next several months, but in January 1840, as the term was winding down, Peirce again referred to "trouble brewing" due to "disharmony" between the steward and the girls. Peirce wrote that it would not matter to him if the steward resigned, expressing the belief that the position was not "essential."[7]

By the following term, the first steward had been replaced, although the next one also proved problematic. Peirce described him to Mann as so lazy it made him angry enough to wish to give him a good kick on "the nether part of his corporality." Not surprisingly, that steward also was replaced. Problems supervising the stewards provide a glimpse into the kind of detail with which Peirce contended.[8]

On July 3, 1839, after only three weeks on the job, Peirce opened the door of the Lexington Normal School. It was not an auspicious start. For one, it rained hard throughout the day. More importantly, Peirce, Mann and the members of the board of education were deeply

Framingham State University Archive

disappointed when only three students showed up for admission; they had hoped for at least a dozen. Eben Stearns, a member of the board, reminisced twenty-five years later that as "they gazed upon the limited capacity of the school building, and thought of the numbers they expected to examine that day, and the greater numbers expected to throng those halls on succeeding days," they optimistically planned how to expand the school and create new normal schools. So, they were dismayed when "Alas! Alas! Three, modest, shrinking girls only were seen...."[9]

These three were Sarah Hawkins, Maria Smith, and Hannah Damon, the first students to enroll in a program to prepare professional teachers in the United States. According to Mann's journal, the young women were "timid" as they were examined in the basic knowledge thought necessary to establish their fitness for admission. "Poor things! No wonder they were frightened," wrote Stearns. "In numbers their examiners surpassed them, and were a presence in which the ripest scholarship might tremble." In addition to Peirce, Mann and Stearns, the examiners included Jared Sparks, the first professor of American history at Harvard (and later its president), and Robert Rantoul, Jr., a lawyer and member of the state legislature. [10] (Note)

All three girls were admitted. But the small number of applicants was disturbing. Mann and Peirce had been certain that there would be many more. They were aware that support for the school in the legislature was fragile and that if the school did not prosper quickly, it would lose its funding. Mann speculated that the fault might have been the dismal weather. He also wondered if the delay in opening the school was a factor. He had originally hoped the school would open on April 19, the date of the Battle of Lexington, but he had not even had a director in place by then. Furthermore, the building had lacked the necessary supplies, furniture and equipment.

Fear of failure haunted Peirce. Filled with self-doubt, he told his wife on that first day that he would "rather die than fail in this experiment" and thought the board of education had made a mistake in appointing him. "Beyond Nantucket I am not known as a teacher and the public have no confidence in me."[11]

Rebecca Viles, a graduate of the school's second year, recalled hearing Peirce talk about his resolve to see the experiment through. "I have put my hand to the plough, the furrow must be driven through, and the whole field turned over, before I will relinquish my effort."[12]

A small student body at the outset did have benefits. For one, there were not many girls to oversee in the dormitory, giving Peirce time to attend to the pressing issues of writing curriculum and procuring materials. Subject to periods of discouragement, Peirce continued to worry about the slow start. However, his workload precluded him from falling too deeply into depression. Being in the classroom helped improve his outlook, and his commitment to the job soon raised his spirits. Working with students, even so few a number, made him cheerful and hopeful. He dove into his work.

The student body grew steadily. By the end of the first week, there were seven students. Two, Mary Swift and Susan Burdick, had been Peirce's former students on Nantucket. Swift was the niece of Seth Swift. The girls brought with them their affectionate appellation, "Father Peirce," by which students called him for the remainder of his life. By the end of the first month, the student body had reached ten, and by the fall, there were twenty-one. Peirce's optimism grew as the enrollment increased and he was pleased that Governor Edward Everett delivered an address to the students at the opening of the second term. By January 1840, the enrollment had risen to twenty-five.

Students arriving at the normal school were plunged immediately into the work and the life of the school. Louisa Harris, who arrived that first September, wrote about her arrival with three other students after a two-hour coach ride from Boston. Lydia Stow had brought her pet turtle along, to the amusement of her fellow passengers. The new girls arrived around dinnertime and that evening attended their first lecture. [13]

Mary Swift kept a journal throughout her studies with Peirce that first year. Her journal provides specific examples of the daily life of the first normal school in America, rich with descriptions of the lessons, lectures, and principles taught by Peirce. Swift's journal was later published in the same volume as a brief journal kept by Peirce during the same time period. Peirce kept another journal, one he often shared with his students, but that journal has unfortunately been lost. Students at the school enjoyed Peirce's readings from the one that is now missing, which is unfortunate because the one that remains provides little detail of the workings of the school. All the students kept journals, but none remain that are as complete as that by Swift.

When Mann visited the Lexington Normal School in September 1839, he was pleased with the progress Peirce and his pupils had made in two months. He wrote in his journal about spending a "pleasant day" visiting the school and he had praise for Peirce's teaching. "Highly as I had appreciated his talent, he surpassed the ideas I had formed of his ability to teach." The confidence of the girls in Peirce as a teacher impressed him. "This surpassed what I have ever seen before in any school."[14]

Mann repeated his views in a letter to board member Jared Sparks, writing that Peirce's teaching style forced students to think critically and deeply, leading them to learn the principles behind facts and to probe assumptions. "The business of education was advancing so systematically, so perfectly, so rapidly." Mann left the school that day confident it would succeed, and optimistic that its success would pave the way for other normal schools. Two new schools were slated to open within two years - one at Barre in the western part of the state and another in Bridgewater. [15]

Much was riding on the success of the Lexington school. Henry Barnard, who oversaw the creation of the first normal school in Connecticut six years later, wrote in the introduction to the journals of Peirce and Swift, "The whole movement depended upon Peirce's success at Lexington."[16]

The girls in the school were well aware of their importance in history. Sixty-two years later, Mary Swift (Lamson) wrote that they knew they were called to "decide the question - "shall there be such schools or not?" Despite the pressure, she recalled that the girls were uniformly optimistic, "ready to work harder than we had ever done before." She attributed their sense of mission to the "power of that remarkable man whom we had yet to learn to love as our Father Peirce." Louisa Harris wrote that the girls felt lucky to be among the "consecrated few," and Julia Ann Smith wrote that she had never worked so hard in her life.[17]

Mann worried about the toll the hard work was taking on Peirce's health, as well as on his pupils. Harriet Peirce, called Mother Peirce by the young women, worked tirelessly alongside her husband in an unpaid and unofficial capacity. Louisa Harris wrote that Mrs. Peirce taught botany to them that first year. Peirce wrote in his journal that she also helped to teach reading. When the model school was opened, Harriet Peirce was also called upon to teach there periodically. Stearns recognized Harriet Peirce's contribution to the school twenty-five years later at a commemoration ceremony. "No sketch of this school, at least, could be complete which did not recognize the modest and uncompensated labor of Mrs. Peirce." Students recalled the dedication and kindness of Harriet Peirce. Rebecca Viles recalled Peirce's "estimable wife was a great assistant to him" as well as a "faithful adviser to the young ladies," and Mary H. Stodder (Loring) wrote "her smile was ever present."[18]

Mann did not want the experiment jeopardized due to the sheer exhaustion of the participants, so when Peirce asked him to grant them a vacation of a week to ten days in the fall, his request was quickly granted.

By October, Peirce opened the first model school in the United States, located on the ground floor of the normal school. Reflecting on its opening over forty years later, Swift described the composition of the school – thirty-three pupils between the ages of six and ten – twenty-one boys and twelve girls. At least five children were drawn from each district of the town of Lexington.[19]

Peirce chose Swift to be the first student teacher in the model school and to be its first student principal, with Mary Stodder as her assistant. Student teachers typically spent one month at a time supervising and teaching in the model school, although its real supervisor was Peirce who monitored the school's day-to-day operation. He also observed the teaching capabilities of his normal school students for a minimum of two hours each school day, often resulting in an eight-hour teaching day. Several times each term he taught in the model school with the normal school students as his observers. In addition, he taught the normal school pupils *all* of their lessons that first year.

The normalites, as they were called, regarded their time in the model school as vital to their training. Viles recalled that teaching the village children under the watchful eye of "Father Peirce" was critical because it allowed for trying a variety of teaching techniques. It also meant that each graduate gained experience in conducting a school, a "very valuable and attractive feature of the institution."[20]

George Emerson, a member of the board of education wrote effusively about the model school after a visit during the second year. "I have never before seen little children so completely under the right influence of their teachers, - so fully awake; I never saw so little of mere mechanical teaching, or greater activity of the faculties of the mind." [21]

Peirce created a broad curriculum for the normal school. Seventeen subjects were taught over the course of the year, ten per term. The courses included "a thorough review of the 'common branches' of learning – spelling, reading, writing, grammar, geography and arithmetic" (including algebra and geometry) and also study of the sciences (including botany and natural history). Peirce and Mann believed that the arts (including drawing and music) were as important as any other academic subject and vital to a well-rounded education. The curriculum was designed to be rigorous so that the women could teach in grammar and high schools.

At the end of each day, Peirce gently rang the classroom bell and closed with the daily motto he had employed while teaching on Nantucket, "Live to the truth." According to Viles, ending the day with these words resonated with each pupil because they knew "it was a symbol of his own daily life." On the occasion of the twenty-fifth anniversary of the school, Samuel J. May recalled those words, "so often on his lips would come with such unaffected earnestness, that they would seem to those, who had heard them most frequently, to have a deeper meaning than every before, and be impressed as the crowning lesson of his life."[22]

Cyrus Peirce

Framingham State University
Archive

Peirce regarded his normal school students as individuals with unique talents and needs. As such, he individualized their instruction as best he could. One way to address students individually was by requiring each normalite to write in a journal every day. Peirce tried to respond to each one, although Harriet assisted in this endeavor as the student body grew. Through these journals Peirce maintained a two-way communication that would have been impossible otherwise, given the demands on his time. Some of these journals exist in various archives.

Rebecca Viles, reminiscing many years later, gave a rare physical description of Peirce, describing him as slightly below medium height with "long, black, silvered hair, parted in the middle, and brushed, painfully smooth, behind his ears, revealing a brow of indomitable will and energy." His very presence and scrupulous conscientiousness, she wrote, "gained the respect of all who came in contact with him." She also praised his high academic standards. He expected students to demonstrate a "thorough knowledge of all the English branches, including music and drawing. He made a specialty of reading, and was singularly successful in teaching it. He never accepted any halfway analysis of a question, and cancelled the word fail from our vocabulary."[23]

The teaching of reading and writing was paramount and students were required to read aloud every day. Peirce often read aloud, too, modeling what he expected. He wrote that while reading aloud was the most difficult art to teach, that writing was even more important. "Most persons in business life have to write," he noted, but "few, comparatively, are called upon to read publicly."[24]

Every Friday, students were selected on a rotating basis to demonstrate something they had learned to the other students. For those comfortable with the subject matter and with public speaking, this may not have been difficult, but for some students, especially early in their studies, it could be a trial. Ann E. Shannon wrote in her journal, "This day of the week I believe is the most valuable to Father Peirce, but most dreaded by his pupils, especially those who know they have got to make a public exhibition of their capacities as teachers."[25]

Geography was a hands-on subject, which often meant trekking around the surrounding countryside. Students were required to draw maps and write about imaginary voyages. They gathered information about other countries, including the history, language, geography, religion and customs of those places. The normalites presented oral reports about their research. Peirce told his students that when they became teachers, they should expect their youngest pupils to begin with the study of their own towns and then expand to other areas. Among the prize possessions of the school were two globes.

Much about the curriculum was revolutionary, incorporating the ideas of Pestalozzi, Lancaster and other progressive educators. Besides the standard academic offerings, normal school students were the first in the nation to study what James G. Carter, as far back as the 1820s had called "the science of teaching." Progressive educators like Peirce and Mann believed people could be taught to be good teachers by studying the science behind learning. Their belief in science was at the core of their experiment. Mann wrote that teaching was "the most difficult of all arts, and the profoundest of all sciences."[26]

Peirce and Mann believed in phrenology, a new science that studied the relationship between a person's character and ability with the morphology of the skull. Phrenology was woven into both theory and practice at the normal school. Books by the leading phrenologist George Combe were required reading. Now discredited as pseudo science, much in the observations by the phrenologists of the period is now accepted. Phrenologists believed that children develop best with fresh air, cleanliness, good food, warmth and exercise, all ideas now widely accepted. Since children who lacked access to such healthy practices could not develop intellectually, phrenologists believed schools should be designed to incorporate as many of those elements as possible. These topics were discussed at the normal school on a daily basis. Swift's journal noted at least fourteen Saturday morning lectures that discussed phrenological principles.[27]

Normal school pupils were also expected to study practical subjects such as bookkeeping, along with proper ways of organizing a school day. They were taught to keep accurate records of attendance and accomplishment.

Rather than resort to physical punishment, students were taught to use positive rewards and "moral suasion" to keep order in their classrooms. In the introduction for the 1926 edition of Peirce's journal, Arthur O. Norton wrote that Peirce recalled his own liberal use of corporal punishment in his early days in the classroom, and recalled questioning its efficacy while teaching in Andover with the stern Simeon Putnam. From that time on, Peirce had become an outspoken critic of corporal punishment, an opinion that would bring him into conflict with the more conservative schoolmasters in the state. Opposition to corporal punishment was in accordance with Peirce's Unitarian beliefs.[28]

Peirce expected teachers to be "firm, consistent, uniformly patient, and uniformly kind," an approach considered dangerously Unitarian to those who believed that sparing the rod spoiled the child. To Peirce, lessons had to be meaningful, challenging, and relevant. Such lessons, he contended, would automatically result in teacher control. Seldom, if ever, was there a role for dull, rote memorization, which he opposed on the grounds that memorization did not require reasoning or deep understanding. According to Peirce's way of thinking, interesting lessons were unquestionably the best answer to classroom management and the maintenance of discipline.

Many teachers blamed students for inattention, Peirce told his students. He blamed the teachers, instead, pointing to their "dull manners." He expected to see dynamic lessons when he observed the normal students teaching in the model school. He emphasized the importance of engaging students in learning with hands-on techniques and experiments, and wholeheartedly embraced new classroom aids or objects such as blackboards and globes. He believed classrooms should be engaging, inviting and comfortable, beliefs contrary to the accepted notion that students needed to be uncomfortable, sitting bolt upright to stay awake and not distracted by things around them.

Peirce taught by example, treating the normal school students as he expected them to treat the youngsters in the model school. Never content with partial answers, he required them to give full oral explanations. He roved the classroom mingling with the students, continually pressing them to explain their answers more fully. He disapproved of teachers standing or sitting in the front of their classrooms dispensing knowledge and symbolizing authority. Teachers were there to facilitate learning, not to dictate it.

Normal school students were required to role-play, alternately acting as pupils or teachers. They discussed case studies in depth and debated ways to handle difficult classroom situations, often taken directly from experiences in the model school. Peirce expected students to explain what they would do in particular disciplinary or academic instances. They had to think on their feet. "What will you do with the perseveringly idle and troublesome? What will you do if your scholars quarrel?" Every Saturday he conducted seminars about educational practices, which graduates described as lively and provocative.[29]

Students at the normal school had full lives, in and out of the classroom. They wrote a monthly school newspaper called the *Normal Experiment* that included humorous observations of their experiences. The paper's motto was "Vast is the mighty ocean, but drops have made it vast." In the only extant copy, editor Mary Stodder begs her readers to "be merciful" while reading it.[30]

Physical activity and socializing were encouraged and required. Long walks in the countryside were promoted. Peirce and Mann were among the earliest proponents of daily physical exercise, believing sound bodies and sound minds were integral to learning. The hour before breakfast, the hour between morning and afternoon classes, as well as two and a half hours after supper were set aside for talking and walking. On occasion, Peirce cancelled classes and took the students on excursions, including sleigh rides, hikes and visits to Boston.

During the evening, there were silent study periods when the normalites were forbidden to communicate with each other, although their journals recount many times when they broke that rule, only to be gently reprimanded by Father Peirce the next day. Louisa Harris recalled that Peirce had to remind them several times not to play cards when they were supposed to be studying. [31]

Peirce believed students needed to enjoy their daily lives and expected them to behave like normal adolescents. Most of them were only sixteen or seventeen years old, and most had never spent much time away from home. Lydia Stow wrote in her journal that she rarely had time to be homesick, but found that she was sometimes homesick on Sundays, when there was more time to think.

They were "a group of giggling girls." At the first reunion, ten years after their graduation, Mary Stodder recalled that they laughingly called themselves the "Old Termites of Normalty." Louisa Harris reminisced that "the love of the ludicrous" was one of their "leading loves." Stodder told of once being tied by her hair to a chair by "Miss D," requiring scissors to be freed. Lydia Morton Drew addressed another reunion recalling individual attributes of her classmates, which included the "mirth" of Louisa Harris who found a way to "provoke a smile" that disrupted the enforced quiet of study hours.[32]

At the twenty-first reunion in 1884, Harris wrote a poem about their lives in the normal school. She described "how pleasantly within those walls we lived, a group of merry girls....we laughed and strove and thought." Over sixty years later, in 1902, Mary Swift recalled they all knew how to play: "a happier, gayer hearted group of girls it were hard to find." Both Peirces believed it was important to cultivate a family atmosphere, and their students' reminiscences make clear they regarded the couple as surrogate parents and themselves as sisters.[33]

The girls at the normal school became part of the Lexington community and participated in local fairs and fetes. Some girls chose to board at various homes near the school. According to Lexington historian Richard P. Kollen, "the girls became a presence in the everyday life of Lexington." Stodder remembered deliveries of "delicious squash pies, apples and pears from our kind-hearted neighbors."[34]

But the school did not always fit easily into the town. On their first Sunday at the school in July 1839, the Peirces and the first five students attended a church service a short walk from the village green. The girls were shown to a pew in the middle aisle with the Peirces a few pews away. The pews were high-backed and un-cushioned, with doors at either end. As the service began, the girls, knowing they were being closely observed, were "anxious to do just the right thing." "All went well until the long prayer, during which the congregation stood." They stood, but found the space so limited that they were crammed together uncomfortably. They did not realize the pews were hinged and that if they had turned around and raised the seats, they would have had sufficient room. When the prayer ended, the minister told the congregation to sit down. There were loud bangs as pews were lowered; the noise startled the nervous girls who jumped and, in their nervousness, laughed out loud, shocking the parishioners. "Alas, that this our first introduction to a Lexington assemblage should have given to these demure old people cause to feel that the town had opened its doors to ill-behaved, irreverent girls!" It took the congregation months, according to the story, before the school was forgiven, "and longer before it was forgotten."[35]

Finding the proper steward for the boarding school continued to be a problem. In the second year, Peirce hired thirty-eight-year-old Dorothea Dix for the job. Both had strong personalities and Dix and Peirce clashed. The estimable Dix had not yet embarked on her crusade to ensure humane treatment for the mentally ill. According to Peirce, Dix was not suited to supervise the young ladies of the normal school. [36]

Dix made it clear that she thought Peirce was far too permissive, and she was determined to hold the girls to a stricter regimen than that to which they were accustomed. For example, she disapproved of the girls walking or riding unsupervised, even in small groups, to places such as the post office, something allowed before her arrival. The girls had also been permitted to have male visitors in the school's parlor as long as a chaperone was present. Dix thought any male in the building was inappropriate unless it was Peirce or a relative of the student. Peirce thought Dix's approach Puritanical and complained to Mann that she was imposing "strait-laced prudery." Girls, he said, had to run and jump and "sometimes laugh loud." Under the Dix regime, he believed the girls were on the verge of mutiny.[37]

Mann, who admired both Peirce and Dix, was put in an awkward position. In the end, he reluctantly supported Peirce. He later said that the loss of Dix to the normalites, had been a gain to the mentally ill. In 1841, just one year after leaving Lexington, Dix presented her famous *Memorial* to the state legislature about the appalling conditions of the mentally ill. She had found her life's calling.

While the normal school was nonsectarian, it was based on what that term meant in the mid-nineteen century. The school was unabashedly Christian. Reading and studying the Bible was mandatory, as it was in all schools of the era. Sectarianism, which then meant adherence to Congregationalism, was a favorite target of the Unitarian convert, Horace Mann. His biographer Jonathan Messerli wrote that Mann "would give it battle wherever it raised its hoary head." Even before appointing the Unitarian Peirce to head the Lexington Normal School, Mann had been attacked for his belief in nonsectarian education. A Congregational minister, Frederick Packard, complained that Mann had not recommended John A. Abbot's book, *Child at Home,* for use in the public schools. Mann responded that he found the book too sectarian. Packard wrote a second letter asking Mann to review over thirty other books that had been rejected for use in the state's public schools. Mann responded that the texts were too Calvinistic and sectarian for the public schools. Preaching to two hundred fellow Congregational ministers in New Bedford, Packard declared the board of education "anti-evangelical." Mann and Packard battled via letters over the rejection of these textbooks for over three months. Edward Newton, a conservative member of the board of education, resigned over the issue as a protest to what he interpreted as Mann's stubborn refusal to include the sectarian texts.[38]

Peirce was equally adamant in his support of nonsectarian education, providing another target for those who believed that it was Congregational dogma that should have been taught and upheld in the public schools. Peirce explained his position in his journal. He wrote, " I wish much to steer clear of all sectarian and party views, ways and measures, but on great principles to speak freely." The intensifying battle over the role of religion in the public schools continued to grow, eventually putting Peirce at the center of the controversy where he was not able to "steer clear" of sectarian views.

Massachusetts had a long history of Christian theocracy. In 1839, when the Lexington school opened, only five years had passed since the state constitution had been amended to separate church and state. Many Congregationalists regarded the amendment as a dreadful mistake and were determined to reverse it.

Therefore, when Peirce and Mann advocated nonsectarian education, it was a raw subject, despite there never being any question that Christianity in its broadest sense would be part of the curriculum. Even the most nondenominational educators of the time believed in the importance of the Bible for educational and moral instruction. The curriculum of the Lexington Normal School included thorough study of the Bible and all normal school students were required to go to "public worship on the Sabbath."

The widening gulf between Congregationalism and Unitarianism had a huge impact on the approach to religion in public schools. Nonsectarians, such as Peirce and Mann, believed in teaching Christianity in broad strokes, avoiding the narrow confines of one Protestant sect over another. However, as both men were Unitarians, many Congregationalists believed they were using the public schools to undermine Congregationalism. To the more extreme Calvinists, Peirce and Mann were heretics. Peirce was attacked throughout his career for undermining Congregationalism and promoting Unitarianism more than for any other aspect of his educational leadership.

It was true that the normal school students were exposed to many lectures from the intellectuals of the period, a preponderance of them Unitarian, providing fodder for those who accused Peirce of promoting his own religious beliefs. Peirce's opponents considered many of the speakers too radical for students to hear. Peirce, however, was determined to take advantage of the school's proximity to Boston and the surrounding area, where many of the intellectuals and activists of the day resided.

A wide variety of visitors came to the normal school, some who were invited to observe the school, and others to lecture. Governor Edward Everett sometimes stopped in to see the school in action and to speak to the students about their mission. Unitarian minister Samuel J.

May was invited to speak about the peace movement. Board of education member William A. Alcott, a phrenologist, lectured about a variety of topics including vegetarianism, classroom design, and the importance of physical exercise. Samuel Gridley Howe, founder of the first school for the blind in the United States, was a frequent visitor and lecturer, often speaking about phrenology, something he believed in fervently. Another frequent visitor was John Augustus Dodge, Lexington's Baptist minister, not known for his liberalism. Dodge had been won over by Peirce, and testified that first winter in front of the legislature in favor of continuing the normal school, despite being desperately ill at the time. (He died shortly thereafter.) Transcendentalist writers accepted invitations to speak, including A. Bronson Alcott. Caleb Stetson, a close friend of Peirce, also spoke to the pupils about temperance. A Unitarian minister in Medford, Stetson was an advocate of total abstinence. Mill owner Walton Felch lectured about grammar as well as phrenology.

Charles Follen, a German immigrant who was an early advocate of physical education in schools was a frequent visitor. Follen opened the first college gym in the United States when he had been a professor at Harvard. By the time he spoke at the normal school, however, Follen had been fired for his outspoken abolitionist beliefs and for clashing with the university's president, Josiah Quincy, over what Follen saw as Quincy's overly harsh disciplinary practices. Follen, an ordained Unitarian minister, was living in Lexington when the Lexington Normal School opened.

Follen oversaw the building of the Unitarian octagonal church there, now the oldest standing church in Lexington. In August 1839, sixteen girls at the school took a stagecoach to West Lexington with the Peirces to raise money for the church at the East Lexington Fair. The fair was held at an observatory on what is now called Follen Hill. Swift wrote in her journal about climbing the observatory from which she could see the White Mountains and Boston Harbor. The next year, she and fifteen of her classmates, unaware of Follen's sudden death in a fire onboard a steamship, took the stagecoach to East Lexington for the dedication of the church. The girls had a festive day, which included dining at the mansion of town selectman Benjamin Muzzey before returning to school.

One controversial topic conspicuously absent from lectures at the normal school was abolition. Although many of the school's lecturers were known abolitionists, when they were invited to speak, it was not about abolition. Despite their own passionate stance on abolition, Peirce and Mann thought the subject was too explosive for the school, and would open them to criticism. Peirce had seen its volatility firsthand on Nantucket. While he continued to advocate for abolition in private, he kept the issue separate from the life of the school. However, Harriett Peirce must not have felt as constricted as her husband because Lydia Stow Adams wrote about attending an Anti-Slavery meeting with Harriet and four other students that first year.[39]

Peirce's health was fragile and the hard work of opening and administering the school had worn him out. The day did not contain enough hours to get everything done to his high standard. One of his later assistants, Electa Lincoln (Walton), wrote about that first year: "Let it be remembered that there was no appropriation for assistance of any kind, and Mr. Peirce took it upon himself to supervise or actually perform most menial services for the school." These included janitorial duties such as wrestling with recalcitrant furnaces and stoves. In one journal entry, Peirce wrote, "No session – cleaning stove funnel." Mann wrote that Peirce "paid a dear price" for the insufficient funding by the state.

"When cold weather came he would stoke the classroom stove at midnight, and then rise again at four in the morning to keep it going. After every snowfall," he recalled, "neighbors recognized his familiar form shoveling the walk between the boardinghouse and the schoolhouse."[40]

In addition, the school was subject to contentious debate as to whether state government should continue to fund the training of teachers. Peirce felt honor bound to answer, or try to answer, all correspondence about the school. The task was time consuming because the school received many letters, including from educators and statesmen in other states who wanted to emulate the Massachusetts model, as well as letters from many of its critics. Peirce sometimes traveled to Boston to lobby at the legislature on the school's behalf.

Peirce worried about gaps in his pupils' background and training. In a letter to Mann in mid-July of the first year, he expressed concern that a single year was insufficient to prepare the girls to be professional teachers. Given how much there was to learn, Peirce wanted to extend their period of training to a second year.

Peirce also worried about students who did not measure up to his exacting standards. In one instance, he complained about the fitness of three pupils referred to as "C", "B" and "K" who he worried had no future in teaching and would not make good teachers. "It is time they were withdrawn from the institution. It is not right for those to continue who feel no interest in its object." The girls withdrew, his records noting that three girls "were connected with the school for a short time only."[41]

Peirce also worried about gifted students whose talents exceeded those of the rest. One of these was Mary Swift. Peirce was troubled by her inability to continue her study of Greek, which she had started on

Nantucket, because Greek was not part of the normal school curriculum. Feeling responsible, Peirce tutored her in Greek three nights a week, leaving his own home to give her lessons in the dormitory. Typical of his way of dealing with students, Swift said that he approached the idea of the tutorial "as if it were a favor to himself" and not to her.[42]

At the end of its first academic year in the spring of 1840, the Lexington Normal School graduated twenty-five young women, the first specifically trained teachers in America. They were justifiably proud then, and throughout their lives, reflecting upon their accomplishments years later. Louisa Harris wrote a poem in 1884 about the "early battle fought" by the reformers. The first normal school students were proud of their role in history. "We helped the planting of that vine."[43]

Mary Swift

Framingham State University Archive

Enrollment increased to thirty students in the second year and the model school and the normal school were both established and running smoothly. Mann wrote in his journal that he was happy with the school and with Peirce's leadership.

Unfortunately, Mann's feelings of success and happiness would be short-lived as the school was about to face stiff opposition from several direction.

Note: Stearns was the third director of the Normal School from1849-1855.

Chapter 8: Threats Against the Normal School

The demanding workload, plus the mental strain from the political aspect of his job, weighed increasingly heavily on Cyrus Peirce. Despite rising enrollment, Peirce became increasingly despondent. Political opposition to the normal school was growing, some from unexpected quarters.

While his students were devoted to Peirce, many on the outside wanted the normal school movement to fail. From the beginning, "powerful enemies" set out to destroy the Lexington school. Enemies in the state legislature were "determined to abolish these schools without delay and lost no time in moving to the attack."[1]

A second normal school had opened in Barre, Massachusetts late in 1839, under the leadership of a more conservative educator, Reverend Samuel Newman, a former professor at Bowdoin College and a Congregationalist. Mann was sensitive that his appointment of the Unitarian Peirce had created controversy, so he chose Newman to balance the equation and placate those who accused him of promoting a Unitarian agenda.

Even in its first winter in existence, a surprise attack on the normal schools was launched in the legislature with a proposal to abandon the entire experiment. This was coupled with support for the attack in the governor's office. Marcus Morton, a Democrat, had unseated Whig governor, Edward Everett, who had supported the creation of the normal schools. Morton thought the responsibility for education should be at the local, not the state, level. Not only did he favor dismantling the normal schools, he also favored the abolition of the board of education.

Mann was stunned and surprised by the nature and scope of these attacks and feared that everything he and others had worked for was in jeopardy. In a speech given several years later, he described the attack on the board and the normal schools as one that combined all their foes into one. "It united them all into one phalanx, animated by various motives, but intent upon a single object."[2]

Mann said the proposal to abolish both the board and the normal schools aimed to "throw back with indignity, into the hands of Mr. Dwight, the money he had given for their support." Surprisingly, many teachers joined the opposition. Mann said their pride had been injured by the implication that their own training had been substandard in their not having attended a teacher-training institute. It was discouraging that even the profession he was trying to help was resistant.[3]

Conservatives in the state warned that the normal school movement had an anti-American agenda because it had copied the Prussian system of teacher training. They pointed out that Prussia was a despotic state and, therefore, not a model for a democracy. In addition, fear-mongers raised the specter of "religious bigotry" as the normal school movement was portrayed as a Unitarian crusade, intent on undermining the Congregationalist underpinnings of New England. Mann's appointment of Reverend Newman to head the Barre Normal School had not succeeded in ameliorating or halting this avenue of criticism.[4]

Even worse, Mann learned that the majority of his own board had decided in secret to abandon the normal school project. This was the greatest blow of all, as he had been given no forewarning. These were the men he counted on, and who were charged with supervising state education. To his great dismay and consternation, a majority on the board was leading the fight against him behind his back. When he read their reasons, it did not seem the situation could get any worse.

The schism on the board resulted in both a minority and a majority report being submitted to the legislature in 1840. The majority report was written in opposition to Mann and the normal schools. Mostly authored by Allen W. Dodge, it argued that the normal schools were an attempt to "Prussianize education in Massachusetts." Dodge, a member of the legislature, had studied at the Andover Theological Seminary, established by the orthodox Congregationalists when the Unitarians took control of Harvard. He argued that the board was a "menace to self-government" because it centralized power in their committee. Dodge claimed that power had been stripped from local school committees where it rightly belonged. The report further claimed that "no benefit" was derived from the establishment of the normal schools and proposed refunding Dwight's donation. The Commonwealth's high schools were "fully adequate" to provide a "competent supply of teachers." They wrote, "every person, who has himself undergone a process of instruction, must acquire, by that very process, the art of instructing others." The normal schools were, in essence, superfluous.

The report further argued that teachers trained at the expense of Massachusetts might take their training elsewhere, and that Massachusetts should not take on the task of educating "teachers for the rest of the Union." In their final sentence, the majority asked the legislature to abolish both the board of education and the normal schools because "the interests of our Common Schools would rest upon a safer and more solid foundation." The report embodied everything Mann stood against and, worse, it had taken him completely by surprise.[5]

The minority on the board who supported the normal schools was also taken by surprise because their fellow members had met in secret. They complained to the legislature that they had not even been given the courtesy of seeing a copy of the majority report before it was submitted. They expressed outrage that even Mann, the secretary of the board, had not been permitted to see or comment on it, all of which led to their having had only two hours to write their rebuttal.

The minority report gave a brief history of the normal school in Lexington, praising its early success. As for problems, it argued that one year was insufficient time to prove the value of training teachers. It rebuked the majority for its willingness to "violate" signed contracts, citing the three-year lease for the school buildings in Lexington. They also pointed out that Peirce had given up a lucrative job on Nantucket to direct the Lexington school; terminating the experiment so quickly would be unfair to him and to the normal school pupils presently enrolled. As for returning Dwight's donation of $10,000, the report claimed it was "now proposed to treat [him] with contempt," casting it "back into the face of the generous donor." As for costs of supporting the normal schools, it was pointed that the amount spent on them paled in comparison to the "hundreds of thousands of dollars" spent by the state over many decades in support of Harvard. In sum, the minority pleaded with the legislature that the current eight-month trial not be "broken off as soon as begun." Since no graduates had yet gone on to teach, it was premature to judge the effectiveness of the school's graduates. "They will have fallen, prematurely, by the hand which should have sustained them."

Two letters in praise of the Lexington Normal School, its students and the leadership of Peirce, were attached to the minority report. Dr. Samuel Gridley Howe, director of the Institution for the Blind, known as the Perkins School, wrote one of them. One of the foremost educators in the world, he pioneered new techniques for teaching those previously considered uneducable. Howe, a fellow Unitarian, was a close friend of Mann's. As a school director, Howe knew firsthand the difficulty in finding competent, well-trained teachers. He wrote of visiting the Lexington school more than once during its first year and sang its praises as "the best school I ever saw, in this or any other country." The discipline at the school was "perfect" and its students "thoroughly understand every subject," their interest in them being "deep and constant." He also referred to the school's ethical culture. "The moral nature is as much cultivated as the intellectual, and the training of each goes on at the same time." He said that hoped the normal schools would graduate hundreds of teachers "to take charge of the rising generation" and argued that future generations of students would bless them for it. In fact, Howe had sent one of his teachers, Eliza Rogers, to attend the school to improve her teaching, and also hired two of the new graduates. They became the first teachers of the blind and deaf Laura Bridgman whose educational progress eventually attracted worldwide attention.

The second letter was from George B. Emerson, a former principal of Boston High School, and long-time president of the Boston Society of Natural History that became the Boston Museum of Science. Emerson also wrote about his visits to the Lexington Normal School. "I spent the day with more pleasure than I ever received from a similar examination." What he observed "far surpassed what I had expected," he wrote, remarking especially on the intellectual rigor required of the normal school students. He also praised the model school, predominantly taught by the student teachers. "Never before," he wrote, had he "seen little children so completely under the right influence of their teachers – so fully awake."[6] (Note)

As the debate raged in the legislature, Peirce told Mann that he was tired, discouraged, ill, and intending to resign. Mann begged his friend to stay on, arguing that his resignation at such a critical point would be "disastrous to the cause." Reluctantly, Peirce agreed to continue.[7]

Fortunately, support in the legislature for the normal schools and the board of education was stronger than Mann expected. When the proposal to abolish them came to the floor of the House in March 1840, it was defeated 245-182. Mann would never again face such fierce opposition in the State House. There would be other attacks, but never again from within his own board. Board members who had advocated the abolition of the board and of the normal schools resigned or were replaced.

Peirce stayed at the Lexington school for two more years. Gratifyingly, enrollment rose each year. Mann also tried to make the job more manageable and more appealing for Peirce to try to keep him at the school. Funds were made available to hire teaching assistants to reduce Peirce's teaching responsibilities. Mann also gave in to Peirce on the mandatory period of training, which was increased to two full years.

The Peirces suffered a personal tragedy in 1841 when their niece, Amelia L. Coffin, a student at the school for five months, died. Amelia was the seventeen-year-old daughter of Harriet's only brother, William, who had died the year the Peirces moved to Lexington. Peirce had written the pamphlet to Nantucket in support of the high school with William Coffin, and it was William who had taken charge of Peirce's private school when he became principal of the high school. The loss of William's daughter was a huge emotional blow to both Peirces.

However, Mann's annual report in 1840 was optimistic. He reported that the model school, then in its second year, had garnered a high reputation in Lexington. More parents wanted their children to be taught in the school than could be accommodated. He further reported that most of the graduates of the normal school had procured jobs and been well received around the state.

Mann's 1840 report included a separate report written by board member Robert Rantoul, Jr. who wrote of the Lexington school's enrollment rising from three to thirty-five women in one year. The students who had graduated and been "universally" successful; he reported that they were admirable for their "zeal and indefatigable perseverance which merit hearty commendation." Rantoul, an influential Unitarian lawyer in Boston, attributed the school's success to the "ability, fidelity and devotion" of Cyrus Peirce. What a difference a year had made.[8]

In the fall of 1840, a third, coeducational, normal school opened in Bridgewater under the leadership of Colonel Nicholas Tillinghast, a retired army officer and former teacher at the West Point Military Academy.

Teachers at the normal schools, such as Peirce's assistant, Electa Lincoln, lectured at state-funded training seminars open to all the state's teachers. The Teacher Institutes gave teachers a chance to talk with each other and to be exposed to new methods and philosophies of teaching. The institutes were well attended and helped to expand the reach and acceptance of the normal schools' methods.

Given their initial success, the legislature voted to continue the normal schools for an additional three years. Two powerful friends of Mann led that effort: Senate President Josiah Quincy, Jr. and Thomas Kinnicutt, Speaker of the House. Support also came from John Gorham Palfrey, a Unitarian minister who had been Dean of the Harvard Divinity

School for five years.

The normal schools seemed firmly established. However, despite the victory in the legislature, and despite growing support from rank and file educators across the state, trouble was brewing, particularly in regard to school leadership in two of the normal schools.

First, Reverend Newman in Barre was on his deathbed; when he died, the school was closed for two years for lack of an adequate replacement, an indication of how difficult it was for Mann to find suitable directors for the new normal schools.

In Lexington, Peirce once again told Mann he intended to resign. Exhausted and in ill health, he wrote in his letter of resignation that he had done all he could, and his "exhausted nature calls for repose." "And now my dear Sir," he wrote to Mann, "let me go." If he were to stay at the normal school any longer, "I must lay my bones here."[9]

Reluctantly, Mann recognized that Peirce was incapable of carrying on and he accepted his friend's resignation. Harriet Peirce wrote to Mann in secret to ensure he accepted her husband's resignation, writing that Peirce was "too ill to teach" any longer. She did not want Mann to pressure Peirce to stay on.[10]

To make matters worse for Mann, Lexington's town fathers had decided to withdraw their financial support for the school, which meant the normal school would have to relocate. "The community says they do not want normal schools, and they will not patronize them," wrote Peirce. In a rare bit of sarcasm, he added, "Well, then, the Lord send them something better which they do not need."[11]

Before he returned to Nantucket, there was a gathering in Lexington in Peirce's honor attended by former graduates and a variety of dignitaries. In his address, Peirce reminded everyone of the importance of the teaching profession and said that his years in Lexington had been the happiest of his life. Students read from the school newspaper and golden pencils were presented to both Peirces. Reverend Robert Waterston of Boston said that he had heard that Nantucket was treeless, but that Peirce, nevertheless, had transplanted a tree from there in the guise of the normal school - a tree of knowledge. "I trust acorns enough have fallen from it to sow the whole continent."[12]

The Liberator Files

Samuel J. May, educator and Unitarian minister, successfully took the helm of the school from 1842-1844. A graduate of the divinity department at Harvard, May resigned as the pastor of a church in Norwell, Massachusetts to take the job in Lexington. Peirce had great respect for May and was pleased that such a man had been tapped to replace him. May and Peirce not only became lifelong friends, but May went on to write an early biography of Peirce. (Note)

Weary and still in mourning, the Peirces packed up and headed back to Nantucket, hoping to lead a quieter life. Peirce planned to return to the classroom and resume his place in Nantucket's society.

Note: Emerson was also instrumental in the establishment of the Arnold Arboretum.

Note: May was the uncle of the writer Louisa May Alcott.

Chapter 9: "A wound of some years" - Nantucket's Continuing Segregation During Peirce's Absence

The controversy over the admission of Eunice Ross to Nantucket High School had continued unabated while Peirce had been working in Lexington. The issue continued to dominate town politics. In a June 1840 town meeting, Edward M. Gardner moved that the "Town will instruct the School Committee to permit coloured children to enter all or any public schools." Had the motion passed, seventeen-year-old Eunice Ross would have been able to enter Nantucket High School. But it was

Nantucket Town Records

defeated.[1]

During 1841, a major outlet for argument and frustration for those on both sides of the issue was in the local newspapers, mostly through letters to the editor in the *Inquirer* and a new paper, the *Islander*. For example, abolitionist Nathaniel Barney, writing under the pseudonym "Thy Friend," attacked the school committee in the *Islander*. "Are your public schools open freely, for instruction of your own children of color? Does your school committee – who should be men of intelligence and moral worth – do they, in school regulations, recognize no oppression?"[2]

As another annual town meeting approached, the abolitionists organized to get their candidates elected to the school committee by printing and widely distributing "Liberty Hall Tickets" which listed their favored candidates. The ethics of this novel approach was questioned for weeks afterward. Two of the so-called "Liberty Hall boys" were criticized for campaigning in the black community of New Guinea "with especial reference to abolitionism" in attempting to garner the black vote.[3]

Samuel H. Jenks

Nantucket Historical Association

One of the most outspoken opponents of admitting Eunice Ross, or any black child to the public schools, was Samuel H. Jenks. In fact, Jenks had been a member of the school committee that originally denied Ross's admission. Re-elected in 1841, Jenks's attacks on the abolitionists became more strident. He repeatedly accused them of plotting "the destruction of our public schools," schools which he reminded them, he had worked for so long to create. On this issue he parted company with his former in-laws, the Peirces, and with many other members of Harriet Peirce's family who were on the side of school integration. Harriet's niece Rebecca, for example, was married to the abolitionist Augustus Morse who had succeeded Peirce as high school principal.

There was more abolitionist activity on the island in 1841 than in previous years, undoubtedly due more to the town's refusal to admit Eunice Ross to the high school, than to off-island events at the state and national levels. At the Annual Anti-Slavery Fair's crafts and handiwork table in Boston that year, the Nantucket chapter raised more money than any other town in the state. At "the head of the host," said the meeting's chairperson in an article in the *Islander*, "stood Nantucket unrivalled."

1841 was also the year that Obed Barney opened his Anti-Slavery Library over his Main Street store in response to the closure of the Atheneum to black people. Everyone in town was invited "free of expense" to avail themselves of an "extensive collection" of anti-slavery literature, as good, he boasted, as could be found anywhere in the country.

In March, the Nantucket Anti-Slavery Society put a cryptic notice in the local papers, announcing a "special meeting" to discuss measures the abolitionists would take "to advance the object which they have in view." The unspecified and unnamed object could have been none other than to integrate the public schools. Daniel Jones, Jr., an abolitionist and a member of the school committee, chaired the meeting. Unfortunately, no records of the meeting have survived, but whatever occurred, it did not "advance the object" in question, and the schools remained firmly segregated.

The Anti-Slavery Association hit the lecture circuit around New England every summer with conventions promoting the cause of abolition. It made the trek to the island every August. In 1841, a month before Nantucket was slated to host the convention, black abolitionist David Ruggles was forcibly evicted from the Nantucket steamship when he refused to ride in the second-class section. Not wanting a repeat of the incident in August, local abolitionists went to New Bedford to escort the inter-racial group of visitors to the convention. Despite an argument on the docks, the abolitionists won the day and the group sailed to the island together and without incident.

The *Islander*, increasingly supportive of the abolitionists, encouraged Nantucketers, to attend the conference, if only out of curiosity. Visitors to the island for the three-day convention that year included William Lloyd Garrison himself, as well as other well-known abolitionist speakers such as Wendell Phillips and Parker Pillsbury. Also on hand was a newcomer, a virtual unknown who was a recent runaway from slavery. William C. Coffin, a New Bedford abolitionist with relatives on the island, had heard the young man speak and invited him to attend the island convention. This man was Frederick Douglass.

While on Nantucket, Douglass was asked to stand up and describe the life of a slave, his first speech to a mixed-race audience, and today there is a plaque at the Nantucket Atheneum commemorating the event. Douglass's eloquence in describing his life as a slave held the audience in thrall, and the Anti-Slavery Association immediately hired Douglass as a speaker on its permanent lecture circuit. Thus, it was on Nantucket that Frederick Douglass's historic career as an orator and spokesman was launched.

Local abolitionists added their voices to those of the off-islanders at the convention. Former African School teacher Anna Gardner spoke, as well as other local leaders Nathaniel Barney, George Bradburn, David Joy, Isaac Austin, and Austin's daughter, Charlotte Austin. It was significant that the convention took place at the Nantucket Atheneum, which had only recently lifted its ban on abolitionist meetings.

A few weeks later, the island hosted the annual Education Convention. Nantucket was a curious choice to hold a statewide conference because of the expense and time required to get to the island, as well as the limited availability of accommodations. Horace Mann chaired it, indicating the importance of the conference. It is possible that it was held on the island that year at the behest of Cyrus and Harriet Peirce to give moral support and assistance to the Nantucket abolitionists in the cause of school integration. Isaac Austin, president of the

Nantucket Education Society, was a leading abolitionist like most of his fellows on the education committee. Unfortunately, no records of the convention have survived, but there was undoubtedly much talk about Eunice Ross and the school committee's continuing refusal to admit her, or any other black children to the high school or any other white public school.

In 1842, the issue of school integration continued to dominate town politics. At the annual town meeting early in the year, the school committee reported that forty-nine students were being successfully educated at the segregated York Street School. They admitted the need for "some plan, whereby the higher branches of education may be communicated to the children of the coloured population, as fully and satisfactorily, as to those of the white citizens." This surprising admission acknowledged that the black children were not receiving education equal to their white counterparts. The committee did, however, not suggest the obvious remedy – to admit black children to the existing grammar schools or the high school. A proposal was put forth, instead, to build a new grammar school in the southern part of the town for the exclusive use of black children, not far from New Guinea, which would result in another segregated school.

The 1842 school committee election was intense, with an astonishing fifty-six men running for the thirteen positions. Ten black men were on the ballot, including Eunice's father, James Ross. None of them won seats, but several prominent abolitionists did win, including Nathaniel Barney. The results, however, were mixed, as several prominent abolitionists were unseated, including Isaac Austin and David Joy. Discouragingly for the integrationists, William C. Starbuck, an outspoken anti-integrationist garnered the most votes. That Starbuck was one of Harriet Peirce's nephews, illustrates how differences over race divided families. The polarized school committee reflected the town's increasing political divide about admitting black children to mainstream schools. Nonetheless, when Nathaniel Barney at the next town meeting proposed, in the interests of "duty and justice," that people "lay aside our party feelings and prejudices, and place the Scholars in that school with reference to their ability to said schools" the motion, strangely enough, passed. For the moment it looked as if victory was in sight for the integrationists. But it was not to be.[4] (Note)

Then, as now, town meetings in New England lasted for as many days as necessary to complete the work on the agenda. The gathering at which Barney's motion had passed had not been well attended. When word got around town about the vote to integrate the schools, many saw it as an example of questionable ethics and trickery by the abolitionists. As a consequence, the meeting the next day was more fully attended and the vote of the day before was reconsidered and repealed, thwarting school integration once again.

The black community responded quickly to the 1842 town meeting's vote to rescind the vote to integrate the schools. A meeting was called at Zion's Church, an African Methodist Episcopal church. The second black church in Nantucket, it stood just up the hill from the African Meeting House. At this meeting, the black community composed a lengthy address to the town that was printed in both local newspapers and in the *Liberator*. First among the resolutions was that, since Massachusetts recognized no racial distinction with regard to education, the Nantucket black community had "the right of having their youth educated in the same schools which are common to the more favored members of this community."

This eloquent address portrayed the black community as "oppressed" and asserted that the recent vote of the town to discriminate against them was not a new practice on Nantucket, but was "a wound of some years' standing, the sensation of which, if it be chafed is apt to become keen." Both the laws of the Commonwealth and of the U.S. Constitution were appealed to, arguing that "complexion" was the reason for the discrimination. They asked "this intelligent and Christian community, is it right, is it just?" The address pointed out the inequity of a having a separate schoolhouse for their children, without the "several gradations" or levels provided for the white children of Nantucket.[5]

This long and persuasive appeal by the black community received no response. Not a single letter to the editor was printed in the following issues of the two local newspapers. In an era when debates on the pages of newspapers were common, not drawing a single response would be significant. The address had fallen upon deaf ears, not even given the courtesy of a single response.

In mid-August of 1842, the annual Anti-Slavery Convention came to the island once again. Instead of the normal three days, however, this one was slated for three additional days, demonstrating the importance of Nantucket's continuing school segregation. Leading abolitionists traveled to the island, including William Lloyd Garrison, and the fiery black spokesman, C. Lenox Remond, a man who came to believe that slavery would only be ended through violence. Frederick Douglass was not present this year.

Reverend Stephen S. Foster of New Hampshire so incensed many islanders with his "Brotherhood of Thieves" speech that riots broke out. Subtitled a "true picture of the American Church and Clergy," Foster spoke in support of a resolution questioning the Christianity of anyone who owned a slave. He described slaveholding as "dreadful libel on the Christian church to affirm that slaveholders" were ever truly Christian, or that Christ, "the Prince of Emancipators" would ever offer slaveholders "Christian fellowship." The resolution, and Foster's speech, were aimed at the established Protestant churches in New England - the Baptists, Episcopalians and Methodists, which all had member churches in slaveholding states and whose congregations included slave owners.

Foster accused southern churches of five crimes: theft of slaves' labor, kidnapping, murder, piracy and adultery. In deliberately inflammatory rhetoric, he called the Southern clergy "pimps of Satan." He claimed that the affiliation of northern denominations of those churches made them complicit in sustaining slavery. He singled out local ministers for their collaboration with horrors of slavery.[6]

Islanders took Foster's attack on their local clergy personally, and his words led to heated discussions all over town the next day. That evening, an unruly mob gathered outside the Atheneum. The next evening, another crowd formed, and the situation quickly deteriorated. Several members pushed inside to heckle and interrupt the speakers. Others milled around outside. Eventually their anger erupted. Rotten eggs and other missiles were hurled into the hall, breaking several windows and the meeting adjourned abruptly in confusion and panic.

The trustees of the Atheneum, fearing for the building's safety, closed their doors to the Anti-Slavery Convention, even though the convention was only mid-way through its scheduled meetings and in mid-debate on several resolutions. The abolitionists hastily reconvened in Franklin Hall on South Water Street. A mob formed again outside that hall, and there was a "shower of rotten eggs, in an exceedingly nauseous and offensive state of putrefaction." Franklin Hall also closed its doors to the abolitionists.

The abolitionists, many of them influential town citizens and officeholders, appealed to Nantucket's town officials to restore order. An emergency town meeting was held to discuss the riots and consider the Anti-Slavery Society's request to use the town hall to finish their convention. A five-member committee was selected to investigate why town authorities had been ineffective in quelling the riots and a vote was taken to censure the rioters.

The abolitionists were allowed to use the town hall on the last day of the convention. The daytime hours were peaceful enough, but at nightfall, another crowd formed outside. Once again eggs and stones were thrown. "An unhatched chicken remained for days afterward stuck to the shingles," recalled one eyewitness. At a town meeting later that evening, Isaac Austin, an abolitionist and school committee member, exhibited a brick and a piece of coal that had been thrown into his house, which he said had endangered the lives of his family.[7]

The off-island speakers and attendees left the island with memories of being the target of violence and of being forced to convene in three different locations. The people of the island were deeply shaken.

Shortly after the Anti-Slavery Convention disbanded, another town meeting was convened. The five-man committee charged with investigating the riots submitted an inconclusive report. No one was blamed for the riots and no one was charged. The sheriff was questioned, but he denied any knowledge of the riots until after the convention adjourned, a highly unlikely claim given the size and intimacy of the island community. But that was his story and he stuck to it. The deputy sheriff reported that he had witnessed the Atheneum riot and testified that he had been injured. He stated that particles of "shivered glass [had]

lodged on the back of his neck." Several island magistrates, he said, had
been at the meeting, but none had given him any orders; he attested that
it was beyond his duty to intervene "in the absence of orders." Two
selectmen also testified they had rushed to the Atheneum upon word of
the riot, but did not think the disturbance serious enough to take action.[8]

There was no further investigation. The riots seem to have taken the
island by surprise. Certainly shock was expressed in the newspapers. A
column in the *Inquirer* called the riots "a blot on the character of the
town." The selectmen were criticized for failing to take action to
suppress the mob when it first gathered. The bulk of the blame, however,
was heaped on Foster for having incited the mobs by his inflammatory
and insulting language. It was easier to blame an off-islander known for
fiery rhetoric than to blame one's neighbors. Just as the black
community's address had been met with silence, the riots, too, were
followed by silence.

Forty years later, discussion of the riots was still a sensitive subject
on the island. When they were brought up in a series of letters to the
editor in 1885, a debate about them ensued, despite the passage of so
much time. One eyewitness, writing under the initials "WRE," recalled
Foster's speech. His account elicited seven responses over a three-month
period by writers who called themselves "Recollection" and "Old
Guard." Both writers asserted that the mobs were not caused by Foster's
attack. "Recollection" said that Foster's speech had been a convenient
excuse for a "well-dressed mob" to attack the abolitionists, an attack that
had been planned well in advance by a group and not motivated by
religious fervor or a desire to defend the clergy, as had been frequently
claimed. In fact, he asserted that the leaders of the mob were not people
known for their religious zeal. Rather, the riots were against those who

opposed slavery. "It was a wicked mob – a heartless mob – a cruel mob." The writer "Old Guard" echoed the sentiments of "Recollection." He wrote that efforts had been made before the arrival of the abolitionists to gather the most nauseating objects to hurl. "Respectable citizens," he claimed, "offered double the price of good eggs for rotten ones." [9]

Although abolition was a contentious issue in the 1840s, the riots concerned something closer to home: the movement to integrate Nantucket's schools and to admit black children to any island school. The quest for school integration brought the issue of race to Nantucket's doorstep. It was expedient for Nantucketers to blame the off-islanders for meddling in island affairs. When the off-island abolitionists had arrived for their six-day convention, islanders who opposed the admission of black children to the schools, were in no mood to be hospitable. Foster's attack on the clergy was just the excuse they needed, giving the protesters the chance to gain the moral high ground by seeming to defend the clergy. In his final letter to the editor, "Recollection" left no doubt as to the real cause of the riots. The mob action simply "grew out of the question of admitting a girl of African descent to the High School."[10]

Throughout the years of debate over school integration, anti-integrationists often referred to Foster's speech at the Atheneum, blaming it for the pressure to integrate the school system. "Every inhabitant of Nantucket knows the origin of this project," stated school committee chairman Jenks. It was "put into the heads of the ultra Abolitionists here by the incendiary Foster." [11]

In the immediate aftermath of the riots, the issue of race continued to be contentious. Local abolitionists were blamed for bringing the radicals to the island in order to disrupt the community. Others defended the abolitionists. Foster's attack on the churches led one writer to the

Inquirer to point out that Nantucket's own churches were mostly segregated. "R" pointed out that black citizens could not sit on a jury or hold state offices, let alone "have his child educated in the common schools, which are established by law for him as well as others."

It was in the midst of this turmoil that Harriet and Cyrus returned to the island, worn out from their hard work in Lexington.

Note: William C. Starbuck was the eldest son of Harriet's eldest sister Betsey Coffin Starbuck.

Chapter 10: Racism: "A By-Gone Folly?"

Tired and ill, Cyrus Peirce returned to Nantucket in mid-1842. He must have thought he was returning to a place where he could rest and take his rightful place as a respected member of the island community. If so, it was not to be. He was aware the controversy to admit Eunice Ross to the high school had not been resolved during his three-year absence. Perhaps he had been so preoccupied in Lexington that he was not aware of how completely he would be engulfed in the firestorm brewing on the island.

Cyrus and Harriet Peirce returned to Nantucket shortly after the August riots of 1842, and they were immediately re-involved in the politics swirling around the admission of Eunice Ross to the high school where he had once been the principal. The couple also became involved in a fugitive slave case causing turmoil in the state. Peirce did not get the respite he sought when he resigned from the normal school. His moral compass, however, would not enable him to sit back and let injustice prevail.

Harriet Peirce quickly resumed her role in the abolitionist movement becoming an officer in the Nantucket Women's Anti-Slavery Society. In January 1841, the Congregational church had barred black women from attending the Nantucket Women's Anti-Slavery Society meeting. With Eliza Barney, Harriet wrote that the church had put "impossible" conditions upon their organization. The women said they had tried to compromise with the church by offering to divide the room in half, with white women sitting on one side. and black women on the other, but when their compromise was refused, the abolitionist women chose alternative sites for their meetings. (Note)

All the abolitionist groups on the island became involved in the case of George Latimer, a fugitive slave who had fled to Boston with his wife Rebecca. He was arrested in October 1842, and jailed under the fugitive slave law, as the state deliberated whether to return the couple to slavery as the law required. The Latimer case became a cause célèbre in Massachusetts with Free Latimer Societies organized across the state to fight the return of the couple. Nathaniel Barney and Cyrus Peirce headed the Nantucket chapter.

In November 1842, Nantucket's Free Latimer chapter held a three-hour rally at the town hall.

Speakers included Barney and Peirce, Henry Clapp, Jr., and high school principal, Augustus Morse. Both were related to Peirce by marriage. Barney told those assembled that he had met George Latimer in Boston and had found him "an intelligent young man." At the same meeting, Peirce criticized New England churches for their apathy, echoing some of the sentiments expressed by Foster earlier in the year. Peirce declared that he had never once heard a sermon preached against slavery in his fifty years as a parishioner. [1](Note)

George Latimer

Nantucket Historical Association

The Massachusetts Anti-Slavery Society organized a massive Free

Latimer petition drive across the state. Anna Gardner, the local secretary, helped to organize the Nantucket effort. Another public rally was held in December to write a second petition to the state legislature demanding the passage of a law to prohibit public officers "from officially lending their aid to slavery, by holding in custody fugitive slaves, in order to secure their return to bondage."[2] Cyrus Peirce was secretary of the rally, which was well attended according to the *Inquirer*. So much for retiring to a quiet island life to recuperate.

Eventually both Latimers obtained their freedom from money raised by the abolitionists to pay their owner. The petition on their behalf successfully altered Massachusetts's law with the passage of the Personal Liberty Act, which forbade judges, justices of the peace, and other state

National Archives

officers from aiding in the arrest, detention, or delivery of a person who was designated a fugitive slave. Massachusetts had taken a bold stance against the Fugitive Slave Act. (Note)

At the annual Anti-Slavery Fair held at the end of 1842, local abolitionists felt a sense of victory because of the success of the Latimer case. Both Peirces spoke at a dinner, he about the success of the Free Latimer petition and she about the "rapid progress of the anti-slavery cause." Harriet Peirce gave a brief history of the Nantucket abolitionists, recalling that the first anti-slavery meeting on the island had been attended by only "two or three" people at a time when the "claims of the slaves were not at all recognized." [3]

Despite their seeming victory, the abolitionists realized that the Personal Liberty Act, while a step in the right direction, was insufficient because it only protected fugitives who made their way to Massachusetts. They also realized that it was not feasible to raise money to buy the freedom of every fugitive. Nor were they comfortable in the ethics of buying a slave's freedom since paying the slave owner validated the ownership of a person.

Another petition drive was launched. This one proposed to amend the Constitution of the United States, that "direct taxes shall be apportioned among the several states . . . according to their numbers of *free* persons." The amendment would eliminate the unfair advantage the South had in the House of Representatives because they were allowed to count each slave as three-fifths of a person. Once again, grassroots abolitionist groups sprang into action, soliciting signatures from around the state. Cyrus Peirce led the Nantucket chapter. Peirce was well known throughout the state because of his leadership at the normal school, so it was no surprise that he was given the honor of delivering the petition to Washington on behalf of the entire state. Nathaniel Barney wrote in the *Inquirer*, "It is a source of no little price to us, and it is no small honor to Nantucket, that our esteemed fellow-citizen Cyrus Peirce had the honor of bearing this noble petition to Washington." [4]

More than 51,000 signatures were gathered and put into a single continuous narrow roll. Peirce wrote in a letter to Electa Lincoln that the large spool of names was as big as a washtub, and attracted much attention from his fellow passengers on the train from Boston.

National Archives

Unfortunately, it is among only a few letters that exist from Peirce, especially as his power of description is compelling and vivid. "I had the Petition enclosed in a large cylindrical box, about 2 1/2 dimensions. Some conjectured that it contained a new invention, for which I was going to Headquarters to get a patent." He wrote that he enjoyed the mystery and drama of the moment, keeping his fellow passengers guessing, and refusing to disclose the contents of the cylinder. He made further adjustments to the contraption in Washington. "When I arrived at Washington, I had a frame fitted to it, so that it would revolve. It looked very much like one of your new-fashioned barrel churns."[5]

He stayed at Mrs. McDaniel's boarding house when he was in the capital with six Massachusetts delegates who lived there, including Nantucketer Barker Burnell, an old friend who was in his second term in Congress. Peirce and Burnell had served on several committees together on Nantucket in the causes of education and temperance.

Peirce met with former president John Quincy Adams who had returned to the House of Representatives as part of the Massachusetts delegation. The two men met to work out a strategy to present the giant petition to the House of Representatives. The problem they faced was the "gag rule." Passed in 1839, the gag rule prevented all petitions regarding slavery from being presented to Congress. So many petitions had flooded the Southern-dominated Congress, that it had put an end to them. How could the Latimer petition get to the floor?

For four days, Adams attempted to get the Latimer petition considered. On the first day, Burnell introduced his fellow islander. He and Peirce carried the contraption into the House and laid it on Adams' table where "unrolled," Peirce wrote, it was "almost 1/2 a mile in length, and rolled up nearly as large round as a barrel." He reported "it nearly hid Mr. A. from the view of the whole House so that in order to be seen and heard he was obliged to step out from behind it." According to Peirce, the petition attracted much attention and "excited more wrath," from Southern representatives.

> Some called it "Wash Tub", others, "The
> Smut-Machine"mand some one thing and some
> another. Bless me! How the sight of that big
> roll did make those Philistines of the South
> rage and foam and stamp and gnash their
> teeth! They threatened and and looked daggers,
> sometimes at me for bringing there, but more
> frequently at Mr. A – for having the audacity to
> present it.[6]

But the gag rule was the law of the land and it could not be overcome. The doorkeeper in the House informed Peirce and Burnell that Peirce would not be permitted on the floor again, even though custom regularly allowed friends of delegates onto the floor. Burnell responded angrily to the South Carolinian representative who had precipitated the complaint. "I shall retaliate," he said. "If he is not allowed on this floor, I shall order the door-keeper not to admit any person whomsoever, unless he has the Speaker's permit." Other members of the Massachusetts delegation registered complaints, but they could not prevent Peirce's exclusion from the floor. [7]

While the giant petition was never officially presented to the Congress, Adams and Peirce made a dramatic statement with it nonetheless. Peirce described the anger of Southern representatives for the petition having been "signed by a d.....m'd runaway nigger feller!" Congressmen who supported slavery cursed those who had signed the petition, wishing them to be "doomed one and all, man, woman, and child to the Southern plantations to taste there the sweets of slavery." The gag rule had prohibited them from officially submitting the petition, but Peirce, Burnell and Adams had forced the House to pay attention. As Peirce described it, "After much bluster and smoke, but no real fire or blood, the Petition was, on the third day, referred by the Speaker to the Committee on the Judiciary." In other words, it was dismissed. [8]

The Latimer Petition was never officially filed into the House records and was left to languish in the unfiled and undocumented files of the National Archives. Today only some pieces of it exist, no longer connected in a continuous roll, taken off its spool. The fragments are in in a metal document box, and include the section with Cyrus Peirce's signature, followed by those of a few other Nantucket abolitionists, including Eunice's Ross's brother, James, and that of Absalom Boston.

Despite not being able to officially present the Latimer petition to the House, Peirce did not feel the effort of the Massachusetts abolitions had been in vain. In a letter to the *Inquirer*, he asserted that the very effect of taking the huge petition to the floor had warranted the effort. "I doubt not, in the least, it has effected vastly more for the great cause of human freedom, which we have at heart, by a hundredfold." Despite the gag rule, he and Adams had not been silenced as they had managed to disrupt the proceedings. "For one humble individual of the goodly company of 50,000, and more, I am entirely satisfied with the good that has been done." [9]

Peirce's rising optimism about the efficacy of grassroots political action was further boosted by his election to the Nantucket school committee early in 1843, along with at least eight fellow abolitionists, including the Barney brothers - Nathaniel and Obed. While absent from the previous battle to integrate the Nantucket schools, Peirce was now fully ready to enter the fray. Healthy enough to represent the state's abolitionists in Washington, he was ready to tackle the cause of admitting black students to the schools on the island.

The outgoing school committee had been so divided by the question of integration that they had filed a minority and a majority report with the abolitionists in the minority. The town's finance committee was similarly divided over school integration, and also presented an unprecedented minority and majority report. All these reports were presented on the floor of the 1843 annual town meeting in January, leading to bitter debate, which revolved around whether to integrate black and white children in the public schools. [10]

Nathaniel Barney read the minority report of the school committee aloud, reminding voters that public schools had been "instituted for the good of the whole people." He asked that the school committee be given the power to place children from the York Street School, as the African School had been renamed, into other schools if "an advantage will be

147

gained to the scholar by such a change." After acrimonious debate, he withdrew his motion.

The voice vote taken to accept the minority report into the official record was inconclusive, forcing the tellers to conduct a written vote, unusual for that time period. In the written ballots, the minority report was rejected by fewer than forty votes, 194-160. It was stricken from the record with lines carefully drawn over it.

Nathaniel Barney was nothing, if not determined, at this meeting. Moments after the minority report's rejection, he moved that black students be admitted to any town school for which they were qualified. The intent of his motion was subverted when pro-segregationist Starbuck amended it to read that the "African School be continued as heretofore." The changed motion passed, the town formally voting that black children would continue to be restricted to the York Street School.

Two days later, the debate shifted to the two reports of the finance committee. The first item put to town vote was a $500 appropriation supporting the segregated York Street School. Intriguingly, the town voted to discontinue the appropriation, effectively abolishing the school by withdrawing all its funding. After that surprising vote, a trio of abolitionists, Charles W. Rand, Edward W. Gardner and Alfred Folger, submitted the finance committee's minority. Their report chastised the town for funding the York Street School, and for practicing racial separation which was contrary to the "letter as well as the spirit of the law." They accused the island of doing a great injustice to the town's children, and recommended the immediate closure of the York Street School. With an appeal to Yankee frugality, they pointed out that the new soon-to-be opened grammar school was costly and that elimination of the York Street School would help defray that expense. As with the school committee's minority report, this one too was rejected, despite the previous vote having stripped the segregated York Street School of funding.

Several days later, the school committee's majority report was brought to the floor. The lengthy report boasted about the impressive progress being made in the Nantucket school system, including the recent building of a third grammar school. The report, full of self-pity, decried how difficult and thankless a job it was to be on the school committee. [11]

Even though a significant number of abolitionists had been elected

Nantucket Town Records

to the school committee, they had not succeeded in integrating the Nantucket schools on the floor of the town meeting. But they had other tricks to play. One week after the annual meeting, the school committee, with Peirce as one of the new members, called for a special town meeting "to consider the subject of the African School." Also included in the warrant, or agenda for the meeting, was the article, "To see if the town will establish a school for all Children having Red Hair." The abolitionists were not above sarcasm.

Debate at the special meeting began on February 25, 1843 with abolitionist Thomas Macy moderating. At first nothing seemed to have changed. Starbuck moved, as he had done at the previous meeting, to continue the "African School" as before. Again, the town accepted Starbuck's motion. Abolitionist Dr. Charles Winslow moved that the school committee be authorized to transfer qualified children out of the York Street School into higher-level white schools, just as Nathaniel Barney had attempted at the previous meeting. Dozens of motions, and many hours later, the abolitionists had once again failed. Starbuck, riding high on his victory, moved to indefinitely postpone all further discussion relating to the schools, in effect asking for a local version of the gag rule.

School committee member and abolitionist John H. Shaw, reminded those assembled that the funding for the York Street School had been eliminated at the previous town meeting and that the town had no choice but to continue discussing schools, as no money was appropriated to run the school. Starbuck retorted that it was within the committee's mandate to be sure that all schools were properly maintained, and the York Street School would have to remain open, as the town had so voted.

An abolitionist in the audience asked Moderator Macy if the town could legally appropriate money to a school specifically designated for black children. Macy replied that, in his opinion, it would be illegal, and he said that the courts would probably agree with him. Starbuck responded that if such were the case, the town had been acting illegally for years and wondered if anyone had "experienced any inconvenience" as a result. Town records dryly note that "replies were made in the affirmative" as the abolitionists and black citizens vocalized their opinion as to the "inconvenience" suffered. On this note, the meeting adjourned. [12]

Not long after the failed attempts to integrate island schools at the two town meetings, C. Lenox Remond, black abolitionist, wrote a letter to Nathaniel Barney that was published on the front page of the *Inquirer* on March 4, 1843.

> On your island of Nantucket, has the
> voice of the people been heard, in
> Town Meeting assembled, refusing a
> well qualified colored girl her place in
> the High School; aye, the citizens of
> an island many miles removed from
> the foul system of slavery; so far, one
> might suppose, that its pestilential
> vapors would become purified; but not
> so; your citizens in their corporate
> capacity conspire against the
> individual rights of a single member,
> and that, be it said to the shame of the
> conspirators in the person of
> a helpless girl!

Undeterred by two votes of the town to keep the school segregated, the abolitionist-dominated school committee resolved to integrate the schools on its own. The majority on the committee decided they had the right to govern town schools as they saw fit.

Ignoring the multiple express votes of the town, plans were drawn up to move some black children into several town schools. Equally determined to prevent them, the pro-segregationists on the school committee called yet another special town meeting. This special meeting lasted four days, even though there were only two articles in the warrant. As it turned out, Cyrus Peirce was a main target at the meeting.

Article One concerned "importing or hiring assistance in the various schools from abroad." This was aimed squarely at Peirce who was being considered as the principal of the new, soon-to-be opened, grammar school. To many Nantucketers, Peirce was from "abroad" as he had not been born on the island, and had spent more time off the island than on it. Starbuck claimed that Nantucket possessed "amply qualified" local teachers and did not need any help from off-islanders. After heated debate, the issue was tabled.

Starbuck's next maneuver was also aimed at Peirce. Starbuck proposed that anyone serving in the public schools be required to resign from the school committee. After lengthy debate, this motion was also tabled. Peirce was a celebrated and famous man who had returned to their community and who had married into one of the island's most influential families. Islanders were reluctant to prevent the eminent educator from being the principal of one of their schools. It did not make sense not to hire him, especially as he had been the first high school principal on the island before he left for Lexington.

Starbuck was not done yet. Next, he demanded the resignation of all school committee members "opposed to conducting the schools agreeably to the wishes of the town." If passed, it would require all the abolitionists on the committee to resign, as it was clear they planned to disregard the town's votes to keep schools segregated. Moderator Macy pointed out that if school committee members were forced to resign, they could not be replaced until the next annual meeting, over ten months in the future.

For three days, debate raged as amendments and counter amendments were put forth, debated and defeated. Two unnamed men engaged in such a heated argument that they had to be called to order by the moderator. The abolitionists were defeated at every turn. On the fourth day, Starbuck's motion calling for all school committee members who supported integration to resign passed.

In desperation, John H. Shaw, school committee member, presented a resolution to force the town to recognize and state clearly the racism of the decision. His carefully-worded motion stated that the African School was be strictly for black children and any child possessing any "taint of African or Indian blood," no matter how qualified, to be educated "apart by themselves." Shaw's motion was defeated. Segregationists were not foolish enough to go on record with their plans so blatantly stated. It seems that advocates on both sides had their eyes on an eventual court case and did not want to pass anything that could potentially weaken their position.

On the last day of the rancorous meeting, another resolution was put forward concerning the hiring of off-island teachers. Shaw moved that the school committee be instructed to give preference to qualified island teachers, but not to limit hiring *only* to them. His motion was tabled. This also related directly to allowing for the appointment of Peirce as principal of the new grammar school.

One final proposal before the meeting adjourned was a last-ditch and doomed effort by Shaw to have the town meeting re-consider its policy regarding segregated schools. He asked those assembled to allow the school committee to keep the African School "for such children as may choose to go there," and to allow those who would not choose to go there to be admitted to other town schools, "without reference to the color of its skin." Unsurprisingly, this was easily defeated and the meeting adjourned.[13]

The Nantucket citizenry had spoken clearly on the issue of school integration. Days had been devoted to heated debate. At the end, it was clear that the men of Nantucket were not willing to integrate the island's schools.

Nevertheless, both sides claimed victory. Abolitionists claimed victory because they had won a majority on the school committee, and the motion to prohibit the hiring of off-islanders had failed.

Segregationists claimed victory because the town had voted to force school committee members to resign if they went ahead with their integration plan.

The segregationists might have believed they had won. If so, they had not counted on the resolve of the abolitionists who were convinced they were morally and legally in the right. As legally voted members of the school committee, those favoring integration were convinced they had the right and responsibility to administer Nantucket schools as they saw fit, and they had no intention of resigning. Peirce and his fellow abolitionists were confident that both higher God-given law and state law were on their side. With enough members on the committee to outvote the segregationists, they chose one of their numbers, Nathaniel Barney, as the chairman. But the minority was also formidable and out-spoken, especially Jenks and Starbuck.

Shortly after the three town meetings, the school committee began to implement its plan. First, it published a notice that they had altered the school districts by dividing Nantucket into North, South and West districts. The line between South and West districts ran through the middle of the black community, placing half of the black students in one district and the other half in the other. Next, Peirce was appointed as the principal of the new West Grammar School, one of the schools whose district included part of the black community.

The York Street School, usually called the African School, was officially renamed the York Street Primary School. Fifty-one black *and* white children were assigned to go there. Fifteen older black children were admitted to both the West and South Grammar schools. It does not appear that any black child entered the high school at that time, probably because none had taken the entrance examination. Eunice Ross, in her twenties, did not choose to enroll.

The independent school committee's integration of the schools led to a spate of letters in the town newspapers. Editor of the *Islander*, Charles Hazewell, previously silent on this particular issue, devoted his final editorial before going out of business to the righteousness of school integration. He wrote that the school committee was acting within the law by distributing the "colored scholars among the other schools, in the same manner that white children are distributed among them." He defended the committee for acting as enforcers of state law. "The School Committee are in some respects state officers, and are not called upon to obey the will of those who elect them only." He broke with the usual norm of anonymity by naming a few of the men who had stood up for integration, including Wesley Berry, a leader in the black community. "The principal speakers on the liberal side were Messrs. Nathaniel Barney, A. M. Macy, John H. Shaw, Henry Clapp, Jr, Cyrus Peirce, Isaac Austin and Wesley Berry," who had "urged their views with great effect, and sometimes with remarkable eloquence, for their hearts were in the matter. High praise is indeed due to all who took part in the discussion on the side of freedom."[14]

Not surprisingly, the next annual town meeting in 1844 was explosive and eventful. The divided school committee once again submitted minority and majority reports. On the first day, Chairman Barney took the entire morning to read the majority report, arguing that the transition from segregated to integrated schools had been smooth, and "the behavior of the children so placed, has been so good." He told the assembly, "the prejudice against color finds no place in the heart of children." The abolitionists defended their actions on moral grounds and by reference to the Constitution, the laws of the Commonwealth, and the teachings of Jesus Christ. Proud of what they had done, they proclaimed grandly that prejudice had been "swept away into the great sea of bygone follies" and that justice, truth, morality, and religion had prevailed. "Freedom and education naturally tend towards each other."

The committee may have been justly proud of its work. The children may have been integrated without incident. Nevertheless, there was a great deal of anger over the arrogance of the abolitionists in defying all those town votes. A furious Jenks filed a minority report lambasting the actions of the integrationists. Reading from the report, Jenks claimed that Nantucket's children had been hurt in the integration process, specifically that the education of white children had been neglected in favor of black children. Moreover, he pointed out that some white children had been pulled out of the public schools by their parents in protest. Praising the former segregated school, Jenks told the meeting that the York Street School had been in a convenient location for black children and that their teacher had provided them better attention than they now received in the larger grammar schools.

Initially the town tabled *both* reports, effectively ignoring them. But, by not accepting the majority report, the voters made it easier for the "experiment" in integration to be dismantled. Jenks was allowed to read the minority report a second time, a highly unusual and unprecedented action. Eventually, the town voted to accept the minority report in its entirety and to accept only the financial portion of the majority report.

An astonishing forty-nine men ran for the school committee in 1844 and the abolitionists paid a heavy price in the balloting for their disregard of the town's wishes. Seven of the eight members who had signed the majority report were voted out of office, including Peirce. The town sent a clear message - don't go against our wishes and our wish is to keep black children in a separate school.

The abolitionists knew the new school committee would re-segregate the schools. True to form, they continued to use reason and persuasion at the town meeting, despite the acceptance of the minority report and the loss of the election. Dozens of motions and proposals were put forth in a desperate attempt to prevent re-segregation. All were in vain.[15]

The abolitionists took their protest to the streets and to the newspapers. They organized a rally in town for those "in favor of admitting the colored children of this town freely" to the public schools. Passions ran high enough that the rally was extended for a second night. A lengthy letter was published on the front page of the *Daily Telegraph*, a new newspaper on the island that had replaced the *Islander*. It offered multiple arguments in favor of school integration. The letter's final argument was a religious one. Simply put, segregation was unchristian, as were the "Negro pews" in many island churches. Moreover it pointed out that many other Massachusetts communities had successfully integrated their schools. But its arguments were fruitless. The letter attempted to shame the islanders into integration, but the arguments fell on deaf ears.[16]

The new school committee elected Jenks as chairman, vindicating the man who had spent the previous year in utter frustration watching his fellow committee members integrate the schools. Now in control, he was intent on undoing their work. His greatest support came from Starbuck, who was also re-elected.

The new school committee's first act was to vote to transfer every black child in an integrated school back to the York Street School. Appalled, the abolitionists called for yet another special town meeting in hopes of preventing the school committee from putting their plan into action. Proposals and resolutions were put forth as had been done so many times before. Thomas Macy and John H. Shaw made separate motions arguing that re-segregation would be found "unconstitutional and illegal." Peirce addressed the meeting at length; unfortunately, his words were not recorded. As principal of one of the schools about to be segregated, he was desperate to keep his students where they were.

All the efforts to prevent re-segregation failed, and the plan proceeded. Once again the name of the school on York Street was changed, this time to the York Street Grammar School, which meant, officially, the town now had four grammar schools. The school committee was playing a name game, suggesting that black children were offered the same levels of schooling available to their white counterparts, even though they would actually be in the same one-room schoolhouse.

In another last-ditch effort to prevent re-segregation, the abolitionist faction called yet another special town meeting which took place on the Friday before the scheduled Monday morning student transfer. Once again, the abolitionists argued that racial segregation was unconstitutional, pleading with the audience not to force the black students out of the grammar schools. Once again, Peirce begged the town to halt the cruel plan of re-segregation in the middle of the academic year. His pleas were ignored. The town meeting approved the re-segregation of the schools to take place in three days.

The disheartened abolitionists' only victory was that the town had voted in favor of a motion specifically approving separation on the basis of skin color. This meant the town had admitted officially, and on the record, what it had been practicing – deliberate racial discrimination.[17]

Sometime during the political maneuverings, Peirce resigned as principal, probably not until it was clear that the abolitionists had been truly defeated. The records do not specify the date of his resignation, but it is clear that he was not the principal when the black students were expelled.

On that fateful Monday morning in April 1844, two representatives of the school committee went to the West Grammar School. Several protesters were also present. The principal, who should have been Cyrus Peirce, but was not, was instructed by Jenks to "call out the colored children from their seats into the aisle."

Jenks pronounced, "Children, you are no longer members of this school, but are dismissed entirely. A school has been provided for you in York Street, you must go there." Jenks then turned to their teacher and told him to no longer regard those students "as his scholars." According to an eyewitness account, the black children immediately left the school, followed by racist taunts of some of their fellow students. "Shout, Shout, the negurs are turned out." So it came about that the actions of their elders were reflected by some of their children. Chairman Jenks later wrote that the protesters got out of hand. One of the parents of an expelled child "exhibited signs of passion in no moderate degree; and actually ordered and sent his child back to his seat."

The next day a similar scene took place at South Grammar School, again with protesters present. One parent of an expelled student asked a school committeeman why his child could not stay in the school. The reply was "because he is colored." An eyewitness to the second expulsion wrote that the nine black children at the school were publicly humiliated in front of their peers, their teacher, and other witnesses. The witness recalled that the nine were seated on a bench in front of their classmates and informed that they had to leave. "During the performance of the ceremony, the children were trembling and weeping." The writer said that he hoped he would never again witness such a heart-wrenching incident. "The bare thought of it is enough to wring any parent's heart." One of the expelled children was Phebe Ann Boston, the daughter of Captain Absalom Boston. As a letter to the editor pointed out, although Boston paid more taxes than many townspeople, his children were restricted to the York Street School because of color.[18]

Two members of the school committee were so upset by the brutal expulsions that they wrote a protest to be entered into the school committee's official records, disassociating themselves from the forced evictions.

Letters to the editor followed the school re-segregation. "Vindex" spoke in favor of integration, "Quidam" in favor of segregation. Vindex, the penname used by Peirce, wrote that the city of Salem had recently integrated its schools successfully and peacefully. Quidam countered that comparing Salem to Nantucket was inappropriate and illogical. For one, he argued that blacks in Salem lived all over town, whereas Nantucket's black people lived "in a neighborhood by themselves." This prompted a long rebuttal from Vindex, who argued that where black families lived in a town was irrelevant and misleading. He pointed out that several white families lived nearer to the York Street School than other schools, and that several black families lived closer to South Grammar School than the York Street School. Vindex, claiming Quidam was a member of the present school committee, suggested he should have a better command of the facts.

Quidam's next letter implied clearly that Vindex was Peirce, suggesting Vindex had once been a preacher and "ex-teacher of common-school discipline." The writer included another hint, writing that he could not "readily *pierce* the mystery of his motives."[19]

Thus, 1844 ended badly for the abolitionists and the children in New Guinea. Peirce was unemployed. With his fellow abolitionists he had been thrown off the school committee, and the children publicly ejected from two integrated grammar schools and returned to the segregated schoolhouse on York Street. It was all very depressing.

The optimism Peirce had felt only a year before was crushed. Nantucket had disappointed and rejected him. Luckily for him, another opportunity soon presented itself. Samuel J. May had tendered his resignation at the normal school and Horace Mann asked Peirce to resume the helm. The Peirces packed their bags once again.

Note: This is a mystery I have never solved; Harriet signed the letter with Eliza Barney months before Cyrus resigned from the school in Lexington. It is highly unlikely she returned to Nantucket without her husband, but how she came to sign the letter is not clear.

Note: Morse was related by marriage to the Peirces and Henry Clapp, Jr. was Harriet's nephew, son of her sister Rebecca. Clapp left Nantucket where he achieved fame becoming the editor of a literary newspaper in New York City that featured luminaries such as Walt Whitman and Mark Twain.

Note: A stricter Fugitive Slave Law was passed in 1850.

Chapter 11: Taking the Reins: West Newton Normal School

When Horace Mann submitted his *Seventh Annual Report* as
secretary of the board of education, thirty-one schoolmasters in Boston's
prestigious grammar schools engaged him in verbal battle. In the report,
Mann laid down in detail what he believed were the principles of
excellent schools and teachers. It stands today as a testament to the core
beliefs of the progressive educators of the time and is relevant today.[1]

Mann's report accelerated the battle between the radically different
philosophies of human nature held by the conservatives and the
Unitarians. It epitomized Unitarian, transcendental reform with specific
applications to classroom teaching. Conservatives regarded the report
with alarm and used it to rally their supporters. Repercussions over the
recommendations laid out in the *Seventh Report* spilled into Peirce's next
tenure at the helm of the normal school and would embroil him in a
lengthy and personal battle which would make his previous battles in
Lexington seem like mere skirmishes.

The *Seventh Annual Report* was written as a result of a six-month
leave of absence that Mann took in 1843. He and his new wife, Mary
Peabody Mann, set off at their own expense to visit Europe, mainly to
see first hand what the Europeans were doing in their schools. The bulk
of his controversial report reflected what he had seen, both good and bad.
(Note)

In the lengthiest of all his annual reports, (approximately 200
pages), Mann meted out his highest praise for the Prussian educational
system because of the "excellence of its schools," which he described in

great detail. Mann claimed that well-trained Prussian teachers could teach material in half the time of teachers in the United States. He ascribed their skill to specific training. Prussian teachers were required to spend three years of preparation for teaching, in stark contrast to the complete lack of requirements necessary in the United States. Mann noted that teaching was a respected position in the German kingdom with teachers earning comparable wages to that of other professions, again in contrast to the poor salaries and low status of American schoolteachers. The Prussian teacher ranks were not filled with those "who have failed in other employments," wrote Mann. If a teacher did not have the "talent, skill, vivacity, resources or wit," the teacher was "deemed to have mistaken his calling" and encouraged to change his profession.

Pages were devoted to the Prussian technique of teaching reading. They had abandoned what Mann called the "abecedarian" approach, popular in the United States. Mann observed a classroom of five-year-olds being taught to read the word "house." The Prussian teacher started with a drawing of a house on the blackboard and proceeded from there. The youngsters were instructed to use a variety of their senses: they drew, read aloud, spelled in the air and on their slates, and conversed in a lesson woven around that single word. Besides being impressed with the result, Mann commented about how much fun the students had in the process.

Corporal punishment was attacked in Mann's report as unnecessary and counterproductive. He wrote that in his six weeks of observation of "hundreds of schools" and "tens of thousands" of pupils in Prussia, he "never saw one child undergoing punishment, or arraigned for misconduct." He added that he never saw a single teacher sit down. They mingled with their students, frequently conversing with them in friendly, supportive fashion. The teachers, he wrote, "have the expression and vivacity of an actor in a play." All these combined, he concluded, in keeping the children so interested in their lessons that they had no motivation to misbehave. He questioned further "whether a visitor could spend six weeks in our own schools without ever hearing an angry word spoken, or seeing a blow struck, or witnessing the flow of tears?"

Some teachers in the state took Mann's report as a stinging and personal rebuke. His praise for Prussian classrooms was taken as insulting, particularly by a group of schoolmasters in Boston.

Led by Barnum Field, a well-respected grammar schoolmaster at the Franklin School, the schoolmasters wrote a 150-page pamphlet that took exception to Mann's report. The masters attacked the progressive techniques he had described in the report, including a direct attack on the normal school movement, still barely five years old.

These schoolmasters were not the itinerant teachers of the countryside. They were formidable foes, men who had dedicated their lives to teaching and were proud of their work. But to educators such as Mann and Peirce, they were hopelessly outdated old school Calvinists who beat and ridiculed their students and clung to outmoded, ineffective, and dull teaching methods.

The schoolmasters defended what they considered tried and true teaching methods, methods Mann had denigrated in his report. The masters maintained that corporal punishment was important to build character, and had an important place in every classroom. They defended rote memorization and denounced object teaching. They claimed that using objects in the classroom, such as globes, blackboards, flowers or coins, made children rely on outward, rather than inward, motivation and stimulus. They found objects to be distractions and gimmicks whose goal was solely to engage children's interest. They claimed that fear was a better motivator than a child's personal interest, which was of little consequence.

The masters took exception to educators like Peirce who lectured and wrote about the best way to teach reading. Peirce believed teachers should put less emphasis on the alphabet and more emphasis on reading whole words in what was called the "look-say" method, just as Mann had described in his report. The masters belittled the normal schools, claiming they would never be able to turn out capable teachers. They insinuated that the methods taught by educators such as Peirce were ineffective and harmful, and further charged that the normal schools were simply conduits to promote a radical agenda.[2]

The battle between Mann and the schoolmasters dragged on for months, extending into 1845, with each side writing multiple responses to each other. Samuel Gridley Howe, George Emerson and Theodore Parker wrote a joint response defending Mann and the techniques described in his report. The trio of Unitarians further bolstered the belief of the Congregationalists that a Unitarian conspiracy was underfoot. (Note)

Samuel J. May wrote a long letter to the *Common School Journal* in 1845, touting the normal school's success in producing good teachers, and countering the Boston's schoolmasters' claim that specific teacher training was unnecessary. May noted that he had directed the normal school in Lexington for two years, but was no longer affiliated with it. He attached eighty-three letters that he had received from graduates of the normal school. "Quite a number have, of their own accord, stated that they have made no use of corporal punishment." He singled out several graduates in particular, including those who had gone on to teach at the

Institution for the Blind. He noted that Rebecca and Eliza Pennell had received praise in their schools, "governed without the rod." He attached a letter from the Fall River school committee commending graduate Betsey Canedy, stating its wish that "every female teacher in town would spend at least one year at the Normal School."[3]

The *Seventh Annual Report* had re-awakened the conservative opposition to the reformers that seemed to have diminished in the early 1840's. New battle lines between the progressives and the hardline conservatives were re-drawn just as Peirce was preparing to leave for West Newton. Never one to fear fighting for principle, he headed off island ready to join forces and support his friend Mann. It would also distract him from the defeat on Nantucket.

Peirce took the time to attend an annual convention of the American Institute of Education in Pittsfield in the summer of 1843 as he prepared to take over the normal school. Introduced as "Reverend Cyrus Peirce of Nantucket," his keynote address, "The Best Methods of Teaching to Read," advocated the very methods Mann had written about in his *Seventh Annual Report.* It did not stray from Peirce's long-held belief that reading needed to be taught in context. While in Pittsfield, he also took part in a friendly debate about corporal punishment where he took on two of its advocates.[4]

During the two years Peirce had been on Nantucket, the normal school had outgrown its space in Lexington, and the town fathers had not renewed its lease. Electa Lincoln wrote that "apathy" about the school had taken hold in Lexington and the town had put forth little effort to retain it. Samuel May surveyed neighboring towns for a suitable place to move the school. May found a building and grounds in the "secluded" town of West Newton where there was a "a manifest desire for the school."[5]

Cyrus and Harriet Peirce arrived in time to oversee the move to the normal school's new quarters in West Newton in the fall of 1844. Neither the Peirces, nor the Manns, owned houses of their own and they decided to build houses close to one another in the town. Peirce found a two-acre wooded site on a hill that he divided with Mann.

West Newton was a town of approximately five hundred people, but it was a growing community partly because a rail line had linked it to Boston in 1834. As he prepared to resume control, Peirce spent time with his friend, the out-going director May. Peirce was returning to the village where he had begun teaching over thirty years before when he had been a student at Harvard, and not far from Waltham, his hometown.

May had found the Fuller Academy in West Newton, which was available for $1500, but no money had been allocated for the purchase.

The West Newton Normal School

Framingham State University Archive

Mann went to his friend, Josiah Quincy, Jr., then mayor of Boston, to ask for a donation. According to Electa Lincoln, Mann said, "Quincy, if you know any man who wants the highest seat in the kingdom of heaven, it is to be had for $1500." Quincy gave Mann the money. Peirce and Mann also contributed $1300 jointly to furnish the school, presumably with Mann paying a larger share than Peirce. [6]

The West Newton Normal School was located on Washington Street on the site now occupied by the First Unitarian Church in Newton, where there is now a stained glass window dedicated to the theme of education that includes the figures of Peirce and Mann. Behind the figure of Peirce is a model of the West Newton Normal School. Mann is holding one of his famous annual reports. [7](Note)

The new school was more spacious than the one in Lexington. Situated on a lot of ¾ of an acre, it was a "three minute's walk" from the West Newton train depot. The *Common School Journal* reported, "a more eligible location could hardly be found." The train from West Newton made it to Boston, only seven miles away, "in less than half an hour," and cost "but twenty cents."[8]

This time managing and running the school would be far easier than it had been in Lexington, primarily because Peirce did not have to do all the work himself. For one, he had competent and enthusiastic young assistants. With the coming political storm, it was fortunate that he had capable educators upon which to rely, because fighting his opponents would consume much of Peirce's time and energy.

Those battles, however, were in the future when Peirce and his wife arrived in West Newton. Coming from a discouraging and disheartening time in Nantucket, Peirce was enthusiastic about training young teachers once again. Teaching always made him happy and optimistic about the future.

One of the assistants who lightened Peirce's teaching load was Caroline Tilden, a graduate of Bridgewater Normal School. Tilden had been hired by Samuel J. May to teach algebra, arithmetic and grammar. In fact, when May had accepted the job in 1842, he had made his acceptance contingent on the co-hiring of Tilden, his former parishioner. According to colleague Lincoln, May considered Tilden "a very brilliant and successful teacher." So important did he consider her appointment, that he paid her out of his own salary his first year. He knew that Peirce had resigned in Lexington due to the crushing workload, and he refused to be put in the same position. According to Lincoln, Tilden's "peculiar genius and talents, high culture and zeal," made her "well-fitted for the post. Her heart was full of kindness, her manners attractive, and her eye was an almost irresistible charm." Mann wrote that Tilden "could be counted upon to do a good job in drilling the teachers on the rudiments of arithmetic." Sadly, Caroline Tilden died in 1848, four years after Peirce's arrival, still a young woman. In a tribute, Lincoln wrote that her friend "preferred to wear out rather than to rust out," and the students at their graduation that year wrote a tribute to their "much respected teacher."

Peirce was also reunited with Lincoln, his former pupil who had been added to the staff just before Peirce had left Lexington. An 1843 graduate of the Lexington Normal School, Lincoln was assigned to teach geometry, reading and drawing. Both she and Tilden helped supervise the boarding students. They also presented seminars together on effective teaching techniques at the two other normal schools in the state, as well as at Teacher Institutes that offered short seminars for working teachers. Lincoln taught at the Newton school with Peirce for five years and remained at the school for one year after his retirement, until she resigned to marry George Walton. She later wrote that she was by Peirce's side, either as a pupil or a teacher, for all but seven weeks of his normal school tenures. Lincoln remained a close friend and confidante of both Peirces until they died.

Other teachers were employed to teach specific subjects over the course of Peirce's five years at the school. For example, Joseph Bird was hired to teach vocal music and Sarah Watson, a Nantucketer, was hired for several years to teach mathematics. Like Lincoln, Watson was a graduate of the Lexington Normal School during Peirce's final year there. Watson was praised in both the *12th and 13th Annual Reports of the Board of Education* in 1848 and 1849 as being a capable teacher.[9]

Enrollment increased with the larger facility, exceeding sixty students every year. In 1847, seventy-five students were admitted, and applicants had to be turned away every year for want of space. The demand for teacher training that Peirce and Mann had once predicted had come to pass.

Peirce once again enjoyed teaching at the normal school. While he had assistants, the student body was large and demanded a lot of work. Just keeping up with the weekly journals of over seventy students every week was a large task. His approach to the girls had not changed; he demanded a high level of work and commitment, but also set aside time for fun, including expeditions.

Portions of "The Second Book of the Chronicles of the Normalites – a Literary Satire in the form of a book of the Old Testament and Hebrew Scripture" by an unknown student, appears in two journals. Probably written in 1848, the lengthy parody makes it evident that the students had fun with Peirce and they felt comfortable sharing the parody with him. It is also evident that the Friday exhibitions were still intimidating, but they did not truly "fear their King."

> Now in the seventh year of the reign of Cyrus, in the
> second month, the tenth day of the month, the spirit of King
> Cyrus was stirred within him, that he made a proclamation
> throughout all his realms....Thus saith Cyrus, all the maidens
> from among my people, both small and great, young and old,
> shall assemble themselves together on the last day of the week
> and shall stand up in the congregation to read their themes or
> to expound to the people some mystery of science.
> Now did this greatly trouble the daughters of Normalty,
> And they knew not what to do, for they exceedingly
> feared their King.
> And Cyrus spoke to those hearts who were ready to
> devise, that such should rehearse the sayings of the
> wise men. And they did so.[10]

When Peirce went to the normal school this time, the model school had its own principal, taking a significant workload off Peirce. Director May had insisted on having a separate principal to run the model school, and when Peirce arrived, the principal was George Walton, a graduate of the Bridgewater Normal School.

Not long after Peirce's arrival, an unwanted problem arose concerning the model school. Parents complained to the school committee that Walton was unable to keep order in the school. The school committee demanded that Walton use physical punishment to establish control over unruly students. Peirce, however, forbade the use of corporal punishment, leaving Walton in an untenable position and he resigned. The community blamed the model school's problems on the liberal Unitarians, May and Peirce. Peirce's increasingly vocal opposition to corporal punishment became one of the main arguments used by conservatives against both him during the course of the next battles over the normal schools.

Peirce needed to find a new principal for the model school immediately. His choice was critical. He had to find someone who could not only reestablish discipline at the school, but also do it without compromising Peirce's strongly held belief that physical punishment represented a failure in teaching. This was not negotiable for Peirce.

At this crucial juncture, Nathaniel Allen entered Peirce's life when he applied for the position. Peirce offered the twenty-five-year-old the job. The two men, thirty-three years apart in age, gradually discovered that they were kindred spirits, and became lifelong friends. Allen's appointment helped stave off a crisis in the model school and allowed Peirce to fight the larger battles that were looming. Allen's success reaffirmed Peirce's conviction that corporal punishment was not necessary and not a good practice.

Nathaniel Allen had grown up in a progressive household in Medfield, Massachusetts. His father, Ellis Allen, was actively involved in the progressive reform movements of the time, including temperance, peace, education and abolition. Allen's parents put their beliefs in action and their home was a stop on the Underground Railroad. William Lloyd Garrison was a family friend and Frederick Douglass a visitor. Douglass wrote, "The world, good and bad, was then opening upon me with vigor. I shall never forget the kindness shown me by the dear Allen family." They "were not ashamed to own me as a brother in Massachusetts."[11]

Allen came from a family of educators. Two of his grandmothers, his mother, two aunts, and four of his uncles, were teachers. Two of his brothers, and one of his sisters, were teachers. But the greatest influence on Nathaniel's teaching came from his Uncle Joseph and Aunt Lucy Allen who operated a successful boarding school in Northboro,

Massachusetts. Joseph Allen was an old friend of Cyrus Peirce; they had been students together at Harvard, both as undergraduates and in the Divinity department. (They also shared a birthdate.) Allen had married their professor's daughter, Lucy Ware. It is likely that Cyrus Peirce and Nathaniel Allen had already met.

Nathaniel and his siblings were frequent visitors to their Uncle Joseph and Aunt Lucy's school when they were young. The school was noted for the love showered on the students by their surrogate parents and for its active teaching style. The students were out and about in the community learning about things first hand. It was not unusual for the Allens to invite village children to their home to let them use their magnifying glasses to look at plants, or to use their microscope.[12]

Lowell Mason, a close family friend and neighbor in Medfield, was also an influential educational reformer and early supporter of Pestalozzian methods of teaching. Mason instilled in Nathaniel Allen a strong belief in the importance of music in the development of children. Mason was convinced music deserved a place in the curriculum of every public school. Mason was hired for a time by Samuel Gridley Howe to teach music to the blind at the Perkins School. The importance of music in the curriculum was a lesson Allen took to heart from a young age, and he played music in his classrooms throughout his lengthy career. (Note)

Nathaniel Allen's first teaching job was in Mansfield, Massachusetts when he had just turned nineteen. Even though he had grown up surrounded by teachers and exposed to modern teaching methods, he was, as was typical of teachers at the time, woefully unprepared for the job. The year before he arrived, the school had been forced to close early because its teacher had been unable to keep students in order. His uncle Joseph warned him not to accept the job, but he took it nonetheless.

After much trial and error, Allen managed to have a successful year, using humor and music to win over his students. On the first day of school, the students drew a disrespectful picture of him on the blackboard, poking fun at his large boots. Allen, when viewing the drawing, labeled the "Teacher's Boot," acknowledged that what they had done was "unpleasant and disrespectful," but countered it with humor. He told the students that if they had tried to make a drawing of his nose, "there would not be room upon the blackboard! This brought a laugh, as intended." He later said that the incident helped him establish "pleasantrelations" with the pupils and the parents on the very first day.[13]

He also won community support by conducting a local church choir and playing the violin there. He taught a singing class in the evenings open to the general public, which earned him an extra $1 per week.

Bridgewater Normal School

Bridgewater Historical Society

These are skills he brought to the model school in West Newton. [14]

Allen's robust physique also came in handy. At six feet tall, he looked as if he could physically tackle the bullies. He worked hard to involve students in their own learning, and even paid them out of his own pocket for good schoolwork. His experiment in paying students backfired when the competition amongst students became too fierce and he never resorted to that particular kind of reward again. Although the school committee in Mansfield asked him to teach a second year, Allen turned them down because he was homesick. He returned to Northboro for two years to work on his father's farm during summers and to teach in a local school during winter terms.

Meanwhile, a brother and a cousin moved to Syracuse, New York to teach. They tried to persuade Nathaniel to join them by telling him what a progressive community Syracuse was. Instead, he enrolled in the normal school in Bridgewater, then in its sixth year. The year that Allen attended Bridgewater there were thirty-eight students, half of them male.

The normal school in Bridgewater occupied two rooms in the town hall. Like Cyrus Peirce, the principal of the school, Nicholas Tillinghast, was a skilled teacher and charismatic character. A graduate of West

Bridgewater Historical Society

Point, Tillinghast had been a private school teacher until Mann tapped him to head the third normal school in the state. Tillinghast was socially and educationally progressive and supported new teaching techniques.

Prospective teachers at the Bridgewater school followed a curriculum similar to the one in West Newton. It included arithmetic, reading, geography, philosophy, chemistry, astronomy, drawing and bookkeeping. Allen's musical talent was recognized and he was asked to teach singing to his fellow students.[15]

Tillinghast, like Peirce, believed children learn best when they study what they like, and when their curiosity is piqued. Neither man believed in humiliating or singling out individual students for their mistakes. Neither believed that punitive measures were effective. Learning by doing was encouraged over rote memorization. Both men believed in taking children out of the classroom to study things first hand.[16]

Unlike the model schools in Lexington and West Newton, the model school in Bridgewater failed. Parents had not supported it, which led to its closure; it was not re-opened for another twenty-five years. The two normal schools, however, attracted a different clientele. Most of the Bridgewater students, unlike most of Peirce's students, were already experienced teachers.

The West Newton school was entirely female, most of them teenagers, whereas the students at Bridgewater included men and women, many of them in their twenties, like Nathaniel Allen. Students at Bridgewater, therefore, were able to draw upon previous experiences, making the lack of a model school less significant than it would have been in West Newton. Students in Bridgewater could talk about what had worked or not worked in their previous classrooms. Another difference was that students were required to complete four terms to graduate from the West Newton School, whereas, the Bridgewater students were only required to complete two terms. This was probably due to the differences in the experience of the students.[17]

While studying at Bridgewater, Allen attended several Teacher Institutes. At one, he recalled a lecture by Mann about the importance of the teaching profession. Mann exhorted the teachers and prospective teachers to have faith and perseverance in their profession. It was at this meeting that Allen met Caroline Tilden and Electa Lincoln, Peirce's two highly qualified assistants, for the first time.

After just one term at Bridgewater, Allen accepted a teaching job in Northfield, Massachusetts. There, he applied the new methods he had learned. He only taught there for one term, because he realized the hard way that he had much more to learn and was not quite ready to teach. Allen was determined to become an excellent teacher and he returned to Bridgewater.[18]

After completing his second term, Allen accepted a teaching job in Shrewsbury, Massachusetts, at another school with a rough reputation. Like his previous school in Mansfield, this one had also been forced to close early the previous year due to student rowdiness. Before Allen even started school that year, students broke into and vandalized their classroom. Because of this, a member of the school committee demanded Allen begin the year by physically punishing his students, even though he had not yet met them. Allen refused. He had become convinced at Bridgewater that physical punishment was not an effective way to engage students in their learning - particularly on the first day of school.

On his third day in Shrewsbury several boys challenged Allen's authority. The physically fit Allen swiftly tackled the ringleader, sending him sprawling into the aisle. He did not hurt the boy, but his quick action had taken the miscreant and his cohorts completely by surprise. Word spread in the community that the new schoolmaster was fully in charge, and for the rest of the year, he had no trouble from the boys. In its year-end report, the school committee meted out high praise to Allen as a "faithful and accomplished teacher," who had taken an "ungovernable and bad school" and turned it around. The report attributed some of his success to the teaching strategies he had learned at the Bridgewater Normal School.[19]

Allen chose not to renew his contract in Shrewsbury. He and several of his fellow teachers from Bridgewater decided to enroll at Rensselaer Polytechnic Institute in upstate New York. Allen intended to study engineering. Some of his professors at the institute used the world as their classroom and took students on hikes to collect specimens. On one such trip Allen hurt his leg, which forced his withdrawal from the school. He went home to recuperate and did not return to Rensselaer. However, he remembered the effectiveness of those field trips, and for the rest of his career, he took his students outside whenever possible.

Shortly after Allen recuperated, Peirce offered him the job as principal of the model school. Probably encouraged by his uncle Joseph, Allen accepted Peirce's offer. A school committee member in Northboro, the elder Allen was a strong supporter of educational reform. In fact, Joseph Allen had been asked by Mann to direct the second normal school, a position he turned down. Little did his nephew know that his acceptance of the model school principalship would change his life. He would find in Peirce a gentle philosopher who would guide his teaching for the rest of his remarkable career.[20]

As a bonus, the job as principal of the model school came with what was then a princely yearly salary for a schoolteacher, $500 a year. Accepting the position turned out to be one of the best decisions of Allen's life, although the wisdom of doing so was not immediately apparent, as the West Newton Normal School became the target of increasingly intense attacks from conservative forces.

Being principal of the model school meant answering to two masters - the local school committee and Cyrus Peirce. It is what had lead to the failure of his predecessor. Pleasing both did not prove an easy task. A friend warned Allen that he would be caught between "two fires," and expressed the hope that "neither will scorch you." It was not an easy position for young Allen to find himself in. [21]

Allen was invited to live for a time at the home of Horace Mann and his wife, Mary Peabody Mann. This saved him money, but more importantly, exposed him to the many intellectual luminaries of New England who frequented the Mann house, including Mann's sister-in-law, Elizabeth Peabody, an early advocate of kindergarten education. Allen found himself in an exceptionally intellectual and stimulating environment where the issues of the day were discussed on a daily basis.

The people of West Newton were wary of Allen; they knew he was from a well- known liberal family, himself a normal school graduate, and yet another Unitarian. They were skeptical that he would be an improvement over the previous principal. The school committee wanted someone to restore order with an iron fist, not another educator reluctant to wield a paddle. When the young schoolmaster moved into the home of the Manns, the people of West Newton were even more skeptical that he was the man for the job.

Fortunately for the normal school movement, Allen was, indeed, the man for the job. Incredibly, he was almost an overnight success in the model school, and his increasing reputation as a gifted teacher, outweighed most of the community's reservations. From a meager enrollment of only eighteen students in September 1848 when Allen opened the school, it grew to sixty-five within a matter of weeks. Parents were eager to pull their children from other town schools and enroll them in the model school. Parents from outside West Newton even paid a fee to the town to place their children in Allen's school. Students had to be turned away because the school was soon full. Allen's success was immeasurably helpful to Peirce, as it also reflected positively on the normal school whose students taught under both Allen and Peirce's supervision.

This does not mean that Allen's task was easy. When he took over, the students were used to getting their own way, and they challenged their new teacher right away. Allen, however, had faced this problem before in Mansfield and Shrewsbury, and he quickly won them over. Privately he reported to his family that he had never seen so many discipline problems in a single school. Once again, Allen used his physical presence to impose himself on his students. A rumor went round the school that the new teacher was so strong that he could lift over one thousand pounds. The rumor seems to have worked, and Allen never needed to resort to corporal punishment to command respect, a fact much appreciated by Peirce. During his seven years at the West Newton school, Allen reportedly only put his hands on one student, and then only to give the boy a firm shaking. Peirce was grateful to have an educator who could put into practice what he preached.[22]

Allen's teaching principles and strategies were compatible with those Peirce held dear, and both men modeled similar teaching techniques for the normal school students. Despite their similar philosophies about students and education, however, they had distinctive styles. The younger Allen was noted for his humor and use of music in winning over students, and was somewhat less formal than the older man. Peirce was appreciated for his genteel and gentle approach, and his penchant for moral anecdotes. Both teachers, however, were firm believers in object education and required students to be active. Students were regularly called upon to demonstrate their knowledge in front of their peers. Both men expected students to keep their classrooms organized and clean, and assigned tasks to that end. Neither believed in reprimanding a student in front of their classmates; when needed, they preferred to speak to students individually. Like Peirce, Allen put his own money into the school. For example, he bought the school a piano.

Allen put to use lessons that he had learned at Renssalaer and took the students outside as often as he could. He introduced botany to the curriculum and gave students individual boxes for planting. Older students were required to take notes, and prepare lectures to teach five younger students. Allen wrote, "so far as I know, the study of plants had never, up to that time, been thus scientifically undertaken in any public or private school in Massachusetts."[23]

Besides teaching the model school students, Allen supervised the normal school students during their student teaching. They were each required to write a weekly letter to Allen reflecting upon her teaching. Allen required his young model school pupils to do the same, paralleling the journals Peirce assigned in the normal school. Thirty-five letters written to Allen from normal school students survive. They reveal that the young teachers had lofty goals, and the desire to become exemplary, not ordinary educators. The letters also reveal gratitude for being able to teach at the model school, and for the critiques Allen made of their lessons. They attest to the time they spent practicing on real students having been the most valuable part of their training. In her journal, Mary F. Peirce wrote, "I learn a great deal in Mr. Allen's room, and have no doubt but it will be useful to me."[24]

Allen worked so hard his first year that he lost fifteen pounds, but his hard work paid off. Both the school committee and Peirce were pleased. Allen had managed to avoid being scorched by, or disappointing, either boss. The school committee publicly commended his successful teaching style, writing that Allen made "his scholars feel that the school belongs to them" and was "for their benefit." Peirce could not have been happier. He and Allen formed a formidable partnership that benefited them both during their long association.

The success of the model school under Nathaniel Allen removed an immense political burden from Peirce's shoulders at a time when he would need all his talents and energy to fight for the survival of the normal school. He was about to be cast into a public, ugly and exceedingly personal controversy that would threaten his professional and personal reputation and that of the normal schools.

Note: In six months, Mann visited England, Ireland, Scotland, various German kingdoms including Hesse, Saxony and Prussia, as well as Holland, Belgium and France.

Note: The battle between the progressives and the Boston schoolmasters continued. In October 1844, Samuel Gridley Howe was elected to the Boston School Committee. The next year, he was on a sub-committee that conducted a three-month examination of the nineteen grammar schools in the city. For the first time, written tests of the students were added to the examination process. The masters were also required to submit to written questions, including the circumstances in which they resorted to corporal punishment. In their final report, the committee concluded that there was too much rote memorization, too much reliance on textbooks, and too little critical thinking in evidence. The committee made the incorrect student responses public, and included examples of particularly brutal corporal punishment. The public was horrified. In the aftermath, four masters were fired and several others re-assigned. To Howe's disappointment, however, Barnum Field's students did well and he remained in his position. From then on, schoolmasters were required to document their use of corporal punishment, and the use of it declined significantly. In addition, written assessment became the norm in Boston.

Note: The stained glass window, created by Connick Associates in Boston, was dedicated in 1956. It was made as a memorial to Mira E.

Metcalf, a life-long member of the church and a life-long teacher. Her wish was to honor the teaching profession.

Note: In 1837, Mason had become the first public school music teacher in the United States at the Hawes Grammar School in Boston. In 1845, he was dismissed because of his outspoken politics. He continued to be active in educational reform and served as a staff member of the Massachusetts board of education for ten years, primarily organizing the Teachers' Institutes. Mason was also known as the "father of American church music, who wrote over 1600 hymns, including "Nearer My God to Thee."

Chapter 12: Heresy and Depravity!

Conservatives were about to launch their most serious attack on what they understood as the liberalization and corruption of Massachusetts. Many of their objections were drawn from Mann's *Seventh Annual Report*, which the conservatives saw as his epistle for change. Arguments over the direction of the schools served as proxy arguments over the direction and future of American society. These battles, long since forgotten, were front-page news then, and frequently involved Cyrus Peirce and the West Newton Normal School.

Conservative Congregationalists watched with alarm as other religions continued to grow in the state. Most disturbing was Unitarianism which was growing rapidly and seen as the most immediate threat. Unitarians were often outspoken moralists who "certainly thought of themselves as heralds of a new and more liberal faith for mankind." In addition, Unitarians were politically active, and for their numbers, were disproportionately influential in state affairs. Unitarians continued in control of Harvard and were leaders and members of numerous reform movements, including abolition, temperance, peace, women's rights and education.[1]

Radical Unitarians, such as Reverend Theodore Parker, held beliefs verging on atheism. Parker and his followers were viewed by conservative Congregationalists as heretics, intent on the destruction of traditional Christianity, if not Christianity itself. Peirce was labeled a "Parkerite" on several occasions, although it is doubtful he ever embraced Parker's more radical views. Peirce did, however, support Parker's freedom of expression and attended some of his lectures. Parker lectured on the importance of education and had penned support of Mann's controversial annual report. Any association with Parker put Peirce in dangerous company according to even moderate Christians, including Unitarians.

Parker came to reject the authority of the Bible as the divine word of God. He questioned the stories in the Old Testament and the Gospels in the New Testament, particularly when they involved miracles, something he did not accept. But, worst of all, in a sermon he delivered in 1840, Parker called into doubt the existence and divinity of Jesus Christ.[2]

than whip him, was zealously inculcated by him; we knew what impressions he, a disbeliever in the Old Testament, left on his pupils in respect to these canonical and sacred books;—we knew that he, a Parkerite in theology, was not careful to disguise his hatred of *priests*, and that he smiled complacently when he read in the journals of his scholars their disbelief in the Bible, their hatred of the clergy and their mockery of the church;—we knew something of the farce daily acted under the name of religious service, the prayer with which the exercises of the school are closed, "*Live for the Truth!*" All this we knew and more, which in good time will appear. But till now we were ignorant of the notions of delicacy and refinement taught in this Pattern State school, by its very accomplished Principal. Mr. J. W. Ingraham, whose friendship for Mr. Pierce none will question, has expressed, what most feel. In allusion to Mr. Pierce's semi-denial, his evasions and prevarications, Mr. I. said in the presence of several gentlemen, "*It would have been better for Mr. Pierce to have owned the truth at once!*"

M. H. S.

Boston Recorder, Congregational Archives

Parker became increasingly vocal on issues of social reform, including as the abolition movement, and Garrison frequented Parker's church in Boston. Unlike traditional churches, Parker's congregation did not keep any records of its members, nor were pews sold to individuals.

People sat wherever they wanted. It was Parker's way of challenging the accepted social order whereby the wealthiest parishioners owned pews at the front of churches. In addition, Parker's church was one of the few integrated congregations in the city. Congregationalists questioned whether his church even qualified as a church.

Another point of controversy which involved Parker and his followers concerned activity on the Sabbath. The Congregationalists had had a monopoly on Sunday conduct since the founding of the Massachusetts Bay Colony with a lengthy list of what was forbidden. Alarmingly to the conservatives, Parker proclaimed that people should be free "to use the Sabbath in the way they felt was best suited to meet their spiritual needs." [3]

Conservatives also regarded the growing transcendental movement with consternation. Transcendentalism has never been an easy movement to define, partly because of its emphasis on the individual and on personal judgment. It embraced a wide variety of people and beliefs, and thus, is difficult to pigeonhole. It is often viewed solely as a literary movement with great writers of American literature, including Henry David Thoreau, Ralph Waldo Emerson, Emily Dickinson and Louisa May Alcott. Transcendentalism, however, contributed a good deal more than literature to American culture, particularly in New England. "Individuals who identified themselves with Transcendentalism did not subscribe to a single, rigid theological, philosophical, and social orthodoxy." Some transcendentalists became social activists; some became utopian idealists; others became naturalists. Some theological historians believe transcendentalism "stands at the turning point in American life when moral questions began to resolve themselves into political ones."[4]

Transcendentalism supported the expansion and improvement of American education, and included many educators in its ranks. It attracted many Unitarians, including Theodore Parker, with their own faith similarly based on personal judgment and observation. Unitarians and transcendentalists believed, like Peirce, in the ultimate goodness of mankind and nature.

Women were important in the transcendental movement, challenging traditional roles of women in society. Some became active social reformers in the movements of their era, from temperance to abolition. Activists included Margaret Fuller, the editor of the most important transcendental publication, *The Dial,* as well as Lydia Maria Child, famous for her work in abolition, women's rights and the rights of Native Americans. Mann's sister-in-law was the transcendentalist Elizabeth Palmer Peabody, who opened the first kindergarten in the United States.

To conservatives, the moral fiber of the nation was disintegrating before their eyes and from a variety of directions and movements. As the power of the Congregational church diminished, its rhetoric against liberal thinking increased accordingly. An area of possible victory was in attacking the progressive educational movement and the perceived threat of its corrupting the nation's youth. Education became a focal point for their attack on all the forces arrayed against them.

Conservative religionists accused Mann, Peirce, Howe and other progressive educators of secretly conspiring to promote Unitarian thinking, while publically professing nonsectarianism. This led to frontal assaults against public schools, normal schools, the board of education, and especially against Mann, Peirce and the West Newton Normal School. By discrediting Peirce and his school, the conservatives thought that educational reform would be irreparably harmed and the spread of Unitarian thinking stopped. Peirce was in their crosshairs, and the attacks when they came, were vicious and personal.

When the Peirces moved to West Newton, the village's only church was an orthodox Congregational one. The entire village attended it and the congregation supplied the town's political leadership. From the beginning, parishioners questioned how this new school in the heart of their village would fit in. From the beginning there were suspicions that Mann and Peirce had a Unitarian agenda that extended beyond the doors of the school.[5]

There was no question that Unitarians ran the school. The Peirces, Electa Lincoln, George Walton and Nathaniel Allen were all committed Unitarians. In their first year at West Newton, Peirce, Mann and Allen attempted to establish a Unitarian church without success. Allen later described West Newton as a "narrow, bigoted community, antagonistic in reality to the union of the District and Model Schools." [6] (Note)

Mann was aware of potential problems that might arise when he re-hired Peirce. Despite his absolute trust in Peirce's teaching ability, he had reservations about Peirce's inflexibility when questions of morality were at stake. Mann worried that political issues might arise, particularly over abolition, with Peirce fresh from the battle over school integration in Nantucket and his association with the Latimer petition. Only ten miles from Boston, the West Newton school was the closest normal school to the state capital, and hence, under the greatest scrutiny by the legislature and the partisan Boston press. Opposition to state-supported normal schools, which for a time had diminished, was increasing once more, despite the success of the three established normal schools, some of the opposition fueled by Mann's *Seventh Annual Report*. Mann knew the experiment was still fragile, and that it would not take much to undo all that had been accomplished.

Mann's decision to build a house in West Newton was seen as an act of solidarity with Peirce. The two families were good friends and two of Mann's nieces had attended the normal school in Lexington. Having a close friend as an employee or an employer can be complicated. Even though their positions on most political issues were closely matched, their friendship would undergo significant strains in the coming years. Of the two, Mann was the more politically savvy. Having held political office, he knew how to build consensus. His job as the secretary of the board of education sometimes called for negotiation with the opposition. Peirce was less willing to compromise.

Reverend Matthew Hale Smith, an Orthodox Congregational minister, led the charge against what he considered the evils represented by the progressive Unitarian educators. Smith was convinced he was fighting a duel with the Devil himself. Blow by blow, the battle was chronicled in the Boston newspapers, especially those that were official publications of the Congregational

Matthew Hale Smith

Church. They published every pronouncement Smith made in his attacks on Peirce and Mann. In addition to newspapers, these fights spilled into church pulpits, street corner debates, schools, lecture halls, meetings of the board of education, and the legislature. Cyrus Peirce, an intensely private man, became a household name.

On October 10, 1846, Smith delivered a sermon at the Church and Society of the Pilgrims in Boston titled "The Ark of God on a New

Cart." He claimed juvenile crime to be on the increase due to a rise in youthful depravity. With no statistics or facts backing his allegation, Smith laid the blame for what he saw as rampant juvenile delinquency squarely at the feet of educational reformers like Peirce and Allen and their practice of coddling school children. Liberal teachers were apt to simply "talk" to children who misbehaved, Smith asserted, instead of dispensing proper and strict punishments. "Spare the rod and spoil the child" was the refrain of conservatives who echoed Smith's views. Smith believed that lax discipline in the schools automatically led to criminality. Liberal education would, therefore, lead to an increase in crime in the next generation.

Smith accused educational reformers, especially Peirce, of diluting the teaching of the Bible in the public schools, which, he said, directly contributed to rising immorality, as did the reading lists promoted by the board of education under Mann. Smith attacked the books read in the public schools for containing "deadly heresy" and atheism. The religiously orthodox asserted that the books eroded belief in the Bible as the ultimate and final arbiter of the truth. In a letter to Mann, Smith asserted that the books recommended by the board of education were "calculated to exert an evil influence," by deliberately including a multiplicity of philosophies and topics. Conservatives complained about children's exposure to books that did not support their own beliefs. To Smith and his followers, the literature recommended for children to read put human intellect over God's word.

Smith also targeted the Washingtonians, the largest temperance organization in New England, of which Peirce was a member. Although Smith was a strong advocate of temperance, he disapproved of the Washingtonian acceptance of members from all religious backgrounds, an ecumenical approach that co-opted the Congregational church's involvement in the temperance movement. Besides, he argued, when the Washingtonians gathered on Sundays, they could be seen as encouraging men to substitute temperance meetings for proper church services. "Washingtonianism has been called Christianity. It has been substituted for the preaching of Jesus Christ upon the Sabbath."[7]

Within several weeks, William Bentley Fowle, a known educational leader and a Unitarian who also lived in West Newton, responded to Smith's sermon in the *Boston Courier.* Writing under the pseudonym "Tremont," Fowle refuted each of Smith's allegations. Calling the sermon "impudent" and "ignorant" of the facts, Fowle labeled anyone who argued that the world was getting worse, rather than better, was "a knave, or an idiot, or both." Fowle pointed out that Smith had publically converted from being a liberal Universalist minister to being an Orthodox Congregationalist in 1843, and claimed that Smith's conversion illustrated his mercurial beliefs. "He has hardly left the Universalists, but he is not ashamed to denounce their chief doctrine as 'the most deadly heresy.'" Fowle described Smith as "blood-thirsty" with an "eye for an eye, tooth for a tooth" philosophy. The teachings of Jesus Christ are merciful and gentle, wrote Fowle, not vengeful as in Smith's sermonizing.

Fowle defended the members of the board of education, who, he claimed, were predominantly Congregationalists like Smith. As proof, he listed those known to be members of conservative churches, including Governor George Briggs, an orthodox Baptist, and other members of the orthodox Congregational church, including Dr. Heman Humprey, President of Amherst College, and Reverend H.B. Hooker of Falmouth. Fowle denied that use of the Bible had been diminished in the public schools. He wrote that in the three normal schools, the only schools under the board's direct control, the Bible was required reading. The rest of the public schools, Fowle reminded readers, were under the control of local town school committees and free to choose whatever books they wanted.

Finally, Fowled defended the Library, the list of books recommended by the board, for use in public schools. He noted that the board lacked the authority to require any school to use any books on the list and denied that any heretical book had ever been included. Smith, the former Universalist, was reprimanded by Fowle for singling out Universalism as particularly heretical. From beginning to end, Smith's sermon was denounced as "falsehood," disconnected from facts and evidence.[8]

Both sides repeatedly returned to these topics over the next three years as each honed its arguments and looked for vulnerabilities in the other. An anonymous letter from "Watchman" in support of Smith's views on the depravity of human nature proclaimed that conservatives "believe in the entire corruption of human nature since the fall." The writer attacked Peirce's friend, Samuel Gridley Howe, for his liberal view of the children under his care. Howe had written that since "almost all children are as pure as Eve," it should be no surprise they were occasionally drawn to "tempting apples." Watchman accused Howe and educators of his ilk, of fostering "liberal Christianity" and mistaken Unitarian beliefs about the goodness of mankind. In a letter from Smith, Peirce was accused of the same misguided thinking. Peirce's approach to children was described as the theory of "no rod - on the native purity of the child, in opposition to his native depravity."[9]

Smith asserted in sermons and letters that the normal school under

Peirce's leadership totally forbade any use of the rod, despite Peirce's repeated response that the rod did, in fact, have to be resorted to on occasion. Instead of a common punishment, Peirce claimed he recommended its use in only in the most extreme situations.

In a letter to Mann in November 1846, Smith defended teachers who frequently used corporal punishment, arguing that Mann and Peirce unfairly criticized and accused such teachers as being poor instructors. He said that criticism of those teachers was unfair because it was the misbehaving children who deserved to be blamed, not the teachers who disciplined them. Smith singled out Peirce as an educator who spoiled and overindulged children, which put teachers at a disadvantage. He quoted Peirce telling a gathering of schoolteachers that his "theory goes to the *entire exclusion of corporal punishment.*"[10]

The use of the Bible in schoolrooms was a key area of contention during the long battle between Smith and Peirce. Despite the fact that Peirce used the Bible every day in his classroom, Smith repeatedly accused Peirce and Mann of attempting to banish it from the public schools. Mann responded that Smith did not have a "tittle of evidence" for his charge about the use of the Bible. The secretary of education wrote, "official reports and letters of the school-committees" confirmed that "the Bible was never so extensively used in our schools as at the present time, and that its use has been constantly increasing." In reading the journals written by the students, it is clear that the Bible was used every day in Peirce's lessons.[11]

What Smith really meant was that the Bible was not being used in the manner he saw fit, but as a way to promote Unitarian theology and to subvert Orthodox Congregationalism. Smith accused Mann of rejecting the Bible as the "inspired Word of God" and of selecting some parts of the Bible as "not proper to be read in school." Anyone who presumed to reject any part of the Bible, Smith declared, must in fact "reject the whole." By his choice of words, Smith accused Mann and Peirce of being followers of Theodore Parker, the most radical of the Unitarian thinkers. [12]

Nor did Smith approve of other texts being used in the schools. If Smith had had his way, the Bible would have been almost the only text given to students. To the orthodox views Smith represented, applying reason, science or open discussion to the Bible was anathema.

In interview after interview, and annual report after annual report, Mann denied removing the Bible from the classroom. He cited facts and surveys of the public schools of Massachusetts as evidence of consistent use of the Bible in state schools. Moderate Congregationalists on the board unswervingly supported Mann and expressed their confidence in the Bible's appropriate use in the Commonwealth's schools. But even arguments from fellow Congregationalists supported by facts, could not appease Smith and his ultra-orthodox followers. They never wavered in their conviction that Unitarians, especially Parkerites, in the teaching profession sought to undermine the Bible and pursue their own heretical agenda.

There was, in fact, some truth to the claims fundamentalists made against Peirce and his approach to the Bible in his classroom. Peirce did use the Bible on a daily basis to illustrate moral lessons, and Biblical stories made up the majority of lessons on how to behave. Those stories and lessons *were*, however, chosen selectively and the Bible was not read from start to finish.

Also true was the charge that Peirce did not believe in corporal punishment. Although Peirce publicly said the rod was sometimes necessary, it was only to placate his adversaries. Privately, he did not believe students ever needed to be punished physically. Ann E. Shannon wrote in her journal in 1847 that Peirce taught that parents and teachers needed to "appeal to the consciences of children." He told the normal school students that, "instead of that, they appeal to the rod and the child is led to think, if I do thus and so, I shall get a whipping." Instead, Peirce said that children should be "cultivated as to ask himself is it right, is it just" before embarking on an action.[13]

It was also true that the educational reformers believed there were other sources of truth than the Bible, and their choice of reading materials and subject matter reflected that. Their curricula included rigorous study of the sciences and mathematics, including chemistry, biology, botany, physics, and pure and applied mathematics. Geography and world culture were also studied.

The Library recommended specific books for children to read on Sundays. Since these were often about nature, conservatives considered them utterly unsuitable for the Lord's Day. Books on the list were also seen as reflecting transcendentalism with its focus on the natural world as opposed to the spiritual. Smith singled out several books as particularly unacceptable, among them *Discovery of Telescope and Microscope, General Aspect of Winter* and *Allusions to the Dew*. "Few Christians," he wrote, "would be willing to place [these] in the hands of their children on the Sabbath." To him, only the Bible was appropriate for Sunday reading.[14]

Smith was asked repeatedly for the titles of books he thought not merely unacceptable, but heretical. In the three years of active debate, Smith named only a few. In late 1846, Mann wrote to Smith demanding that he name specific heretical books or withdraw his charges. Smith

195

then named, *Sequel to Popular Lessons* by Eliza Robbins, a book of moral lessons used by many schools in the state. Robbins had written "the religion of Moses spoke of this life only," an interpretation Smith cited as an example of heresy. Robbins also had written, "Sabbath is the day when men go to the house of God in company, and *meet in pleasant walks.*" As Smith did not approve of recreational walking an appropriate Sabbath activity, he was horrified. A book advocating walking on Sunday had no place in the schools, or in the hands of children. Worse yet, Robbins had written that Jesus promised, *"all men shall never die, but have everlasting life."* She had dared to promise everyone could enter Heaven. To Congregational dogma, this was heresy, plain and simple. "Here is bald, blank, undisguised Universalism, taught by a most palpable perversion and alteration of the words of the Savior," Smith wrote. The orthodox view was that only the Elect would enter the Kingdom of Heaven; the rest of humanity would be damned for eternity. In contrast, a major tenet of Smith's former religion, Universalism, was the belief in the possibility of universal salvation. Robbin's book stood as incontrovertible proof to Smith that the board of education was determined to undermine God's truth.[15]

Smith claimed there was as much wrong with what was excluded from the Library's list as what was in it. The absence of texts supporting orthodox Congregationalism was more proof of a Unitarian-Universalist conspiracy at work. The Library, he declared, "excludes books as sectarian that inculcate truths, which nine-tenths of professed Christians of all names believe." He failed, however, to specify a single book that had been excluded.[16]

Debate about how Christians should behave on the Sabbath intensified when it was learned that Peirce encouraged the normal school students to go for walks that day. This revelation gave Smith more ammunition to fire at the West Newton school and added to his charge that Peirce was Parkerite. Peirce, he charged, "made it a *duty*" for his students, "wind and weather permitting, to attend church a half day on the Sabbath, and do their walking for recreation on that day, in the morning and evening." Peirce's laxity about church services were compared by Smith to those at Harvard, which required students to attend services in only the morning and afternoon. Smith believed that the entire day should be spent in church, in prayer and contemplation. *Any* other activity was inappropriate.[17]

Peirce responded to Smith's accusation about the Sabbath on March 26, 1847 in the *Christian Register*, calling what Smith had written an "unpardonable slander." Normal school students, he write, were never encouraged to be morally lax. A highly moral man, Peirce set a high standard of morality from his students. He was sufficiently disturbed by Smith's charges that he felt it necessary to write a personal letter to Mann defending himself from the charge of moral laxity. He had never, he wrote, equated walking as "recreation," which might suggest something inappropriate. Smith had "grossly misrepresented" what Peirce allowed students to do on the Sabbath – "in both the *spirit* and the *language.*"[18]

Smith fired back a few weeks later in the *Boston Recorder* with more allegations about what Peirce allegedly allowed students to do on Sundays. Normal school students, he insisted, routinely violated the holiness of the Sabbath and made it "a sort of gala day." He claimed he knew for certain that some girls "washed and others ironed" clothes, in direct violation of the strictures for keeping the day holy. Furthermore, Peirce requiring the young women to attend church services for even half a day was in itself a compromise, he wrote, implying Peirce would have preferred his students to ignore church attendance entirely. "And this is the model State school – supported by funds paid out of the treasury," Smith exclaimed. He lamented that normal school graduates would be going into the community spreading their anti-Christian views and practices.[19]

Unwilling to allow these fresh allegations to go unanswered, Peirce wrote directly to the Congregational *Boston Recorder*. He denied allowing the Sabbath to became "a gala day." There had also never been a time when his students "except one or two educated as Quakers" did not attend church, he wrote. Smith, he argued, dealt in unsubstantiated rumor and slander rather than facts. The claim that students had used time on Sundays to wash and iron their clothes was "destitute of truth."[20]

It was a relief to Horace Mann that the board of education stood behind Peirce and the school. In its annual report for 1847, the board defended Peirce and the school unanimously. They wrote that the "school has uniformly maintained the character which may be justly required of such an institution, and that the charges referred to can only be attributed to a culpable ignorance, or perversion, of facts."[21]

Nothing that the board wrote, however, had any influence on Smith, and he continued his attacks unabated. Another practice that Smith held against Peirce involved the writing of the student journals, something Peirce had required since his teaching days on Nantucket. The journals were turned in for correction and comment, a not uncommon practice in schools today. Keeping journals, however, was not commonplace in Peirce's time. Progressive educators like Peirce and Allen promoted journal writing as a way to teach self-expression, penmanship, and reasoning. They considered the journals an appropriate way for students to communicate with their teachers. Peirce's comments were generally positive in nature. He applied what he taught to his students. "Avoid scolding and fault finding." "Make it a point to speak of the good, rather than the bad."[22]

Smith completely misconstrued the intent and the content of the daily journals. He accused Peirce of inappropriate behavior, implying the journals were personal diaries, not meant for a man's eyes. It was a sordid accusation making Peirce appear as a voyeur. "We knew that he inspected daily their private journals," Smith wrote in the *Boston Recorder* in June 1847. This

> We had some knowledge of the West Newton School before this. We knew that the Principal held a sway over the minds of his pupils that has never before been assumed in a seminary of learning, save in the institutions of the Jesuits. We knew that he inspected daily their private journals; took newspapers into the school to read and comment upon articles in respect to West Newton.

Boston Recorder, Congregational Archives

accusation, with its implication of sexual impropriety, especially stung the upright Peirce to the quick. Smith accused him of using his journal responses as a way to communicate sacrilegious views to the vulnerable teenagers under his care. Whenever a student wrote about "their disbelief in the Bible" and about "mockery of the church" Peirce "smiled complacently," Smith charged. No proof accompanied these charges. In the journals that are now in existence, it is possible to sample Peirce's comments in the journals. They are the standard fare of correcting grammar and spelling with an occasional comment about the progress of the student's writing or thinking. (Note)

With all that was going on about the school in the newspapers, Electa Lincoln, writing over forty years later, recalled that the daily life of the school was undisturbed. "Nothing that was said outside the school disturbed the peace within or hindered its progress." It was not that the students were unaware of the accusations; Peirce and the teachers ensured that they were shielded from it as best as possible through hard work and focusing on their studies. Lincoln recalled that the girls were as "a unit" in their "hearty repudiation of the charges made whenever opportunity occurred." Early in 1847, Peirce talked to the students about the "Roaring Lion" that roamed the street outside the normal school taking a "gentle peep in." Ann E. Shannon wrote in her journal that the lion "has come this time in the form of Matthew Hale Smith.[23]

Smith's accusations about the propriety of their journal writing in June 1847, however, elicited a response from the student body. Lincoln wrote, "what a stir those cruel words made among the pupils." The thought of Father Peirce "smiling complacently" about disbelief in the Bible and "hatred of the clergy" made them angry. That attack by Smith, with its implication of moral decadency on the part of their principal, had prompted a student body meeting within two days of its publication. They met without the knowledge of any school administrators "entirely upon our own responsibility." The girls passed a series of "resolves," one addressing the practice of "journalizing." The journals, they wrote, were a form of "regular exercises," with the full understanding that they were scholastic writing assignments, not private diaries in any sense of the word.

This extraordinary letter defended all their teachers. "All honor to them for their goodness," they wrote. "Resolved, That the conduct of *all* of our teachers has been such as to inspire us with confidence and affection; that they labor to advance the cause of truth, and to promote the best interests of education." They expressed "sincere gratitude" for the "kindness and patience" of their teachers. Every student signed the letter, which they sent to a number of Boston newspapers. The conservative *Boston Recorder* was the only paper that refused to print the letter.[24]

The letter from the students did not end the attacks on their Father Peirce. In fact, the attacks intensified and reached a climax in 1847 when Peirce was attacked for immorality and depravity.

Note: Several years later, in 1847, the group was successful in establishing a Unitarian church in West Newton, the nucleus of the church consisting of the Allens and the Peirces. In fact, Peirce was chosen as the congregation's first Moderator. Fewer than half of the parishioners were old-time residents of West Newton.

Note: I have read through many of the surviving journals and have not found even one response by Peirce to any religious comments written in them.

Chapter 13: Allegations of Immorality, Depravity, Licentiousness and Bowling!

Matthew Hale Smith's attacks grew ever more strident and personal. In the spring of 1847, he made his most serious attack yet on Peirce and the West Newton school, accusing Peirce of allowing and encouraging licentious and inappropriate sexual behavior, involving not only Peirce but his wife Harriet, and his teaching assistant Electa Lincoln.

Smith's damning accusation centered on an evening of *tableaux vivante* at the normal school at the end of the fall term of 1846. A tableau is a dramatic frozen picture. Participants dress in costume and hold fixed positions as if in a still-life portrait. Tableaux were popular, often staged in churches to represent scenes from the Bible. School children performed them for classmates and parents to represent scenes from books, both fictional and historical. Smith asserted that the content and presentation of the tableaux in question were inappropriate for young ladies.

A series of five tableaux had been organized to celebrate the end of the term by Electa Lincoln and Harriet Peirce. Smith wrote, accurately, that students had dressed in men's clothing in several scenes. To Smith, young women dressing as men constituted indecent and shocking behavior. He described the evening vividly in an exposé in the *Boston Recorder*. About the first scene, titled "Before Marriage," he wrote there was "a young lady of the senior class, dressed in a *complete suit of gentleman's apparel.*" He described the third tableau as even more lewd. A girl dressed as a man "elevated" her heels "as high as the chair, or higher." The most shocking scene of all, according to Smith, was when

Electa Lincoln portrayed Pocahontas in the final tableau. Her shoulders were "bare," her arms and neck "naked" and her clothing indecent, reaching "*just* below the knees." Even more incriminatory, she had worn stockings of "Indian skin color" and daubed herself with "paint." The evening ended with dancing, another ungodly and inappropriate activity in his judgment. Smith wrote that Peirce had praised the "ladies for acting their parts so well!" To the conservative minister, it was evident Peirce condoned flagrantly immoral behavior.[1]

These were serious and specific allegations. Smith wrote in graphic language meant to shock his readers, and he succeeded. The debate over the tableaux resulted in unwelcome headlines and scrutiny of both the school and its instructors. These accusations of immorality, combined with Smith's earlier attacks, represented a serious threat to the continued existence of the normal schools.

A shaken Mann wrote to Peirce: "How far are the statements of Mr. Matthew Hale Smith, in regard to the School under your care, correct?" Peirce replied that Smith's allegations were "a compound of malevolence and falsehood." He said that Smith's characterization of the tableaux was "the blackest of calumnies" and "the most devilish of them all." Above all, Smith's public slander of the names and reputations of his wife and Electa Lincoln angered and alarmed him.[2]

In his defense, Peirce wrote that the tableaux had not been an official school event, but a private evening party. He acknowledged it had taken place on school property and that several men, though not specifically invited, had been present. He defended the suitability of tableaux vehemently, arguing they had been neither indecent nor inappropriate. Peirce admitted not having seen the tableaux himself, but said he had made inquiries of those who had attended. A woman known for her "notions of propriety and delicacy," had assured him nothing untoward had taken place.

Peirce vigorously defended Lincoln, writing that Smith had besmirched her reputation for the sake of attacking the normal school. Smith "wantonly dragged before the public gaze a young woman of fair renown," he wrote. He accused Smith of "licentious imagination and enthusiasm for falsehood" in his descriptions of the tableaux. The arms of the young women were "not more exposed than has been common" in the short-sleeved shirts and dresses in vogue at the time. Further, he wrote that Smith's description of Lincoln "daubed with paint" was

> Again: The piece makes the impression that the positions and attitudes assumed at the Tableau representation, especially by the lady assistant, were grossly indelicate and disgusting. Nothing could be farther from the truth. What is a Tableau? I apprehend many to the *very word* attach the idea of *indelicacy,—action*, and *histrionic gesticulation*. There is nothing of this. Tableau is a *living picture simply*, in which the person represented, appears at a distance, perfectly motionless, and only as long as he can hold his breath and refrain from moving a muscle. But, it may be said, a "*living picture*," motionless, and lasting but for a moment, *may be* a very indelicate thing. So indeed it may: but was *this* such? Mr. Smith says it was. From inquiries that I have made, I believe every lady present at, and witnessing the same, is ready to deny this assertion.

Boston Recorder, Congregational Archives

totally fictitious.[3]

Mann was concerned enough by Smith's unrelenting and repeated allegations to publish a pamphlet of responses in mid-1847. The persistent flow of charges, however, was difficult and delicate to handle. The continual defense of Peirce gave Smith's allegations more credence as the issues were kept in the public eye. Mann knew that charges once made are difficult to erase, despite facts that later disprove them.

Mann realized it was not enough to react to Smith's allegations. Moreover, he didn't have the time. He had to find a way to discredit Smith himself. In an effort to do so, Mann reminded readers of Smith's religious inconstancy and instability, his recent rejection of Universalism, and his becoming one of its sharpest critics. Mann pointed out that Smith's change of faith indicated that his views were unreliable and inconsistent. He accused Smith of zealotry, and of imposing his own newly-found orthodox beliefs on everyone else. In short, he declared Smith a man not to be believed. [4]

Smith was wounded enough by this attack on his religious conversion to write a responding pamphlet against Universalism, *Universalism Not of God, an Examination of the System of Universalism; its Doctrine, Arguments, and Fruits, with the Experience of the Author, During a Ministry of 12 Years*. In it, Smith defended and described his difficult decision to leave the faith of his father, a Universalist minister, writing that the decision "cost me almost my life." Smith confided that, although he had become a Universalist minister at the tender age of fifteen, it had not taken him long to doubt basic tenets of Universalism. He had found his fellow Universalists did not live up to his high moral expectations of them. This included his first congregation which he wrote had not been religious enough. He accused many of its members of drinking alcohol, and of being bigoted and profane. Some, he said, even conducted business on the Lord's Day. When he saw they were unable to change their behavior, he began to question the religion itself. "My faith did not reform men," he concluded.

Disillusioned, the young minister moved to Hartford, Connecticut in 1832, hoping to find a more pious community that would welcome a zealous minister. "But the moral aspect of things in Connecticut was worse," he wrote. He was shocked to discover the congregation did not have sufficient knowledge and regard of the Bible. "They had no more faith in the Bible than they had in the Koran."

The Universalist belief that God promises all men, even sinners, eventual salvation most disturbed Smith. He began to believe the Calvinist idea that only the Elect will enter Heaven. "I was compelled to reject ultra-Universalism, or that form of Universalism which limits all punishment to this life." Discouraged and demoralized, he decided to leave his Connecticut congregation, too.

His next assignment was as the Universalist minister of a congregation in Salem, Massachusetts. Within a short time he judged that congregation as unworthy as the previous two. He threw himself into his work, desperately trying to change his congregation's thinking and behavior. He wrote an open letter to the congregation with an ultimatum. He told them that he "could not serve them, unless I could do so without being considered a Universalist." Unsurprisingly, they did not abandon Universalism to please their new minister, and Smith resigned from the Universalists for good.

When he left Salem, he said that he was at the lowest point of his life, disillusioned, discouraged and lost. Most of his friends, and all of his family, were Universalists. To leave Universalism was to detach himself from everything and everyone that was familiar. Wrestling with his beliefs, he embarked on an intense study of the Bible, seeking evidence to refute Universalist beliefs. He made his objections public, renouncing his former friends and relatives. Fortunately, his Universalist wife shared his doubts and joined him in his rejection of their former faith.

Smith and his wife joined an evangelical Congregational church. He compared himself to St. Paul who had repented his former beliefs to become a disciple of Jesus Christ. He wrote that he made it his life's goal to destroy beliefs and tenets contrary to orthodox Congregationalism, especially the beliefs of the Universalists and the Unitarians. Both, he claimed, were thinly-disguised atheism with "the marks of being the doctrine of Satan." The Universalist religion "does evil, and only evil," he wrote, accusing the Unitarians and Universalists of conspiring to weaken the teaching and belief in the Bible.[5] (Note)

After the publication of Smith's pamphlet, Mann had had more than enough of Smith's accusations. He decided to use information that he had previously obtained about Smith, but which he had been reluctant to reveal, not wanting to stoop to Smith's level of attack. Mann was loath to ruin the man's reputation, but felt he had no choice but to use the information he had attained.

Mann's counter attack concerned Smith's involvement with nine or ten pin bowling, a game considered inappropriate by many people because of its association with gambling and crime. In fact, the state of Connecticut banned nine-pin bowling in 1841. (Bowlers there circumvented the law by simply adding a tenth pin as the law had specifically outlawed only *nine*-pin bowling.)

Mann had discovered a skeleton in Smith's past that he had not wanted to use against the minister, knowing the impact it would have on him. He tried subtly to let Smith know that he had this knowledge, hoping Smith would cease his attacks on Peirce. Mann hinted in a letter to Smith that he knew Smith had something to conceal when Mann defended Peirce for allowing the normal school girls to go for walks on Sundays. Mann wrote, "I said, you might as well have foisted the word *'bowling'* as *'recreation'* into Mr. Peirce's allowing the girls to walk for exercise." Mann later said his allusion to bowling had been included to let Smith know that Mann knew about his connection with bowling. Meant to be a warning shot, it was either lost on Smith or he decided to ignore it.

Smith continued to attack the normal school and Peirce. Mann finally decided he had no choice but to expose Smith as a secret bowler. To modern sensibilities this seems a benign charge. But in conservative circles in the 1840s, this was a serious allegation against an orthodox minister, particularly against one as righteous as Smith.

Mann publicly charged that while Smith was an ordained orthodox Congregational minister of a church in New Hampshire, he had participated in the game of bowling. Not only had Smith participated in bowling, he had preached against it at the same time, exposing him as a hypocrite. When his congregation learned their minister had bowled in public, according to Mann, Smith had been compelled to "confess it to your church and people."[6]

Mann's pamphlet included a letter from Jesse Bowers, a state senator in New Hampshire, and the former sheriff of the city of Nashua. Senator Bowers testified that he had personally seen "the Rev. Mr. Smith rolling at ten pins" at Hampton Beach. Furthermore, Bowers observed that Smith was no novice at the game, but rather a "practiced and excellent roller, from his style of rolling then exhibited." Bowers noted that he had seen the minister bowling during the time Smith was "settled over a church in this place." This letter supported Mann's claim that

Smith continued to bowl at the same time he was condemning it as an immoral activity. Bowers testified that he heard that when Smith's congregation discovered him to be a bowler, he had confessed to them and "promised to sin no more in that particular."

Mann also included a letter from Franklin Munroe, a member of Smith's congregation. Munroe wrote that he had heard the minister deliver several sermons "condemning the practice of bowling" prior to Smith's exposure as a bowler. Monroe wrote that when Smith was unmasked, he gave an emotional, tear-filled sermon confessing his sin, promising to sin no more. According to Munroe, the minister told his flock, "the ball-room was no place for a professed Christian, and the bowling alley no place for the minister of the Gospel."

The evidence was printed for all to see. Smith was caught red-handed. The charges were substantiated with irrefutable evidence, unlike the allegations and insinuations Smith had leveled against Peirce. Mann wrote that he regretted exposing Smith in such a brutal manner. He had hoped his earlier allusion to bowling would have warned Smith to cease his attacks. "It is painful so to expose a fellow-being," he wrote, "but you have left me no other alternative." Mann pressed his argument; once a liar, always a liar. If Smith had concealed and lied about his own weaknesses, it followed that he was not to be believed in his accusations of others, from his charge that the teaching of the Bible was suppressed in the normal schools, to his claim of having witnessed the tableaux at the normal school.[7]

Mann's pamphlet went a long way toward discrediting Smith, turning him into fodder for the partisan press. Testimonials appeared in newspapers in support of Mann and Peirce based on the exposure of Smith as an unreliable source. It was gratifying to Mann when Emerson

Davis, a former member of the board of education, and a Congregationalist, wrote that he was certain the "whole orthodox community" was convinced that "neither the board nor yourself have ever had any secret purpose or desire to convert the people to any particular system of faith or to undermine the faith of the orthodox." Davis underscored his belief in the importance of the public schools for the future of American democracy. "Abolish this system and it would not be strange if one-half of the next generation of voters should be unable to read."[8]

Smith was incensed by Mann's assault on his character and his exposure as a bowler. The shoe was on the other foot, as Mann had hoped. Smith was now in the position of having to defend himself. His immediate response was to categorically deny the bowling allegation "as false as it is infamous." He called Mann a liar who had dragged out "vile and rotten calumnies" against him in order to divert attention from the unsuitable doings at the normal school. [9]

Despite the exposure and shame he suffered, Smith did not give up easily or retreat quietly. In May 1847, he wrote a lengthy rebuttal in the *Boston Recorder* calling Mann's pamphlet "a curiosity in its way." He claimed Mann had been unsuccessful in his attempt to prove that Mann himself was a "very good man," and that Smith was "a very bad man." He tackled the accusation about bowling as best as he could. He denied that he had preached against bowling while continuing to bowl, ignoring the testimony of Bowers and Munroe. He admitted he had bowled for "exercise" at Hampton Beach "at the invitation of some townsmen," but claimed he had bowled "purely for purposes of health." Further, he asserted that it was not uncommon for other orthodox ministers to bowl.[10]

It was not until five months later that Smith reproved himself, admitting to "having once been caught in the devil's society." Continuing to keep his attacks personal, and attempting to shift discussion away from himself, Smith wrote that Mann had been forced to turn to politics because he had been such a poor lawyer, "scarcely able to

> PERSONAL TO MYSELF.
>
> On page 12, I find the following:—
>
> MR. SMITH'S "BOWLING:" *First preached against; then committed; then confessed to his Church; then denied to the world.*
>
> That I preached against bowling and then practised it, is a falsehood. That I ever confessed to my church what I denied to the world, is another falsehood. In his Sequel, Mr. Mann insinuated that I was in the habit of " bowling Sunday mornings and evenings." He intended to make such an impression; he did make it. Now, he pretends to have had no such intentions. He presents two other falsehoods more infamous than the first.
>
> In the early part of August 1843, I was at the famous watering place at Hampton Beach. At the invitation of some townsmen, I went out and rolled at ten pins, for exercise, a short time. At that time I had not given the question a consideration, whether such an exercise, under such circumstances, purely for purposes of health, was, or was not, proper. I knew it was no unusual thing for gentlemen of my profession to take such exercise. In the winter following, I found it necessary to rebuke certain professors of religion, who

Boston Recorder, Congregational Archives

get his own bread" in that profession.

In that letter Smith repeated his assertion about the impropriety of the tableaux in West Newton almost verbatim with new attacks on Electa Lincoln. He wrote, that if he had been there to see her, he "should then, as did the men of old, have spied out the 'nakedness of the land.'"

Furthermore, he claimed that she had admitted to the general truth as Smith had written it and had brazenly defended her participation in the evening's performance. He wrote that Lincoln had told people "she should not hesitate to do the same thing again, under similar circumstances." Smith repeated his familiar allegations about the desecration of the Sabbath by Peirce and the normal school students, not altering his former accusations despite evidence to the contrary. He ignored anything that contradicted his own view of matters.

Smith wrote that Mann, as secretary of education, posed a grave danger to American society. He alleged that Mann was adept at tricking people about his true nature, making himself appear good and pious, while actually being the human embodiment of evil. "Satan is most to be feared when he puts on the garb of an angel of light." He repeated his belief that Mann and Peirce were part of a Universalist conspiracy against him. He claimed that his former Universalist friends had "commenced an assault" on him ever since he had left their ranks. Though Mann and Peirce were not Universalists, he claimed they had become "allies" with them. Smith ended his long letter with a reference to Psalm 109, the 8th verse. "Let his days be few; and let another take his office." Was Smith hoping that Mann, that "officially bad man," would die? Or was he only hoping that he would be removed from office? He left it to his readers to interpret as they wished.[11] (Note)

Peirce wrote to the conservative *Boston Recorder* to refute Smith's latest letter, furious that Mann had been compared to the Devil. He chose the Congregational *Boston Recorder* to "expose and refute his slanders" as that paper had published most of Smith's attacks over the years. Unlike the letter of the normal school students defending their school, the paper chose to print Peirce's letter. Peirce quoted Smith's brother who described his brother as "religiously insane," and suggested his slanders "be regarded as the fruit of a mind diseased – a spirit bereft of reason."

Peirce reiterated earlier arguments. He defended his students' use of the Sabbath, defended Lincoln, and explained the educational benefits of student journals. He repeated his support of using the Bible in public schools, and wrote of being deeply insulted by Smith's claims that he had "smiled" when reading journal entries of students who wrote about disbelief in the Bible. "I charge upon Mr. S. the malicious slander both of myself and my pupils."

> I am acquainted with the school's history. I know on what foundation it stands. I feel that it is secure. You may continue to concoct your falsehoods and bruit them abroad—you may defame and oppose,—you may vilify and falsify; it will be all in vain. The cause of education and Normal Schools, as its efficient aid, have taken fast hold upon the public sympathies and confidence. Heaven is smiling upon them, and you will find it hard to curse " what God has *not cursed.*"
> Yours truly,   C. PEIRCE.
> *West Newton, June 5, 1847.*

Boston Recorder, Congregational Archives

Peirce took offense at Smith's mockery of his motto, "Live to the Truth." Smith had claimed Peirce's signature phrase was a mockery of prayer. While this may seem a minor charge set against the other allegations this one involved something especially dear to his heart. "Live to the truth" was central to the daily life of his classroom and integral to his self-image. (Note)

Peirce ended his letter demanding Smith cease his slanders and insinuations. If Smith had facts, Peirce wrote, he should lay them before the public. "I fear them not. You will find me always 'face to,' never on the *retreat.*" Peirce confidently asserted that public education would eventually triumph, despite the lies of people like Smith. "You may continue to concoct your falsehoods – you may vilify and falsify; it will all be in vain." Public sympathy, he wrote, was on the side of the progressive educators. "Heaven is smiling upon them."[12]

Peirce was concerned about the continuing attacks on the school and the effects it might have on his students, especially the insinuations of impropriety and lax morality. He invited Governor George Briggs to observe the school and to address the students in 1848. After his observation, the governor said he had enjoyed and benefitted from what he had seen that day. He acknowledged the "enemies of the normal school" and wished that they had been able to witness what he had that day. He testified to the students' abilities as "the next corps of teachers" and to their high "moral qualifications."[13]

The board of education decided it had no choice but to instigate an investigation of the tableaux. A committee was appointed which included three conservative Orthodox ministers including Dr. Heman Humphrey, president of Amherst College. Humphrey was no supporter of Cyrus Peirce and had, in fact, wanted Peirce replaced a year prior to the investigation. With such a group in charge of the investigation, it was of supreme importance when they "completely cleared" Peirce of any wrongdoing in March 1848. No one could accuse Mann of stacking the deck in Peirce's favor. The governor and the entire board signed the document exonerating Peirce. The board hoped that the investigation and exoneration would put an end to the unfortunate episode.

The quarrel died down for several months - until Mann published his *Eleventh Annual Report*. Unfortunately, the report, which referred to the controversy, returned it to the headlines. The editor of the *Boston Recorder*, unhappy his paper was mentioned, responded with a long and critical editorial, liberally quoting passages from Smith, repeating some of his assertions almost word for word. The editor repeated Smith's allegation that the board of education opposed the use of corporal punishment in the classroom. He accused the board of sectarianism, and of promoting Unitarianism and Universalism. He also expressed disappointment that the board had "found no evidence" of impropriety when it investigated the "offensive" tableaux at the West Newton Normal School. There was no doubt, he claimed, that the performance had been "indecent" and that Lincoln had worn "savage dress."

Finally, the editor reasserted Smith's charge that the Sabbath was regularly dishonored by the "Parkerite" Peirce. Evidence for this, according to the editor, was that Peirce attended Parker's lectures and had invited him to speak at the normal school. The editor claimed that Peirce supported a radical Parkerite to be the first minister of the recently established Unitarian church in West Newton. The editor also alleged that, at yet another end-of-term exhibition, normal school students had presented essays that included references both to Parker and to transcendentalism.

Finally, the editor reminded his readers that the board of education was an expensive undertaking for the citizens of Massachusetts. "No less than ten thousand dollars a year is expended to sustain it." He reminded them that $1300 had been spent on the West Newton Normal School alone and he claimed that many of the students trained in the normal schools were "unfit" to teach[14].

Fortunately for Peirce and Mann, the editorial was almost the last salvo in the long battle. The school at West Newton had more applicants that year than they could accept and the two other normal schools in the state continued to flourish. Actions spoke louder than words, and even the negative words began to fade away.

Sporadic accusations against Peirce and the school in West Newton continued to appear, but they were short-lived. J.S. Clark, the Congregational minister in West Newton, led one attack, borrowing heavily from Smith's writings. Peirce answered Clark's allegations briefly, not giving them more credence or publicity than he felt was necessary.[15]

In most of Peirce's letters he accentuated positive developments. He wrote that over "a *thousand* improved teachers" had already gone forth from the state normal schools. He proudly pointed to "sister states" copying the Massachusetts model of teacher training that he had been most responsible for developing.

In only one letter did Peirce express bitterness over the attacks against him, those he loved, and his school. In a lengthy letter to the *Christian Register* in July 1848, Peirce wrote about the history of the normal school. He described how it had flourished in Lexington "surrounded by a genial and healthful atmosphere." He lamented, however, the move to West Newton, which he described as a "region of bigotry, narrow-mindedness and intolerance." Many in West Newton would "rejoice" in the failure of the normal school, he wrote, singling out a local minister [Clark] as the leader of critics who from "a convenient distance, misunderstood, misrepresented and exaggerated" incidents at the school.[16]

Peirce's letter prompted the *Boston Recorder* to write its final editorial against Peirce and West Newton school, but it was the most personal and nasty of all the attacks ever written against Peirce. Peirce was described as a "rabid" man who "foams at the mouth, runs round and round in very extensive circles, and bites, snaps and barks at every decent person he sees." The editor accused Peirce of being "blind with the rage and spite of the bigotry of liberalism, which is the worst kind of bigotry there is."[17]

Another attack on Peirce came from the Reverend Clark in the *Christian Register*. Clark described himself as one of " the orthodox portion of the community [in] West Newton" attacked by Peirce. Clark expressed surprise at the "grave charges" made by Peirce, a man he had

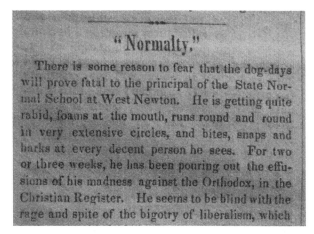

Boston Recorder, Congregational Archives

he previously found to have a "meek and quiet spirit." Clark reminded Peirce that West Newton had cheerfully consented to send students to the experimental model school. Peirce, he asserted, had divided West Newton along religious lines, and had aligned himself exclusively with fellow Unitarians, which was not the "prevailing faith" of the community. He wrote that his fellow citizens had been uncomfortable with the controversial tableaux. For these reasons, he suggested the board of education replace Peirce as the principal of the school.[18]

Peirce wrote a short letter in response to the attack in the *Boston*

Recorder, but he chose to ignore Clark. He reverted to his usual positive attitude, focusing on the success of the normal school movement. "We cannot meet more than half of our applications for teachers," he boasted, and predicted that future teachers would come from the ranks of normal school graduates.[19]

With these last letters the battle between the orthodox Congregationalists and Peirce came to an end. Matthew Hale Smith had been silenced and there was nothing new to report. The episode faded from the headlines.

In February 1849, before the controversy had come to a close, Peirce wrote to Mann that he was thinking of resigning. Mann responded that Peirce was thinking too much of himself and not enough of the school and their cause, encouraging him to stay on the job. In October, however, Peirce again wrote that he was ready to retire.[20]

The board of education accepted Peirce's resignation with regret, expressing "their high appreciation of his services." Their annual report said, "Mr. Peirce had literally worn himself out in his arduous office. He had, for many months, been suffering from rheumatism, sleeplessness, and the other usual consequences of excessive and long-continued mental labor and care."[21]

Peirce's last months at the normal school were peaceful. He had faced down the controversy and had been exonerated by the governor. He concentrated on the school's day-to-day management, confident the normal school concept was well established. The railings of Christian conservatives could not hurt him or the normal schools any more.

Mann recognized that Peirce's health was fragile. In a private letter, he wrote that he regretted that Peirce's body had given out before his mind. "Why could not the old soul transmigrate into another body?

Lame, cold and numb as he is, there are few young men that could equal him in the race." He recognized Peirce's important role in American history as the director of the first teacher training institution, describing him as responsible for "the planting and early culture of a seed which will grow."[22]

A factor in Peirce's decision to retire was that the normal school had once again outgrown its facility. Tired and in pain, he lacked the energy to oversee the move, even though the school was only relocating to a bigger facility in West Newton. It was the right time and the right place to retire. He was fifty-nine years old and ready to give up the rigors of running the school, worn out by the years of battle.

Peirce decided that the summer term would end with a series of tableaux. The decision may have been an attempt on his part to prove how innocent they were or a final gesture of defiance. Reverend Clark and other conservatives objected to the tableaux beforehand, and the *Boston Recorder* added its disapproval, proclaiming, "Model artistes are an offence to good morals."[23]

Mann publically recognized Peirce's vital contribution to the professionalization of teachers and to the study of how best to teach. Peirce had become the father of teacher education in the United States. Both men were proud of their accomplishments and a job well done. But it was time for both to move on. Mann was elected to the House of Representatives to take the seat of John Quincy Adams who had recently died. Mann resigned as secretary of education in 1848. (He served in the House for two terms, from 1848 to 1852.)

In his twelve years as secretary of education, Horace Mann had transformed the public schools in the state and established three normal schools. The status and salaries of teachers had improved. He had fostered outreach to classroom teachers from Teacher Institutes to the creation of a professional journal for teachers. Under his leadership thousands of schoolhouses had been repaired or replaced. Taxes had been increased to improve the schools, the teaching year had been lengthened, new texts were published, and libraries established.

To honor their beloved principal, students at the normal school organized a huge retirement celebration. Dignitaries from around the country were invited, as were all the school's graduates. Mann secretly solicited money to send Peirce to an international peace conference in Paris, seeking donations from around the state. For example, he solicited Nathaniel Barney on Nantucket asking Peirce's colleague from the school integration fight. He wrote to Barney of his hope "the voyage might conduce to the restoration of Mr. Peirce's health broken down by his long and exhausting labors." Barney made a liberal contribution and solicited funds from other Nantucketers. Students, past and present, donated as well as prominent citizens such as Senator Charles Sumner, a fellow Unitarian, abolitionist and member of the peace movement.

On July 26, 1849, over 200 former pupils descended on West Newton to pay tribute to Father Peirce and to celebrate the graduation of his last class of educated teachers. Peirce delivered the welcoming address, followed by a speech from Lincoln. Other dignitaries, including conservative members of the board of education, praised Peirce to a crowd that filled the normal school hall to capacity.

In the afternoon, the celebration moved to the West Newton town hall for more speeches honoring Peirce and the normal school movement. Speakers came from as far away as Louisville, Kentucky. Students and teachers were praised throughout the festivities and Peirce was lauded for his dedication. Only a passing reference was made to the trials and tribulations of the previous three years, calling them "the late unworthy attempt to excite popular prejudice against the institution."

The focus was where it should have been – on the contributions of Cyrus Peirce. Peirce was proud the normal school had not only survived years of controversy and opposition, but had thrived and prevailed. The gift of money to enable Peirce to travel to the international peace conference in France was overwhelming to him, a dream come true.

To add to his satisfaction, his most recent critic, Reverend Clark, was discredited that same month for having misrepresented Peirce and the normal school in what he had previously written. The *Christian Register* wrote that the "wound" Clark had tried to inflict on Peirce "is now as the surgeon's say, 'healed' and without a scar."[24]

The *Common School Journal* devoted three pages to Peirce's retirement ceremony and to his contributions to education. It quoted from Mann's touching speech about his friend who had "stood by him through sunshine and shade." Mann talked about the toll Peirce's hard work had taken on him. Mann's speech, it reported, "touched every heart, and should have been heard by every school committee man and parent who ever grudged his wages to a teacher, on the ground that teaching is not hard work."[25]

Cyrus Peirce's Passport application

National Archives

So, Cyrus Peirce retired in style, vindicated, honored and loved. He had fought a long, personal and important battle and had prevailed. It was a grand way to end his association with the normal school. He began to plan his trip to Paris.

Note: The Universalists, who based their religion on belief in universal salvation, did not merge with the Unitarians until 1961.

Note: Curiously, the same psalm has surfaced by those opposed to President Barack Obama.

Note: "Live to the Truth" is engraved on Peirce's headstone and is the motto of Framingham State University.

Chapter 14: European Adventure: International Peace Congress in Paris

After his retirement, Cyrus and Harriet Peirce chose to stay in their home on Cherry Street in West Newton where they lived until Cyrus's death. Whatever controversy or bitterness had existed between Peirce and the town faded. He was never again the center of the kind of political maelstroms that had consumed his life for twenty years and was able, for the most part, to settle into a more peaceful life.

First, he had an exciting trip to take, thanks to the generosity of his students and other benefactors. He prepared to travel to the International Peace Congress in Paris as an official delegate of the United States less than two months after his retirement ceremony.

The American peace movement had been formally organized in 1815 when peace societies were formed in Massachusetts and New York. The founder of the first society in Massachusetts was Unitarian minister Noah Worcester who believed disputes between nations should be settled by international arbitration. By 1818, the Massachusetts Peace Society had grown to over 1,000 members.

The national American Peace Society was formed in 1822, and the Massachusetts Peace Society was absorbed into it. Formed just seventy years after the American Revolution, many members of the peace movement, including Peirce, questioned the morality of the American Revolution, challenging the wisdom of even the Founding Fathers in resorting to violence in their pursuit of independence.[1]

The peace movement included progressive religious leaders, transcendentalists, abolitionists and utopian idealists. Early supporters of the peace movement were predominantly Unitarians and Quakers. Their belief in nonviolence influenced the tactics they used to promote many other reform movements.

Another early Unitarian who embraced the peace movement was Ellery Channing. Like Peirce, Channing had been a Congregational minister, but had left the Congregationalists in 1820 becoming an influential and outspoken Unitarian leader. The popular minister's participation in the peace movement drew others to the movement.

Samuel J. May was also prominent in the peace movement. Like Peirce, May was a Unitarian minister, an abolitionist, a temperance advocate, a leader in women's rights, and a leader in educational reform.

The leaders of the peace movement put their faith in the role of public education to promote their principles, believing that an educated public would be a peace-loving public. They optimistically believed that war could be eradicated and, as civilizations developed, good would prevail over evil.

This was something Peirce believed whole-heartedly. As far back as his 1824 sermon in North Reading, he had advocated nonviolent resistance and the hope that war would be eliminated. He supported pacifism in a letter to his Nantucket students in 1839, the year he left to take over the school in Lexington. He singled out and admonished two students, John and Charles, for warlike leanings. He admitted his misgivings about the American Revolution to them, particularly living in a place where the Revolution was commemorated. "To be candid, I think our forefathers ought not to have resisted unto blood. They should have endured until God had pointed out some other way for their deliverance."[2]

Despite the setbacks he had experienced, Peirce believed that humankind was making progress. Idealism and optimism were central to his philosophy. Teaching the principles of nonviolence to youngsters was part of the value system that he was certain would lead to a better world. Peirce envisioned a world without slavery, without the abuses of alcohol, without cruelty to others, and without war. To Peirce, all these goals would be accomplished in the classrooms of America.

In 1837, the American Peace Society accepted an amendment proposed by William Lloyd Garrison and Reverend Henry C. Wright stating that the group was "founded on the principle that all war is contrary to the spirit of the gospel." Total opposition to war was a radical viewpoint that many in the peace movement were uncomfortable with, and the proposal caused the peace movement to splinter. The radicals opposed all forms of militarism; whereas the moderates argued that some wars were justifiable especially those in self-defense. Some moderates withdrew from the American Peace Society because of its extreme stance.[3]

In 1838, Garrison formed the separate New England Non-Resistance Society. Amongst its earliest members was Nantucket-born Quaker Lucretia Mott. Garrison went on the lecture circuit speaking about both nonresistance and abolition. He lent the support of his newspaper, the *Liberator*, to the cause of nonviolence, believing nonviolent resistance would bring down slavery and end racial segregation in the north.

Abolitionists across the nation practiced nonviolence through their spending power. They boycotted slave-produced products, such as sugar and cotton. Nathaniel Barney was a trustee of the Boston and Taunton Railroad which continued to segregate black passengers after most railroads in Massachusetts had discontinued the practice. When the company refused to integrate its cars in 1842, Barney declined his dividends for over a year and a half, saying he did not wish to "profit from evil." When the railroad capitulated and stopped its discriminatory practice late in 1843, Barney wrote to the railroad's treasurer for the dividends that were owed to him. He directed the funds, $22.50, sent as a donation to the *Liberator.* This was the kind of protest the Garrisonians believed was most effective in the battle against discrimination.[4]

Political nonresistance was also practiced. Garrison and Barney, for example, refused to vote in state or federal elections in a symbolic gesture of nonviolent resistance. Both believed that voting indicated support of a government that continued to allow slavery and to count slaves as three-fifths of a person in determining the number of politicians states sent to the House of Representatives.

Nantucket was a shining example of successful nonviolent resistance. The nonviolent methods employed by the islanders during their fight for school segregation produced a historical result when Massachusetts passed Bill 214 in 1845. This important law prohibited discrimination in the public schools of Massachusetts and guaranteed equal education to all students. The law gave parents or guardians the right to sue their towns for damages due to segregation. This was the first civil rights law for equal access to education in the history of the United States, and was heralded as a success story for nonviolent resistance.

To achieve their stunning victory, the Nantucket opponents of school segregation had employed a variety of nonviolent strategies. When the island schools were re-segregated in 1844, the black community organized such a successful boycott of the segregated African School that the school committee was forced to assign white students to the school in order to keep it open.[5]

Petitions were ultimately effective in pressuring the legislature to pass the civil rights law. When town meetings failed to integrate the schools, Nantucket abolitionists submitted petitions to the state legislature including a petition from Eunice Ross, the young woman who had been denied access to the high school. After receiving the petitions, the State House in Boston passed its groundbreaking law. (Note)

Not surprisingly, transcendentalists embraced the peace movement. They believed in the power of individual choice and encouraged Christians to refuse to go to war, even at the risk of imprisonment. They believed that if large numbers of men refused to participate in the military, war would inevitably disappear. Prominent among these influential thinkers was Ralph Waldo Emerson of Concord, Massachusetts, original founder of the Transcendental Club.

The Mexican War in 1846 presented the American peace movement with a challenge as war fever swept the nation. Abolitionists viewed the war as a barely-disguised ploy by slave owners to extend the reach of slavery. Many Unitarians and Quakers opposed the war on Christian principles of nonviolence. Emerson wrote that war was "abhorrent to all right reason." In a lecture to the American Peace Society, he said war is "an epidemic insanity, breaking out here and there like the cholera or influenza, infecting men's brains instead of their bowels."[6]

One of Emerson's closest friends, Henry David Thoreau famously refused to pay his taxes to protest the Mexican War, choosing jail instead. While he only spent one night in jail, Thoreau wrote an important essay about his motive and rationale. Originally called "On Resistance to Civil Government," it is now known as "Civil Disobedience." Thoreau's essay had minimal impact during his lifetime, but it has been a major influence on nonviolent resistance ever since. "Under a government which imprisons any unjustly, the true place for a just man is also a prison." Like Garrison and Nathaniel Barney, Thoreau believed that voting was ineffective. He said that if slaves had to wait for the American people to vote against slavery, generations would pass before they would be freed. Thoreau argued that bolder approaches, such as refusing to pay taxes, would be far more effective.

Another staunch abolitionist from the radical wing of the peace movement was Senator Charles Sumner of Boston who donated money to enable Peirce to travel to the Paris Peace Congress. In 1845, Sumner gave a speech supporting the idea of a league of nations where nations would have the chance to cooperate and settle their disputes peacefully. Sumner also spoke in favor of a world court of arbitration where countries could submit their disagreements for resolution. In addition, Sumner called upon the United States to completely disband its standing army, navy, and all state militias, an extreme stance.

The American peace movement was in contact with their international brethren. World conferences were organized sporadically, the first convening in London in 1843. When Peirce was given the money to enable him to attend the 1849 Peace Congress, he was elated. He had never been out of the country and this was a great opportunity. The trip was an unexpected surprise and he quickly applied for a passport. On his application, certified by Horace Mann, Peirce described himself as having dark hair, a "darkish" complexion, blue eyes and a large nose. Despite their long association, Mann consistently misspelled Peirce as Pierce. [7]

The Paris Peace Congress was almost cancelled before it began. First, there were violent street protests in Paris, resulting from a French attack on Rome in an effort to restore the Pope who had fled during a populist uprising. Then, cholera broke out in the city. Luckily for the congress, French authorities quickly quelled the riots and the epidemic petered out.

Although Peirce left no account of his trip, one of his traveling companions, his old friend, Joseph Allen, did. They had attended Divinity classes together and had kept in touch through Allen's nephew, Nathaniel. Allen and Peirce supported the same causes and had lived their lives in similar fashion. Both had been ministers for a short period, but with similar educational philosophies, chose teaching instead. It is likely that his friend Peirce shared the experiences described by Allen in his memoir.[8]

The sailing packet *Plymouth Rock* left Massachusetts in early July with most of the New England delegates aboard, including Peirce and Allen. They joined a select group of twenty-three men who comprised the American delegation. Peirce was reunited with Henry Clapp, Jr., also a delegate from Massachusetts. Clapp was related to Peirce by marriage and had served with Peirce on the school committee when it had tried and failed to integrate the Nantucket public schools. Clapp had left the island, and was living in Boston when he was selected to go to Paris.

According to letters sent home by Allen, they had a pleasant trip crossing the Atlantic. Delegates organized evening discussions onboard about topics to be discussed at the peace congress, including arbitration of disputes between countries. The other passengers were invited to join in the evening seminars. Allen and Peirce, both teachers, probably helped lead the discussions.

The delegates arrived in England after "a most delightful voyage," stayed overnight in Liverpool, and then boarded a train to London. En route, the train stopped in the industrial city of Birmingham, described by Allen as "a smoky and uncomfortable-looking place." The train continued to Leamington where the delegates took in some sights. For sixpence, they went by carriage to see Warwick and Kenilworth Castles.

After their long day of sightseeing, the delegates arrived in London around 9 p.m. where lodging had been arranged for them at Radley's Hotel in Fitzroy Square near Regent's Park. Their English counterparts arranged for the Americans to see some sights in London during their visit. Several delegates observed the House of Lords in session. Undoubtedly, Peirce was one of the observers as he was determined to learn and see all that he could on his once-in-a-life time journey. On their second morning in London, the Americans toured St. Paul's Cathedral, climbing the 600 stairs to the Whispering Gallery in the dome. Allen, despite being fifty-nine, chose to climb even higher. He described the ever-narrowing stairwell in great detail, writing that he was lightheaded when he finally reached the golden ball at the top of the dome. "It made me dizzy to look from such a vast height, - more than four hundred feet."

The majority of the American and English delegates left together from London Bridge Station in two trains hired specifically for them. Six or seven hundred strong, they traveled to the port of Folkestone where they boarded two steamers, the *Queen of the Belgians* and the *Princess Clementine*. The party had a pleasant journey in mild weather across the English Channel, landing in Boulogne where they were greeted with great cheers.

It is possible that Peirce was with the bulk of the delegates, but it is more probable he stayed with Joseph Allen who had chosen to leave England several days earlier than the majority of the delegates. Allen had decided to take advantage of the opportunity to see more of Europe before heading to Paris. He and some other unnamed Americans sailed to Ostend, Belgium in a smooth eleven-hour journey across the English

Channel. From there, they journeyed into Switzerland.

Regardless of whether Peirce took the side trip or not, eventually all the American delegates converged on Paris where they lodged in "good quarters." Charles Sumner's brother, George, who lived in Paris, welcomed his fellow Americans. He had assisted the organizers in getting everything ready for the congress beforehand.[9]

The congress convened on August 22, 1849 in the Hall of St.

Paris 1850s

Cecilia, a space that could accommodate approximately two thousand delegates. The hall was decorated with the flags of the delegates' nations. The doors opened at 11 a.m. and by noon, the hall was filled to capacity. At 1 p.m. the members of the organizing committee convened the congress. Loud cheers filled the hall. Victor Hugo, novelist, social activist, and member of the French National Assembly, presided.

During the first session, American Elihu Burrit, one of the secretaries of the congress, read the names of the American delegates. Among them was Amasa Walker, a member of the Massachusetts legislature, Joseph Allen and Cyrus Peirce. One can imagine it was a thrill for the delegates to hear their names entered into the official rolls.

Hugo addressed the congress with optimism, predicting the abolition of war. "A day will come when the only battlefield will be the market," he said in his opening remarks. "A day will come when bullets and bomb shells will be replaced by votes." Hugo spoke about the massive expense of nations maintaining large militaries, as well as the cost of war itself. He mused about the wonderful public projects that could be accomplished with the money then spent on the military diverted to things such as the building of canals, and the extension of railroads across the globe. "Misery would no longer be found."[10]

Allen described Hugo as "one of the handsomest men I have seen." He wrote a vivid and humorous description of what he thought was the strange style of French public speaking. "It is vehement, the voice rising at times to its highest pitch, the speaker rising on tiptoe, raising his hands to the utmost extent of his arms."[11]

Auguste Visschers, leader of the Belgian delegation, reminded the audience the state of Massachusetts had voted five years earlier that "arbitration ought to take the place of war." The Belgian singled out Elihu Buritt as the "ring of that chain which will indissolubly unite the old and the new continents." He praised early members of the peace organization from Massachusetts: Ellery Channing, Noah Worcester and William Ladd.[12]

On the second day of the Congress, it was announced that "all the national palaces and other public establishments in Paris" would be open to the foreign delegates. Likely Peirce took advantage of the opportunity to visit the sights of the city.

Education was a major topic on the second day. Vice President of the congress, W. H. Suringar of Amsterdam, said that obstacle to the progress of disarmament and peace was "bad education." He lamented the way history and patriotism was taught to young people. "They are shown the glorious trophies of victories by sea and land; warriors are held up to them as the most worthy models for their imitation; and they are told that to die on the field of battle is the most glorious and enviable lot that can befall a mortal." Remedying the way history was taught, he said, should be a high priority of the peace advocates, a view shared by Peirce.[13]

The subject of public funding of schools also came up that day. A member of the French Assembly, Frederic Bastiat, spoke in favor of publicly funded schools, again pointing to Massachusetts. He said he knew of "only one country in the world where all the public expenses are covered by a direct and proportional taxation. I refer to the State of Massachusetts." This was music to Peirce's ears, having fought long and hard for public schooling. After the morning's lectures, a resolution was passed recommending all countries "endeavor to eradicate from the minds of all, those political prejudices and hereditary hatreds, which have so often been the cause of disastrous wars."[14]

By the third and last day of the congress, even more delegates and visitors had arrived, making it the most heavily attended day of the convention. Resolutions about disarmament and peaceful arbitration had been passed in previous days. The major topics on the third day concerned the creation of a "Congress of Nations" and the vast expense of maintaining the militaries of the world.

Speakers from Massachusetts took center stage on day three. An essay by Burritt was read concerning a league of nations. He wrote that the idea had been discussed more in the United States than in Europe. The American delegates believed a congress of nations was "indispensable for the order and peace of nations." The Americans favored an international court of arbitration and the writing of "well-defined international law" to settle disputes between countries. Burritt said writing such a code of law was the "first and most important step to be taken" in the quest for "permanent and universal peace."

Getting down to specifics, Burritt proposed a league of nations made up of two legislative bodies, similar to the bicameral U.S. legislative branch. One body would be based on world population with a delegate per every million people. The second body, which he called a "High Court of Nations," modeled on the U.S. Senate, would be composed of two judges from every nation, appointed for life. He also envisioned an international tribunal similar to the U.S. Supreme Court to which every nation could appeal for justice and redress on an equal footing, regardless of the size of the country.

Burritt, who was later appointed by Abraham Lincoln as consul to Great Britain, did not believe his dream of international cooperation farfetched or overly idealistic. He thought its establishment hinged on getting the support of the populations of the various countries, a task with which he charged the delegates. "We need the sympathy and support of the popular mind," adding he was hopeful because the English Parliament had been bombarded with more petitions about peace that year than for any other single cause.[15]

Another leader from Massachusetts, Amasa Walker, followed Burritt to the podium. He repeated Burritt's claim that Americans had championed the idea of a congress of nations "for more than twenty years." Massachusetts, he told them, had passed a series of resolutions "commending the matter [of a league of nations] to the attention of the National Congress" with "great unanimity." Such a measure had been introduced by Massachusetts to the federal Congress at its last session, he said.

The subject of slavery came up on the last day as well. Walker said the United States had disgraced itself "by tolerating a system of chattel slavery." He said a world court could have had an impact on the issue had one existed. Addressing the argument that countries might not abide by a world court's decision, he noted that the Supreme Court of the United States made rulings between arguing states, and had never had to call in the militia or the army to enforce them. He predicted that squabbling countries would follow suit, accepting unfavorable rulings of the world court.[16]

Two American fugitives from slavery addressed the peace congress that day. William Wells Brown reminded the audience of the millions of enslaved peoples in the world. He told them he had been a slave for over twenty years, and undoubtedly showed them the slave collar that usually accompanied his lectures. He told the audience that if he were to give a similar talk in the United States, his life would be in danger. "It is impossible to maintain slavery without maintaining war," he told them. He said that it was as important for the peace congress to abolish war as to "proclaim liberty throughout the world, break in pieces every yoke of bondage, and let all the oppressed go free."

James Pennington

The second former slave to address the congress was James W.C. Pennington. He talked about the danger of patriotism. Love of country "is capable of great abuse," he said, adding that people are not said to truly love their country unless they are wiling to fight for it. Pennington talked about the violence of slavery, but said he believed the best way to defeat slavery was through nonviolence. "We are wronged, but we do not wrong others." He said that no group of people "has suffered more unqualified and unprovoked wrongs than we." He stated that African descendants constituted "full one-fifth of the whole population of the Western continent" with over half of those "in servitude to the whites." Despite such gross injustice, he said American slaves had been remarkably peaceful and patient, looking to God for ultimate justice. "The sword settles nothing," he concluded.[17]

Allen described that day's speeches as ones "which lifted me off my seat." The "immense audience again and again rose from their seats and made the air ring with the bravos and hurrahs."[18]

Victor Hugo thanked the delegates and lecturers in his concluding address. He praised the "wisdom and dignity" of the discussions, and said he had been stirred to see former enemies sitting in concert. It was marvelous to have witnessed "England shaking the hand of France, and America shaking the hand of Europe." He could "conceive of no sight more grand or sublime." Lengthy cheers followed his address.[19]

The next day the delegates toured Paris. That evening the Minister of French Foreign Affairs, Alexis de Tocqueville, invited the delegates from England and the United States to a grand soiree at "his magnificent house on one of the boulevards." Allen wrote that the rooms and gardens were brightly illuminated and the guests were "regaled by a band of as many as forty or fifty musicians" who "made glorious music." Refreshments were served in "silver cups with golden spoons."[20]

The next day being Sunday, the delegates attended one of several church services. The Quakers held two meetings. William Wells Brown spoke at the Wesleyan Chapel and, Reverend Pennington delivered a sermon to a large gathering at another church.

On Monday, the American delegation went by train to the Palace of Versailles on the outskirts of Paris where they were given tours of the many galleries, apartments and opulent gardens. A luncheon was provided by the English delegation in one of the grand galleries. After the luncheon, more speeches were delivered.

A member of the English Parliament thanked the Americans who had traveled so far. He said the English delegates did not want their American friends to leave without "tendering their sincere thanks," and each American delegate was presented with a copy of the New Testament in French, inscribed with a thank you "for the purpose of expressing their respect for the zeal manifested by their brethren in crossing the Atlantic to attend the Great Peace Congress at Paris."[21]

Reverend Dr. Allen of Massachusetts, on behalf of the Americans, thanked the English for their hospitality. As there were two Reverend Allens from Massachusetts at the congress, it is not clear which one addressed the crowd. He talked about the shame of American slavery saying that he came from a state that had abolished the wicked institution and he hoped the rest of the states would be persuaded to do the same. Another American added that his generation "rejoiced" the steamboat had been invented so they had been able to travel to Europe so quickly.[22]

Henry Clapp Jr. spoke and told them that words were not sufficient to express what was in his heart about the privilege of attending the Paris Peace Congress. He and his fellow American delegates would return home "taking with them the principles and sentiments which they had caught," determined to further the cause of "universal brotherhood of peace and love."[23]

The meeting ended with another round of cheers. Delegates next went into the gardens to view a grand exhibition of the fountains. The display was special, as the "waterworks at Versailles are put in operation only four times in the year." In honor of the delegates the fountains were turned on for two days in a row. The official report indicated that over 30,000 people were on hand to see the displays, mostly French citizens having come to see the spectacle. Allen wrote to his family: "But the cascades, the enchanting, illuminated cascades in the evening! Oh, how I wish you could have seen them." He struggled to put the sight into words, writing simply that they reminded him of "descriptions in the Arabian Nights."

The delegates were also invited to the Palace of St. Cloud, the residence of the French president, said to have been a favorite retreat of Napoleon Bonaparte. Allen wrote that the palace "seems made for comfort more than for show."[24]

Most of the American and English delegates left for London the next day. A large peace rally was held in London to welcome them. Speakers described the congress to a cheering crowd. Undoubtedly, Peirce and Allen attended the jubilant gathering with their fellow delegates.

Several American delegates took carriages to Aylesbury, forty miles outside of London as guests of British delegate Dr. John Lee. They were invited to his observatory to look at Saturn and the moon. Allen described Lee as "a great scholar and antiquarian as well as a philanthropist and reformer."[25]

After the visit to London, most of the Americans traveled to Liverpool and sailed back to the United States. Peirce may have been with them, although he probably threw his lot in with Allen, who delayed his return home to tour the Lake District of northwestern England for several days.

Regardless of the route Peirce took home, the trip to the Paris Peace Congress had been the trip of a lifetime, made all the more satisfying in its having been made possible by his friends and students.

Note: The Nantucket petitions reside at the Massachusetts State Archives.

Chapter 15: Cyrus Peirce of West Newton

Cyrus Peirce spent most of the last ten years of his life in West Newton, a town he once criticized for narrow mindedness. The town had changed significantly since his early years as a raw inexperienced teacher in 1807. While he may have been known as "Cyrus Peirce of Nantucket" throughout his life, it is fair to say that he could justifiably have been called "Cyrus Peirce of West Newton."

The normal school had been responsible for bringing changes to the village, just as the old timers had feared. Where once there had been a single church, there was now a thriving Unitarian congregation where he and Harriet worshipped surrounded by friends. They had failed in their first attempt to establish a Unitarian congregation in 1844, but the "new population coming from other towns," demanded the establishment of a Unitarian church. The Peirces were instrumental in the founding of the church, and when the Unitarians first celebrated the Lord's Supper in 1849, the Peirces were among the fifteen present, along with Nathaniel Allen. The Peirces, the Manns, and the Allens were active members of the new church, serving on a variety of committees. The establishment of a Unitarian church was directly related to the many newcomers who moved to West Newton.[1]

Both Cyrus and Harriet visited Nantucket periodically during their retirement years. Harriet Peirce visited her hometown alone on several occasions. When they were on the island, they visited the high school where he had been the first principal.

An influx of influential intellectuals settled in West Newton drawn to the circle of Horace Mann and his sister-in-law Elizabeth Peabody. Many people visited the pretty New England village for the first time when invited to speak at the normal school. Others came to observe the famous school in action.

George B. Emerson, influential publisher and longtime friend of Peirce and Mann, moved to West Newton. Emerson had been involved in the battle to establish the board of education and the normal schools, and had helped found the influential American Institute of Education in 1830 to improve teaching in the state. Emerson served on the board of education and had been a staunch supporter of Peirce and the normal school where he was a familiar lecturer and visitor. After his move to West Newton, he served several terms on the town's school committee.

Caroline Healey Dall, an early champion of women's rights, also moved into the village. The first woman to preach in a Unitarian church, Dall was a follower of Theodore Parker, and a close friend of Mary Peabody Mann. In 1853, Dall founded the first newspaper in the United States dedicated to women's suffrage. She wrote about economic rights for women, convinced that middle class women were underemployed.

William B. Fowle, who had defended Peirce against Matthew Hale Smith, also settled in West Newton in the early 1850s where he was active in the Unitarian church. In 1852, Fowle co-edited the *Common School Journal* with Mann, which had been founded by Mann in 1838. The journal featured articles about the teaching profession, including sample lesson plans. Peirce contributed numerous articles to its pages before and during his retirement.

Peirce was also reunited with Seth Swift, his friend from Harvard and Nantucket, where Swift had been the first minister of the Second Congregational Church. Swift moved to Newton in 1850 and served for a year on the school committee with Peirce.

Another close friend living in West Newton was Electa Lincoln, who should, in fact, be recognized as the first woman director of a normal school. After Peirce's resignation, Lincoln was asked to head the school until a replacement could be found, a task that took three months. Lincoln was in charge of the beginning of the next school year, responsible for the examining all thirty-seven candidates. She admitted all but one, commenting that it was the second largest class enrolled in the school to date. She took over the full administrative and teaching duties of a director.

In her journal Lincoln wrote that she had two wishes as she took over the leadership of the school. One, she hoped she would do a good job, and that members of the board of education would find her satisfactory. "Many people think <u>women</u> can't do much. I'd like to show them that they can keep a normal school and keep it well too for one term at least. My motto shall be "<u>succeed or die</u>" …I rather it'll be succeed. I have <u>strong hope</u>." In a more practical vein, she hoped the board would see fit to pay her the equivalent of Peirce's salary.[2]

Shortly thereafter, Lincoln married George Walton, former principal of the model school who had resigned when he had been unable to maintain order. Whatever bad feelings might have existed between George Walton and Cyrus Peirce disappeared, and the couples became close friends. Electa Lincoln Walton named her first child Harriet, and was later in charge of executing a part of Harriet Peirce's last will and testament.

Most importantly to the Peirces, though, was the presence of Horace and Mary Mann in the neighborhood. The two families spent much time together, including sharing Thanksgiving dinners. Mann maintained his house on Chestnut Street in West Newton during the two terms he served in the House of Representatives in Washington. He did not seek a third

term, choosing to run for governor of Massachusetts. On the day he lost
that election, he was offered the presidency of Antioch College, a
progressive new college in Ohio, which he eagerly accepted. In 1853,
Mann became the school's first president, and he sold his house in West
Newton to move to Yellow Springs, Ohio. Although happy for his
friend's opportunity, Mann's departure was a blow to Peirce. They had
been neighbors and friends since 1839 when they both lived in
Lexington.

Nathaniel Allen, thirty-three years younger than Peirce, replaced
Mann as Peirce's best friend, and, in fact, bought Mann's house. The two
had forged a close relationship based on mutual respect. Allen credited
Peirce as his most important educational mentor. Their political views
were similar, both committed to world peace, temperance, women's
rights, racial integration, and the immediate abolition of slavery.
Neighbors since 1848, they had both married Nantucket women and
helped found the Unitarian church in West Newton. Allen had rescued
the model school when it looked as if it would fail, and Peirce was
grateful to him for that. Allen had gained early acceptance in West
Newton in a way Peirce had failed to do. Peirce was gratified that Allen
had implemented Peirce's style and philosophy of teaching, and
recognized that Allen had added his own valuable imprint. Allen was, in
turn, grateful to Peirce for having given him the opportunity to make his
mark in a larger sphere than would have been possible if he had
remained a country schoolteacher.

Allen continued as the director of the model school at the West
Newton Normal School for three years after Peirce's retirement. The
successful public school swelled to 128 pupils and outgrew its old
building, moving to a new facility in the center of the village in 1850.

Students from the normal school continued to practice their teaching there under Allen's supervision. Every senior was required to spend one week observing, and two weeks teaching, at the model school, the system that had worked so well during Peirce's tenure.

The school committee praised the model school for its "good order, good government, good feeling and good improvement in the various branches of study" in its 1850 annual report. As an indication of Peirce's eventual acceptance in West Newton, he was elected to the committee that year, and was partially in charge of monitoring Allen and the model school. Allen was commended by the committee for "making his scholars feel that the school belongs to them," noting parents were satisfied with the school.

The school committee also noted how pleased they were with Allen's practice of requiring students to write letters to their teachers. The letters "encouraged [students] to communicate feelings, trials, joys or sorrow, make explanations, give excuses, or communicate any other thought which he wishes, to his teacher." The irony of praising the practice of journal writing could not have been lost on Allen or Peirce who could recall Matthew Hale Smith's attacks on the reading of the normal school journals.

In the years Allen remained as head of the model school, more praise was heaped on it and on Allen. In 1851, the school committee, which no longer included Peirce, noted that pupils in Allen's school behaved better than those in other village schools. They attributed the exemplary student behavior to Allen and to the normal school student teachers. Students behaved well because they wanted to do so, something the committee found remarkable and unique. Despite the school's strict rules, students obeyed "with great pleasure." They seemed determined "to refrain from noise" because they were so involved with their own learning.

Allen incorporated physical education into the curriculum the year before he left the job. The taxpayers in West Newton raised money for a "good Gymnasium" to be built on the second floor of the model school, which was "profitably used by the boys and girls alternately." Peirce, a lifelong advocate of exercise, saw another of his once-controversial ideas accepted. Allen also added singing and music to the daily curriculum during his last year at the model school. [3]

The model school in West Newton under Allen's leadership had become world famous. The school register in his last school year alone recorded over one thousand visitors, including educators from other states and countries, as well as normal school students from other schools, such as the one in Bridgewater. The notion of a school kept for the practice of student teachers, which had been initiated by Cyrus Peirce, had become accepted as a valuable tool in teacher training.[4]

Peirce soon realized that his years in public service had not made him financially secure. Just one year into his retirement he wrote to Mann complaining about his poverty, writing that he was inclined to "take to the field" again. Less than two years after his retirement from the West Newton Normal School, Peirce accepted a job in East Machias, Maine.[5]

It is unclear why Peirce accepted a job at Washington Academy in the remote community in northern Maine. There were Peirce families in the area, although the kinship was not close. East Machias, with a population of only approximately five hundred when Peirce moved there, was reachable only by boat. There were no highways or roads, just forest tracks. Mail arrived twice a month by horseback, but the predominant form of transportation was small packet ships which plied the coast.[6] (Note)

Washington Academy was a progressive school established in East Machias in 1793. In 1850, the school had thirty-five students, drawn from seven towns. The sole teacher boarded at the school. Inexplicably, the academy decided to become a normal school. Who better for the post than Cyrus Peirce, the first-ever director of such a school? One of the few available

Washington Academy, E. Machias, Maine

accounts says that "under the direction of Joseph Dow, Cyrus Peirce and W.J. Corthel, the trustees voted to hire new teachers and make Washington Academy a Normal School" in 1853. "The needed teachers were not available, however, so the Academy was forced to close its doors for approximately one year." When it reopened in 1854, it resumed its previous high school curriculum without Cyrus Peirce and "without Normal Courses."[7]

It appears that Peirce stayed in East Machias for parts of two calendar years trying to organize a normal school. It does not appear that Harriet accompanied him. In September 1852, when he had just arrived in Maine, Harriet attended the annual reunion of the first class of the Lexington school without him. In his place, Peirce sent a short letter in which he expressed enthusiasm for his new job. "The old gentleman has renewed his youth, put on his working dress, and gone into the field again. To speak without a figure, I am literally and actually here keeping school." And from his attendance at a conference in Connecticut during the summer of 1853, it seems likely that Peirce was in Maine for just under a full year. [8]

Peirce's sojourn in East Machias is a puzzle. He wrote that he was keeping school, but records in East Machias indicate that the normal school never opened. Possibly he started teaching there, but the school either did not attract enough applicants, or there were not enough staff available. The latter seems unlikely, as Peirce had taught his first normal school without assistance. The reference to "teachers" not being available is cryptic, as it could refer to either the applicants or the staff.[9]

Regardless, when the Washington School re-opened its doors a year and a half later, it resumed its former high school curriculum, and Peirce had returned to West Newton. He picked up where he left off, continuing to be active in the Unitarian Church and in various causes, especially abolition and temperance. Both he and his wife attended the yearly reunions of the first graduating class of the Lexington Normal School whenever they could.

In 1853, Peirce submitted a controversial essay to the American Institute of Instruction which sponsored a yearly essay contest about education, and he won first prize. As the winner, he was invited to read the essay at the Institute's annual convention that summer in Connecticut. Unexpectedly, he found himself at the center of debate.

Once again, criticism came from his fellow educators. In his essay, *Crime: Its Cause and Cure*, Peirce argued that secular and mandatory education would *not* and *had not* decreased the crime rate, contradicting a cherished and commonly held belief of his fellow progressive educators. Peirce provided statistical data as evidence that crime had actually *increased,* even as mandatory education increased. Surveys were cited that showed convicts were often better educated "than the generality of their class."

Peirce's lecture sent shockwaves through the audience of educators, who were appalled at what appeared to be an attack by Peirce, of all people, on public education. Many of those present concluded that his remarks were aimed at undermining one of their most firmly held beliefs – the belief that public education would reduce crime. It was conventional wisdom that crime would decrease with the upward mobility predicted by higher educational attainment. It was believed the lower classes would not have to resort to crime, because better education would have lifted them out of poverty. Unlike in his previous battle with the Boston schoolmasters, this argument was with liberal educators like himself. The progressive educators believed that Christian morality taught in the schools would inevitably improve public ethics. It was a belief that Peirce himself had often expressed, which is why his essay came as such a shock.[10]

The progressive teachers felt betrayed. Educational historian Michael Katz contends that teachers at the time "knew they were above the rest of mankind; they knew that, in the last analysis, they alone were responsible for the future of civilization; whatever statistics might show, they knew they were succeeding." To them, "Peirce had not only denied the moral efficacy of the common schools but had implied that they contributed to crime."[11]

Because of the instant controversy created by Peirce's speech, the Institute decided to withhold the essay from the public. Normally it published the winning essay, but in this case, the members voted to return it to Peirce unpublished, although he was allowed to keep the prize money.

Peirce was hurt by the vote to suppress his essay. Once again, he found himself on the defensive, subject to attacks he considered unfair. He decided the only way he could resolve the issue was to publish the essay himself. In the preface to the slim forty-five page volume, published in January 1854, he wrote, "I am induced to publish it, chiefly for the reason that I think its character was misunderstood and misrepresented by many of the gentlemen who took part in the discussion which followed the reading of it."

He defended his essay in the preface, writing that he had been unjustly accused of professing things he had neither said nor implied. He vigorously and categorically denied that he had made accusations against the schools. His long, carefully-crafted, and eloquent essay supported the idea that schools do, in fact, hold the key to the nation's conscience and morality. Contrary to what his critics had interpreted from his lecture, he built a case for more emphasis on the teaching of morality. He acknowledged that it had been difficult to resist making "sundry verbal alterations to improve the phraseology. But to prevent all doubt and cavil," the essay had been published exactly as he had read it to the Institute.

In his essay, Peirce agreed with his colleagues about the link between crime and moral education. Where he parted company with them was in application and practice. Peirce contended that the schools had neglected moral education, and were doing an inadequate job of teaching right from wrong. "Facts will show, that, to make men *good*, we must do something more for them than teach them how to read and write."

Peirce criticized the public schools for their superficial treatment of

249

values. He wrote that he would love to find a school "in which sound principles and good manners are inculcated; where the cardinal virtues of purity, integrity, truth, temperance, justice, and righteousness, occupy the same platform with grammar, geography, history, mathematics, and the languages. I hardly know the school where they occupy equal ground, either in regard to time or attention or expense."[12]

On Nantucket, his hometown newspaper gave the book rave reviews, although it was less well received elsewhere. The *Inquirer* wrote, "This is a subject which should be commended to the attention of every teacher and parent through the length and breadth of the land."[13]

Eventually the furor abated and Peirce was accepted back into the fraternity of educators. He never wavered on his firm belief that moral education was of equal importance to the teaching of academic subjects, nor from his belief that the public schools did not devote enough time and resources to it. He continued to believe that crime and education were intrinsically linked.

Peirce was elected to the West Newton school committee again in 1855, the last public office he would hold. As a member of the school committee, he was required to visit the village schools, a task he enjoyed. He was responsible that year for the supervision of the schools in District 4, a big task, as the district included the town's new high school, a grammar school, an intermediate school and at least two primary schools.

Peirce's report about District 4 focused on the quality of the teaching staff, consistent with his belief that good teachers were essential to good education. He was not entirely happy with the progress of the district, reporting that while "very much good teaching" had been done in the high school, there was a "deficiency in discipline and order." Two primary school teachers were singled out for praise. Of Mary Russell, he wrote, "Let her works praise her. Few have ever made so hopefully a beginning." Of Miss S.J. Cowles, that she was "endowed with a more than ordinary share of the qualities of a good teacher."

Peirce saved his highest praise for a teacher at the intermediate school. He wrote that the school had made good progress under the direction of Sarah Fuller, and predicted she would become "one of our best teachers." Peirce's prediction about Fuller was correct, as she went on to become a noted teacher of the deaf, and the principal of a school for deaf mutes in Boston in the 1870s. An associate of Alexander Graham Bell, Fuller was present when the first telephone message was sent.[14]

While Peirce was embroiled in defending his views about crime and education, Nathaniel Allen resigned as the principal of the model school. Once more, the normal school had outgrown itself, and it was decided to move it to Framingham, where it is now Framingham State University, tracing its roots to the oldest public normal school in the nation, and the oldest school in the University of Massachusetts system.

Educational institutions were eager to hire Allen when they found he was available. Samuel Gridley Howe invited him to be his assistant at the Perkins Institute for the Blind, and the Troy Institute in upstate New York offered to make him head of their preparatory department, responsible for preparing students to enter universities. The school committee in Newton also tried to recruit him to be the first principal of the new high school.

He turned them all down because he had decided to open his own private school. Although he had devoted himself wholeheartedly to public education, he was tired of the oversight of meddlesome school committees, the board of education and the fickle nature of public opinion. He was keenly aware of the suffering Peirce had endured during his career in the public schools - from the failure to prevent the Nantucket public schools from re-segregating, to his battles at the normal school. Allen wanted to be freed from political constraints and teach how he saw fit. He decided to involve his beloved mentor in the venture. Finally, Peirce would have a school based on his principles.

Note: The 1870 census lists several Peirce families. Among these are Jonas Peirce who had one of the most valuable properties in the village and Frederic Peirce, manager of one of the local saw mills.

Chapter 16: Teacher Emeritus

Cyrus Peirce was about to enter the most satisfying phase of his teaching career thanks to good friend and protégé, Nathaniel Allen. Fresh from his work in Maine, Peirce was ready to embark on a new project where he could rejoin his wife and his friends in West Newton. Allen offered him the opportunity to design a school based on their shared educational principles and Peirce accepted gratefully. Allen and Peirce dreamed of opening a new school where they could freely implement their vision of education. Both men

Nathaniel Allen

Courtesy of Historic Newton, Newton, Ma

were tired of reining in their political views and curtailing their activism to conform to the more conservative mainstream desired by school committees. Because it would be independent, their new school could be politically active. Both men looked forward to the prospect of designing and administering a school where they had to answer only to the students and their families. They were also aware that opening a private academy was a risky venture even with their reputations.

Their grand collaboration, officially known as the West Newton English and Classical School, was popularly known as the "Allen School" during its forty-seven years of operation. From the outset, Allen involved Peirce in the planning and vision of the school, making the sixty-four-year-old his co-principal. The two men made up half of the board of trustees. The other two were Allen's brothers, George and James. [1]

In their partnership, however, it was Allen who dominated, even if he and Peirce were officially co-principals. It was Allen who purchased the former normal school building to house the academy. It was Allen's youthful energy that made the school into one of the most successful and important academies of the era. There is no doubt, however, that Peirce played a critical role, especially in the planning stages. Allen had, in fact, offered Peirce the perfect job, and he settled happily into the role of respected advisor and teacher emeritus. The stress of day-to-day management was left to the younger man. It was a time for Peirce to do what he loved best: teach.

At the core of the school's philosophy was an emphasis on moral education which received as much attention as intellectual development. Much of the planning took place while Peirce was defending his essay on crime. Helping to design the curriculum gave him a chance to vindicate himself and his beliefs to his fellow educators.

The opportunity also offered Peirce financial stability. He had made little money in his career, often contributing his own funds to various projects. He hoped this venture with Allen would ensure him a comfortable income. Allen shared the profits equally with Peirce once the building expenses were deducted. In addition, Harriet Peirce was employed to teach botany. Allen had offered his mentor and friend financial security.

Horace Mann, normally opposed to private academies as threats to public education, fully supported the endeavor. Two of Mann's nieces had studied under Peirce and one of his sons had attended the model school in West Newton under Allen. Mann appreciated the talents of both men in the classroom. He was also well aware of the difficulties of operating in the public sphere. He, too, had recently left the public sphere to head Antioch College.

Other public school advocates encouraged Allen and Peirce, including George B. Emerson. As a member of the West Newton school committee at the time, Emerson may have been disappointed to lose Allen, but he wholeheartedly encouraged him to pursue his dream. Others who lent their support were their political, religious and educational friends, including Theodore Parker, Samuel J. May, Samuel Gridley Howe and Charles Sumner. They all looked forward to the creation of a progressive school they hoped would serve as a model for

Caroline Bassett Allen

Nantucket Historical Association

all schools.

Before the school opened its doors in January 1854, Allen married Caroline Bassett of Nantucket. "Carrie" Bassett had been a student at the West Newton Normal School, graduating at the end of Peirce's last year. She had, therefore, been a student teacher under the supervision of her future husband.

After graduating from the normal school, Bassett returned to Nantucket where she was hired as an assistant in the high school under Augustus Morse, the principal who had taken Peirce's position when he left the island. Bassett taught at the high school for three years. However, she became increasingly unhappy in the position. According to papers in the Newton History Museum, Bassett kept a journal for those years, although it is in private hands and not available to the public at this time. When she was in graduate school researching Allen, Lynn Cadwallader was able to see Bassett's journals. According to her, they show that Bassett was frustrated in Nantucket because she was "under a male supervisor who did not let her participate in the examination process." Presumably, she was referring to Morse.[2]

During those three years, Allen courted Carrie on frequent trips to Nantucket. Records on the island show that he visited the high school several times as an observer, sometimes in the company of Harriet Peirce who encouraged their courtship. On one trip, Bassett and Allen went with the noted Harvard geologist and zoologist Louis Agassiz to collect specimens around the island. Several years before, Agassiz had nominated the celebrated astronomer Maria Mitchell to the American Association for the Advancement of Science.[3]

In 1853, Caroline Bassett resigned her teaching position on Nantucket to marry Nathaniel Allen. Harriet Peirce wrote to her about her future husband. "He is a true Nathaniel of old 'in whom there is no guile'." When the couple married on March 30, 1853, she was twenty-two and he was thirty. Over fifty years later, Carrie Allen remembered being welcomed to West Newton by Horace Mann who joked that she needed to have a "tub of water, well salted, lest she pine for her native sea-girl isle."[4]

In Carrie, Allen had found his perfect partner. Both dedicated teachers, the couple made it their life's work to make the school in West Newton a success. Both were keenly interested in the art of teaching, and both were committed to the same political causes, including that of women's suffrage. Carrie was the president of Newton's Woman Suffrage Association for many years, and her husband lectured at, and attended, meetings.

In addition, both considered the Peirces as mentors. Like the Peirces, both Allens were Unitarians. Like the Peirces, the Allens were a team in the true sense of the word. Carrie Allen moved to West Newton ready to devote herself to her husband and to the new school. Because the school was private, she was exempt from the prohibition of married women being employed as teachers.

From the outset, Allen decided it was imperative the school be a boarding school. A boarding school would give teachers the necessary time to implement their philosophies, and to exert a greater influence on their pupils than a day school would. Allen remembered the successful and progressive boarding school that his Uncle Joseph and Aunt Lucy Allen had operated in Northboro decades before. The younger Allen emulated many of their techniques, particularly by insisting that boarders be folded into family life. Allen bought Horace Mann's house where he had lived briefly during his first year in Newton and moved in with his family and about a dozen boarders.

Carrie Allen's main responsibility was to oversee the lives of the boarding students. They were expected to become part of the families where they boarded, and were assigned household chores. They were allotted garden plots to put into practice the hands-on learning in which Peirce and Allen so firmly believed. Gardening taught students basic farming techniques and provided lessons in botany, some supplied by Harriet Peirce. Students were encouraged to keep pets, which ranged from barnyard animals, including pigs and ponies, to conventional domesticated pets like dogs, to more exotic animals such as pet monkeys.

Cyrus and Harriet Peirce also took boarders into their home on Cherry Street, next door to Nathaniel and Carrie Allen. One of their first boarders was thirteen-year-old Arthur May Knapp. At a reunion of the school seventeen years later, Knapp recalled that he had lived with the Peirces for two years "in intimate relations as a sort of adopted son." Knapp went on to an illustrious career. A Harvard graduate, he worked as both a teacher and a minister, and spent three years as a missionary in Japan.[5]

The West Newton English and Classical School opened its doors in January 1854. A student from the first class recalled that day: "Father Peirce asked God's blessing on the new school, a prayer which has been so signally answered."[6]

One of Allen's advantages in opening a private school was his exceptional reputation in the town for his work at the model school. His reputation stood him in good stead over the years, especially as the school bucked educational conventions, implemented radical innovations in curriculum, and solidified the school's unorthodox approach to

West Newton English & Classical School
258

children.

The West Newton English and Classical School was coeducational from the outset, revolutionary at a time when the vast majority of boarding schools catered to a single gender. The education of girls was considered as important as that of boys. The Allens and Peirces favored woman's suffrage and all of them were active in the Woman's Suffrage Association. One of the school's advertisements stated their rationale for coeducational education: "It is believed that the union of the sexes in family and school, conduces, under proper management, to a better moral development, and offers a more healthful mental stimulus, than the education of either sex alone." When the school opened, thirty six

Allen School class photograph

Courtesy of Historic Newton, Newton Ma.

percent of the student body was female. Even more remarkable, the girls took the same classes as the boys.

Students who formed the core of the student body were children of wealthy liberal New Englanders. The school, however, also admitted children from less privileged backgrounds. Donations from Theodore

Parker were used to give scholarships to those who would not otherwise have been able to attend.

From the beginning the school admitted black children. It was important to the Peirces and the Allens to integrate their school. Committed abolitionists, they were determined to practice what they preached. Both couples continued to participate in the American Anti-Slavery Society; Allen was the president of West Newton's chapter, as well as an officer in the parent organization in Boston. He sometimes acted as a bodyguard to abolitionists like Charles Sumner when they appeared in public, and the Allen home was a stop on the Underground Railroad.

Some of the school's black graduates became famous in their own right, or were the children of famous black Americans. For example, Elizabeth Smalls attended the school. Her father, Robert Smalls was the slave famous for commandeering the Confederate ship, *CSS Planter*, in 1862 and sailing it to Boston. Smalls later represented South Carolina in the U.S. House of Representatives, serving five terms during Reconstruction. He wrote the bill that established the first free and compulsory public school system in the United States and founded North Carolina's Republican Party.

Two black women graduates became well known. Ethel Shaw became a teacher at Booker T. Washington's Tuskegee Institute, and Lizzie Piper became the Colorado editor of a black women's newspaper, *The Women's Era*, that championed progressive causes, such as the equalization of the state's divorce laws.

In 1851, Allen had led a successful fundraising to build the first gymnasium in a public secondary school in the United States. It is, therefore, no surprise that physical education was an important part of the curriculum of the Allen School. He and Peirce believed exercise was important for overall health, equally important to children's development as the teaching of reading and mathematics. Students were expected to be up early, and it was not unusual for Allen to lead a three-mile walk before sunrise. Within five months of opening, the school had "gymnastic apparatus erected in the school yard."[7]

In addition, exercise was fun, something Peirce and Allen thought important in every school day. Dances were permitted, rare at that time, and every year at least one sleigh-ride was organized. The students of the school were among the first to experiment with newly-improved roller skates invented by James Plimpton, another of Allen's cousins. Eventually the school built its own bowling alley, ballpark, stage and pond. Students went boating on the Charles River and took hikes, sometimes camping overnight in the woods. They went on numerous field trips to historical sights in Boston, Lexington, and Concord.[8]

None of this meant that academics were given short shrift. The curriculum was rigorous, and students who fell behind were required to attend Saturday classes to catch up to their classmates by Monday morning.[9]

As the fame and success of the school grew, it attracted students from farther away. By 1870, over 250 students from other states had attended the school. The school had also enrolled seventy-five foreign students. Eventually, the school's alumnae represented thirty countries. They included Tanetaro Megato, who became the Minister of Education in Japan, and Jujoi Atzmori Shimidz, the Japanese Prince Royal.[10]

Students from outside Newton brought in significant revenue. Local students paid from $150-$200 per year in tuition, and students from other parts of Massachusetts paid $350. Out-of-state students paid

$1000, and students from foreign countries paid $2,000 every year to attend.

Peirce and Allen gathered the best teachers they could find to staff the school. Not surprisingly, as many as one-third were their former students. Graduates of the other normal schools were also hired. Guest lecturers were regularly invited to speak to the student body, a practice Peirce had established at the Lexington Normal School. This time, however, abolitionists were welcomed. William Wells Brown, who had traveled with Peirce to the Paris Peace Congress, was a guest speaker. Besides being an abolitionist lecturer, Brown was among the first African-American novelists.

Allen enlisted many of his own talented family members during the course of the school's history. Brothers James and Joseph taught at the school and their families took in boarders, and their Uncle Phineas Allen, a linguist, conducted a multi-lingual household for foreign students in his home. Cousin William Francis Allen taught the classics; he is also credited with compiling the first book of American slave songs.

Carrie Allen also brought family members into the school. Her two sisters married men from West Newton, and both taught at the Allen School. Anna Bassett, the middle sister, married Joshua G. Nickerson in 1863. Their youngest sister, Sarah Bassett, was the victim of a terrible accident the year Carrie moved off island. Visiting West Newton, Sarah stepped off the train and caught her foot under the carriage; her foot had to be amputated. Only two months later, however, she enrolled in the first class of students attending the West Newton English and Classical School. After graduation, Sarah moved back to Nantucket and taught at the Polpis School, outside the town of Nantucket. The school had the reputation of having unruly students and uncooperative parents. Sarah

Bassett, however, did well there. A memoir of one of her students, Abbie Pitman Ray, recalled her teacher using crutches to get around the classroom. After several years of teaching on the island, Sarah resigned to join her sisters as a teacher at the Allen School. She married Asahel Wheeler in 1869. Because all of his children had moved to West Newton, James Bassett, their father and a widower, left the island in 1856 to join the family where he continued in his trade as a hardware dealer.[11]

Forty years later, student John Ricketson remembered the first year's faculty members: "I can see, as if it were yesterday our teachers in their accustomed chairs, Father Peirce on Mr. Allen's right, on his left Mr. George Allen, Miss Dresser, Mrs. Urbino, while on the right of Father Peirce sat at the piano Mr. B.F. Baker, our genial teacher of music." It was a small staff that first year, but it quickly grew as the school expanded.[12]

In a time when a teacher's tenure at a private academy was only one year, the average teacher's tenure at the school was three or more years. The school also attracted teachers from Europe, usually hired to teach foreign languages. The school pioneered the practice of scheduling teachers' meetings when teachers gathered to discuss individual student progress, problems within the school and to talk about pedagogy.[13]

Visitors, particularly from the nearby Framingham Normal School, frequently came to observe. Both Peirce and Allen continued to lecture at Teachers' Institutes held across Massachusetts and other New England states. Allen was a member of the American Institute of Instruction and an early vice president of the Massachusetts Teachers' Association.

Within a few years, the school expanded to include a comprehensive program for children as young as three years old. The Allen School was the first to include kindergarten as part of a larger school. Allen's belief in the importance of kindergarten education came from his close association with Elizabeth Peabody, Horace Mann's sister-in-law, whom he had met while living with the Manns. Peabody had volunteered in the West Newton model school when Allen was its principal.

Students from ages four through eight studied reading, simple prose, mathematics, natural history, and French. In addition, they took music, singing lessons, and physical education. Students from ages nine through thirteen attended what was called the "Training School" where they studied the same subjects, but as preparation to enter the high school.[14]

High school students chose between a college preparatory program and a business program. Both groups studied a modern language and drawing, painting, or music. In later years, an industrial training program was added to the curriculum with an emphasis on agriculture. In a lecture given in 1997 by John Hillison, a professor at Virginia Polytechnic Institute, Cyrus Peirce was credited for being a pioneer in the field of agricultural education, an addition to the many educational innovations attributed to Peirce.[15]

Many features from the model school and the normal school were incorporated into the curriculum. For instance, students were required to write one page every day in daily journals. They were required to record the daily weather, including temperature and barometric readings. The journals were collected every two weeks and corrected for grammar, penmanship and composition.[16]

Natural science was part of every student's course of study. The out-of-doors was a steady resource, from individual garden plots to the woods, fields and hills of the surrounding area. Students were taken outside as often as possible. Nathaniel Allen was an enthusiastic geologist with a huge mineral collection of twelve thousand specimens.[17]

Unsurprisingly, moral education was at the heart of the curriculum. Ethics permeated every subject, and the everyday lives of the students and faculty. Each morning, students attended a devotional exercise before starting their classes. During the time that Peirce was co-principal, he spoke to the student body every morning "to offer a 'Sentiment." John H. Ricketson, spoke about that daily assembly at the school's fortieth reunion. Ricketson, said that Father Peirce chose a "brief selection in prose or verse, embodying some truth he was anxious to impress upon our minds." He recalled one vividly: "When human policy fastens the chain to the ankle of the slave, Divine justice rivets the other end around the neck of the master." Ricketson recalled the importance that Peirce attached to the daily moral lessons in his quest for living to the truth. Morning assembly was not a time for levity. Ricketson remembered "but one instance" when the sober Peirce broke into laughter at the morning gathering. Once, a "great, big, good natured schoolmate from Ohio" called out: "Hungry men call the cook lazy." Discussing that phrase in a serious manner was too much "even for the gravity of Father Peirce."[18]

Current events were part of the curriculum and students were expected to keep abreast of what was happening in the country and world. The 1850s were tumultuous as the United States was drawn inexorably into the Civil War, and the Allen School did not shy away from controversial topics. Students attended lectures in Boston by the great speakers of the era. They attended the funerals of such people as Ralph Waldo Emerson and William Lloyd Garrison. Teachers at the school were unapologetically radical when it came to the topic of immediate abolition and the injustice of returning fugitive slaves to bondage. Later, they supported Radical Reconstruction.

For students who wanted even more involvement in current affairs,

Allen and Peirce formed a Lyceum that met one evening each week in Allen's living room. At the fortieth reunion, Ricketson recalled the first meeting of the Lyceum when the group framed their constitution. He recalled that, although female students were not allowed to join the Lyceum at first, it took only one term to remedy that situation. From then on, girls were members on an equal footing. Ricketson remembered discussing the Kansas-Nebraska Act and the possible extension of slavery. Together, the group read Harriet Beecher Stowe's *Uncle Tom's Cabin*, and Henry Longfellow's poem about a slave's dream of freedom. The tough fugitive slave law of 1850 that resulted in the return of several hundred runaways to slavery was a frequent topic. Ricketson said, "no school in the country was more closely in touch with it than our own." Forty years later, the Lyceum at the school was still active.

Ricketson recalled that, in 1854, some of the older boys asked Allen if they could attend the rally scheduled in Boston to protest the pending return of Anthony Burns to slavery in Virginia. Allen, who planned to attend the rally, agreed to let the boys accompany him. Over 50,000 protesters showed up to vent their outrage. The students from West Newton were in the thick of it, getting a close up view of "Burns closely guarded by Marines from the Charlestown Navy Yard." Allen became separated from the students, and they had to make their way back to West Newton without their principal.

That night they met at the Lyceum with Father Peirce, nervously waiting to hear the fate of Allen. No one knew what had happened to him. The scheduled topic that night was: "Ought the North to aid the South in returning fugitive slaves?" In the midst of their discussion, Allen came in and sat down quietly next to Peirce. He said nothing right away, indicating that the discussion should continue.

"Later Father Peirce told us what had happened," Ricketson recalled. Allen, "unable to restrain his indignation at the scene he had witnessed, had cried "shame!" as Burns was marched by where he was standing." A policeman "clothed with a little brief authority had laid violent hands upon him." Allen was detained and questioned for several hours before being released.

Ricketson recalled how angry the group was that the authorities had mistreated their headmaster. "I assure you that, had it been in their power, the members of our Lyceum would have anticipated the Emancipation Proclamation and then and there have abolished slavery by unanimous vote."[19]

There were no public examinations or graduations during the administrations of Peirce and Allen. Both men regarded them as too showy, although the end of each year was celebrated with student performances of music and drama. Parents were kept apprised of their children's progress through descriptive reports, rather than the standard numerical marks. The goal was to form "a sort of mental and moral photograph of the pupil as he appeared to his teachers."[20]

The school prospered and expanded. Peirce kept Mann informed of their progress in letters, and after the first year, he was pleased to write to his old friend that the school was going well. Rebecca Pennell Dean, Horace Mann's niece and a first-year graduate of the Lexington Normal School, continued to have a close relationship with Peirce. One of the school's most famous graduates, she became the first woman professor in the United States when she accepted a teaching job at Antioch. Whenever she or her husband returned to Massachusetts, they tried to stop in to see Peirce.

Peirce settled in nicely to his life at the school, doing what he loved, active and respected in the community. Students from his days at the Allen School remembered him fondly. At the fortieth reunion, Ricketson recalled an anecdote which he thought revealed Peirce's somewhat old-fashioned character. He said that as Peirce was going home for lunch one day, two young women were sitting in front of the schoolhouse opening their lunches. Seeing their teacher passing by, they invited him to share their lunches. He declined their invitation in verse:

> "All the world would stare
> If wife should dine at Edmonton
> And I should dine at Ware"
> (*The Diverting History of John Gilpin* by William Cowper)

Ricketson reminisced about Peirce's teaching style and mannerisms. By that point, years after Peirce's death, Peirce had become a legend at the school. Ricketson knew that many in the audience had not had the privilege of having been taught by Peirce. "All you have heard of him, all the traditions that have been handed down concerning him, can give you but an imperfect conception of that singularly gifted man." He pondered what it was about Peirce that made him such a remarkable teacher. It was, he said, "sympathetic nature, that drew his pupils closer to him and inspired them with the love of knowledge," as well "his infinite patience."

Ricketson remembered Peirce's high standard of morality, but did not remember him as austere or judgmental in any way when it came to student conduct. "And, even though he often spoke about serious topics, Peirce "did not overlook the gentle graces, and was equally at home in his lectures on politeness and courtesy, of the old fashion type of which he himself was the embodiment."[21]

Peirce taught at the West Newton English and Classical School for as long as his health permitted. In December 1856, he wrote a lengthy emotional letter in response to a letter he'd received from Horace Mann. The letter revealed that he was an elderly gentleman facing mortality. He wrote that he feared he would never see Mann again, and wanted to be sure that Mann knew how important he had been to him. "I am more indebted [to you] for whatever good I have done, or reputation I have acquired as a Teacher, than to all others whosoever." Peirce reminisced about their years together when they "toiled for the good cause of Education" and told him how privileged he felt to have been at his side. Peirce congratulated Mann on making Antioch College a success, but rued the day Mann had left Massachusetts. He blamed the politics of the state for driving him away. "Massachusetts couldn't afford to lose such a man," he wrote. He correctly predicted that Mann's name would go down in history at the top of the list of educational leaders.[22]

Despite the fact that the two men could point to a lifetime of accomplishment, Peirce was convinced that the battle over public education and teacher training that he and Mann had waged, was not over. In fact, he complained that ground had been lost since he and Mann had retired from public education. Although old and in declining health, he wrote that he had no intention of retiring "while so much ground remains to be conquered from the enemy."

Peirce, however, was also optimistic about the cause of education. He wrote to Mann that they were naïve to expect that the work that they had started would be done within the "short compass" of their lives. He was proud of those in whom they had instilled with their philosophy of education. He expressed faith in teachers like Nathaniel Allen and other normal school graduates. Peirce was confident those teachers would carry on their teaching philosophy and build upon the "foundation" that he and Mann had laid together. [23]

Despite failing health, Peirce taught at the West Newton English and Classical School until two years before his death. Allen reduced his old friend's teaching load in the last years. When he was too ill to teach, he would often sit in the back of a classroom to watch lessons. In 1857, Peirce wrote to Mann twice, recommending Mary C. Pike, a student at the school, for admission to Antioch. In his second letter that year, the sixty-seven-year-old Peirce referred to himself as "old and infirm." He wrote that had hoped to be well enough to travel to Ohio for Antioch's spring commencement, but doubted he would be able to make the journey. His prediction was correct, as he was not well enough to travel.[24]

During the Christmas season that year Peirce reunited with his old friend when Mann was on a visit to in New England. Mann described the visit in a letter to Dr. Samuel Gridley Howe.

> One cruel night, I went out to see Father
> Peirce, or what is left of him, - weak, paralytic,
> and almost coming within Shakespeare's
> description of old age, with each of the *sans*.
> But what a glorious old wreck he is - What
> rising sun is comparable to his setting one?
> Without him, as well as without you, where
> would the Normal Schools have been?

Mann encouraged Howe to hurry to visit Peirce because of their friend's precarious health. Despite Mann's gloomy description, however, Peirce did not die until almost three years later, early in 1860. In fact, Mann died before Peirce the previous summer. Rebecca Pennell Dean described her uncle's illness and death, noting that, even while he was dying, Mann thought about his old friend, Cyrus Peirce. In his delirium, she said that he "spoke to Mr. Peirce."[25]

Cyrus Peirce died in the spring of 1860 spared from witnessing the tragedy of the Civil War. Committed to the abolition of slavery, he was also committed to the principle of nonviolence, and the war would have posed a moral dilemma for him.

The Graves of Cyrus and Harriet Peirce

After Pierce's death, over one hundred of his former students raised money to erect a monument over his grave on Nantucket. A white marble cross on a marble plinth was erected within several months with "Live to the Truth" carved on it.

Peirce was honored in the annual report of the American Anti-Slavery Society in 1860 as an "early, earnest, and ever-faithful" friend of abolition, praising his courage as an early officer of the Massachusetts chapter. "He accepted an office when to do so brought upon him derision and reproach." The report reminded members that it had been Peirce who had attempted to present the Latimer Petition to the U.S. House of Representatives. Peirce was praised as a "man of sterling worth, exceedingly modest and retiring, amiable in disposition, gentle in speech and manner, but firm and uncompromising whenever principle was involved." Finally, they praised Peirce as a teacher with "rare tact and eminent success" who was called Father Peirce out of the affection of his students.[26]

In 1871, thirty-one years after their graduation, a two-day class reunion was held on Nantucket of the graduates of the first graduating class. Nine of the original twenty five women made the journey. They decided to meet on the island so that they could visit Harriet Peirce and "visit the grave of Father Pierce."[27]

Chapter 17: Harriet Peirce

Harriet Peirce, despite having lived in West Newton for many years, chose to sell the big house on Cherry Street after the death of her beloved husband, and move back to Nantucket where she spent the rest of her long life.

The island Harriet returned to after a sixteen-year absence was very

Nantucket Historical Association

different from the one she had left in 1844. Nantucket had fallen on hard times. In 1846, a fire gutted much of the downtown, burning businesses and residences. Many families left the island rather than rebuild. Economically, Nantucket had been eclipsed by New Bedford, where the railroad allowed whalers both to dock, and get their oil to market immediately.

The Gold Rush of 1849 further decimated the island population. Unemployed young men left Nantucket to seek fame and fortune in California. Idle Nantucket whale ships used to transport the 49ers were abandoned by the dozens in San Francisco Bay, their wood stripped to construct houses.

Whales had become harder to catch due to overfishing. The discovery of oil in Pennsylvania in 1859 sealed the fate of the whale oil industry, as the industrial age turned to petroleum. The few Nantucket ships that remained in whaling were forced to venture on longer voyages to more distant realms. The Bering Sea was one of their dangerous destinations.

Harriet Peirce arrived home on the advent of the Civil War in her mid-sixties. She joined a sisterhood of friends - strong, independent, intelligent women who had fought for abolition, for temperance, and for women's rights. They were "universal reformers," women who were confident they could affect change. They had spent their lifetimes challenging the status quo, and were skilled at organizing clubs, rallies, petition drives, and fundraisers. They were capable writers, and not too shy to speak in public. Some of the credit for that may be given to the Quaker heritage of the island, as Quaker women were free to speak at Friends Meetings. Over their lives, these women had scored victories that allowed them to be optimistic about the effectiveness of grassroots protest. On Nantucket, they had fought successfully to integrate the public schools, and prodded the state into passing an important civil rights law. They had helped push

Harriet Coffin Peirce

Nantucket Historical Association

the state to pass the Personal Liberty Act which had forbidden judges and other state officers from returning fugitive slaves to slavery. Accomplished women, they had never let the island isolate them from national or international affairs. Most were past the age of sixty when Harriet rejoined them. There was still a lot of work to do. The woman's suffrage movement regained strength after the Civil War, and the group welcomed the return of Harriet Peirce, glad to add her voice and intelligence to their causes.

During the Civil War, Harriet was a founding member and the president of the Nantucket Soldiers' Relief Society. After the war, she wrote about the group's beginning. "A meeting of ladies was called in the Atheneum to see what could be done for men in the army." The women, whose ranks grew to sixty-two, met regularly throughout the war, sewing bandages and clothing for wounded soldiers, as well as raising funds for their aid. They sent parcels containing blankets, soap, and medicinal brandy directly to Nantucket soldiers. Harriet's final report concluded the group was happy to be no longer needed "for soldiers in the tented field, or in the gloomy hospital," but reminded Nantucketers that there were still many men "whom the terrible scourge of war has thrown back upon us" who would continue to need help and support from the community.[1]

Most of the Nantucket volunteers were members of the legendary 20th Massachusetts Volunteer Infantry, sometimes called the Harvard Regiment. Over eighty islanders joined that regiment before it left for duty in 1861. By the time of Robert E. Lee's surrender, seventy-three Nantucket men had lost their lives, and scores returned wounded. Many others chose not to return home, as there was little work to be had on the island. Many houses were vacant, and parts of downtown were like a ghost town.[2]

Harriet had fought for the rights of women throughout her life. She had been a Garrisonian abolitionist where women were accepted as equals. She and her husband championed equal education for girls and fought for parity in the salaries of men and women teachers. When she returned to the island, she served on the executive committee of Nantucket's Women's Suffrage Club with friends from her childhood.

Eliza Barney was a close friend and an important member of the club. Barney's credentials in the women's rights movement were impressive. In 1839, she attended the critical meeting of the American Anti-Slavery Society in New York City as a delegate. She went there expecting to be allowed to fully participate with the men for the first time in the organization's history. The proposal to include women had sparked a two-day debate at which she addressed the

Eliza Barney

Nantucket Historical Association

assembly, urging them to accept the women as equals. Eventually the Garrisonian faction won, and she was seated as a delegate alongside her husband, Nathaniel. In 1851, she attended the first women's suffrage conference held in Massachusetts with her husband and their daughter, Sarah.

Both the Barneys and the Peirces had been committed to multiple progressive reforms. Widows now, Harriet Peirce and Eliza Barney were determined to see the day when women gained the right to vote.

Anna Gardner returned to the island a dozen years after Harriet's return. By then, the island's population had plummeted even more. In the 1870s and 80s, the population of the island numbered less than 4,000, with more women than men. The graduating class of Nantucket High School in 1877 had no boys and only four girls.

Gardner, the former teacher at the African School, had left

Anna Gardner

Nantucket Historical Association

Nantucket in 1862 to volunteer as one of the first teachers to travel to the South to teach the freedmen. Gardner had an illustrious career with the Freedman's Bureau, bravely teaching in the South until 1873 in adverse circumstances, often close to enemy lines. In Charlottesville Virginia, she started one of the first normal schools for freedmen, believing education was imperative for the advancement of blacks in the South. Gardner helped to educate black teachers who carried on heroic work during the bleak years of Reconstruction and beyond. Gardner's normal schools and her educational philosophy were greatly influenced by Cyrus Peirce and his approach to students and teaching. Thus, Gardner carried on Peirce's important legacy, affecting at least a generation of new teachers in the South.[3]

In Massachusetts, the battle for women's suffrage was first waged over the right to vote for members of local school committees. The push for that vote on Nantucket heated up just before February's annual town meeting in 1875. Anna Gardner spearheaded the fight. The suffragettes had reason to be encouraged. The Atheneum had recently named its first two women trustees, and the Atheneum wielded considerable political influence on the island.

Gardner wrote a long letter to the newspaper addressing the issue of women being given the right to vote for, and hold positions on, the school committee. She noted that the representation of women on the school committee was particularly pertinent on Nantucket "where women constitute so large a majority of the inhabitants, and where there are so many ex-teachers, who have proved their fitness for the position by their complete success in their profession. They understand the needs of the schools from their own experience."[4]

This campaign was a partial success. Two women, Judith J. Fish and Mrs. Elizabeth C. Crosby, were elected to that 1875 school committee. Women, however, had not been allowed to vote in the election and would not be allowed to vote for school committee members for another four years. Nonetheless, during those four years, the men of Nantucket elected at least one woman per year to serve on the school committee.[5]

The women continued to push for participation in politics. The *Women's Journal*, published in Boston, reported in 1876 that Nantucket women had taken part in a local Republican Party committee meeting at the Atheneum. The magazine reported that "about an equal number of either sex" attended the party meeting and that both sexes had chosen delegates for a statewide convention in Worcester. It noted the chairman was "very cordial" to the women. The journal singled out Eliza Barney, Anna Gardner and Harriet Peirce, as "veteran Anti-Slavery laborers."[6]

It was not until 1879 that Massachusetts passed a law requiring towns permit women to vote in school committee elections. After Harriet Peirce's death, almost five years later, Gardner reminisced at a meeting of the Women's Suffrage organization about the day when women were finally allowed to cast ballots on Nantucket.

> My mind has gone back to the time when we were
> first allowed to vote for School Committee, and
> how some of us, although determined to do what
> we felt to be our duty, dreaded to go to the polls to
> deposit our votes on account of the ridicule and
> the sarcastic remarks that we thought were sure to
> be expressed by some of those who felt women
> were out of their sphere in so doing – but when the
> time came, and we found we had for our leaders
> Eliza Barney, Elizabeth G. Macy, and Harriet
> Peirce, three women who had shown throughout
> their long lives such purity of spirit united with so
> much zeal and courage, who had, in her own way,
> and to the best of her ability, done all that she
> could to help every noble reform…..we took
> courage, and thought with these three women to
> lead us, we could do anything.[7]

At age eighty-five, Harriet Peirce had proudly been one of the first women in Nantucket to vote. She was one of only thirteen women who took advantage of their newly won right at that town meeting. With so few taking advantage of the opportunity, the newspaper reported that the presence of the women had not caused disruption. "There was a respectful exhibit by the gentlemen in the hall as the ladies filed in, and a seat was soon vacated for their use."[8]

Because so few women had availed themselves of the ballot, the Sherburne Lyceum chose to debate the possible reasons for their absence. One side argued that the lack of women voters was proof that women did not really want to vote. Not surprisingly, Anna Gardner was one of those who spoke in opposition to that point of view. Gardner exhorted the women of Nantucket to vote at the next election.[9]

Before the next election in 1881, the women published the following in the local newspaper:

> *To the Women Tax-payers of Nantucket:*
> The law of the state gives us the right to vote
> for School Committee, and, small though this
> crumb of the loaf may seem to some of us,
> we feel that it forces upon us a responsibility
> that we, as mothers and citizens, interested
> in the welfare of the young of our island,
> dare not thrust aside. Will you, then,
> at the coming election, aid the cause by
> voting for a woman to fill one of the
> vacancies that will occur.[10]

Their plea was effective. The number of women voting that year almost doubled, going from thirteen to twenty-five.

The temperance movement underwent a revival after the Civil War, and Harriet Peirce was an active member, often serving as an officer in the local chapter. Not reticent to speak in public, she was often called upon to do so. The *Inquirer* reported on one lecture where she "addressed the meeting, recalling many interesting reminiscences of the manners and customs of half a century ago, when alcoholic beverages were considered indispensable to true hospitality."[11]

At the end of 1876, Harriet participated in a well-attended debate at Nantucket's town hall about the legalization of alcohol. She advocated total prohibition, speaking against those who favored the regulating or licensing of alcohol. She helped lead a petition drive to convince the selectmen to refuse licensing alcohol distributors, and was disappointed when the town granted alcohol licenses to various boarding houses and druggists.

Harriet Peirce also helped to lead a drive to obtain signatures on a pledge to abstain from alcohol. "Taking the pledge" became an important component of the temperance movement of the era, with people publically signing to abstain from alcohol. The newspaper reported, "Mrs. Peirce almost regretted having signed the pledge of the society, because she experienced such pleasure in doing so that she wanted to do it again."[12]

Harriet Peirce continued her life-long involvement in charity work. She was an officer of the Unitarian Children's Aid Society that raised money for children in poverty and served on its executive committee with Eliza Barney. In 1867, the society opened a home for "young girls that are exposed to such influences as to render it desirable to remove them from their present homes." During the first year, six children were taken in. Harriet served on the subcommittee that selected the children; the next year, eight girls lived in what was called "the Home." [13]

Harriet Peirce was also a member and officer of the Ladies' Howard Society which provided help for sick and poor families on the island for over seventy years. The women collected clothing and shoes for the poor. They also became involved in the quest to establish a home for the island's elderly. Harriet was on the Committee for the Old Peoples' Home that raised money to establish a home for the elderly, separate from the Island Home that was predominantly a home for the indigent. She knew how hard it was to live alone in old age, having lived in a variety of lodgings after her return to the island.

Harriet Peirce took part in public forums of the Sherburne Lyceum that sponsored well-attended debates every two weeks throughout the winters in the late 1870s. In 1878, she took part in three. The first concerned whether women who wished to pursue intellectual careers ought to marry. She argued alongside several others, including Eliza Barney, that marriage should not be an impediment to women who wished to have a professional career. In their opinion, women could have both. Harriet was a good example of the possibility, having taught alongside her husband in the normal schools, as well as in the Allen School. A vote of the approximately sixty spectators at the end of the debate showed that "a large majority" sided with the feminists.[14]

The second debate concerned a topic near and dear to Harriet Peirce's heart: whether coeducation was "inexpedient." Harriet spoke emphatically, again from personal experience, that it was better to educate the sexes together. Anna Gardner, whose classes were also always coeducational, was slated to be one of her partners on this occasion. Unfortunately, Gardner was unable to attend the debate in person because she was on crutches, having suffered an accident when visiting a nephew in New York City. She sent a speech in her place. Once again, the side argued by the progressive women received the most votes.[15]

The last debate of the season concerned the propriety of preachers using graphic pictures to illustrate sermons against vice. Again joined in argument by friends from abolitionist days, Harriet Peirce argued in favor of the use of such illustrations as necessary for good causes. Her side won by a slim margin.[16]

Peirce was an active member of Nantucket's Sorosis Club, a national women's intellectual society. Anna Gardner organized the Nantucket chapter in 1874. The members met to discuss books and intellectual topics, sometimes inviting guest speakers, although usually a member prepared an essay for discussion. Gardner wrote many essays for the club, a number preserved at the Nantucket Historical Association. They cover a wide range of disparate topics that give us a glimpse of the scope of their discussions - the life of Marie Antoinette, the importance of keeping the mind active, universal suffrage, temperance, the philosophy of Spinoza, and the poetry of John Greenleaf Whittier.

Sorosis Club provided Nantucket women with an organization that was social, intellectual and fun, less serious than organizations devoted to a single reform or to charity. Gardner composed several poems extolling its importance to the women. In one, she wrote

> What is a school that aims to teach
> The highest good that it can reach,
> And draws us nearer each to each?
> Sorosis[17]

The group usually met in each other's homes where they ate a meal and discussed a chosen topic. In 1885, Frederick Douglass and his wife were invited to one of the meetings where he spoke about his long association with Nantucket. (Note)

Sorosis Club also organized outings and picnics. Every summer the women traveled by carriage to Siasconset at the end of the island, where they visited the beach and had a picnic, joined by off–island Sorosis members vacationing in Siasconset. Frequent guests were Dr. and Mrs. Benjamin Sharp who had a cottage in the village. Sharp was a world-renowned zoologist who accompanied Robert Perry on his first trip to Greenland.[18]

Harriet Peirce died on September 29, 1884 on Pearl Street, at the age of ninety, having outlived her beloved husband by twenty-four years. Her death certificate indicates she had been sick for "two weeks and three days." The cause is listed as "general debility," a common notation for those who died at an advanced age.[19]

Note: Frederick Douglass visited Nantucket five times during his career, the first in 1841, and the last in 1885.

Chapter 18: "And being dead, he yet speaketh"

Cyrus Peirce left a legacy that endures. He was an activist in the true sense of the word, having been involved in the peace movement, the temperance movement, the woman's suffrage movement, and the abolition movement. Unitarianism provided the principles by which he lived.

It is for his impact on educational reform, however, that Peirce must be recognized. Horace Mann justifiably deserves credit for his political expertise as the first Secretary of Education in the United States. It was through Mann's efforts that the first teacher training schools were created. But Mann's contribution has been well recognized; schools and other institutions bearing his name dot the American landscape.

Although Cyrus Peirce is the father of teacher education in the United States, there are only two schools that bear his name - one a middle school on Nantucket, and one a primary school in Newton. Yet through Peirce's efforts, teaching began to be a profession in its own right. Although it took somewhat longer than his lifetime, it is to his credit that specialized education and practice are now required for would-be teachers.

Peirce was one of the founders of the state universities in this country, most of which began as normal schools, and the model he created in Massachusetts was copied by many other states. Many of the great universities and colleges of the United States had their origins as normal schools.

Peirce was steadfast in his belief that prospective teachers required specific instruction in child development and in the art and science of teaching. Every prospective teacher needed to teach real students to learn how to craft lesson plans suitable for their particular classroom. This practice, known as student teaching, is now taken for granted. but it was an innovative idea when Peirce insisted on creating the first model school in the United States alongside the first normal school. Student teaching, then as now, serves many purposes. It weeds out those who, for various reasons, are not suitable for the classroom, whether by their own judgment or that of supervisors. More importantly, it provides teachers with hands-on learning. Peirce believed that specialized instruction for teachers was critical for the creation of a professional teaching corps. Furthermore, a professional teaching corps would result in higher salaries as teachers gained professional status. A professional teaching corps, in turn, would improve education and improve American society socially and economically. Simply, it would ensure the survival of American democracy.

Peirce's child-centered approach in the classroom endures, although the role of teachers and students is still subject to lively debate, both within the teaching community and without. Over 150 years later, the kind of child-centered classrooms advocated by Peirce are sometimes accused of pampering children. Peirce argued against authoritarian approaches whereby teachers dispense knowledge to passive learners. He maintained that children learn best with kind and thoughtful teachers, and lessons that require them to be active learners. He believed such classrooms would result in mutual respect between teachers and students, minimizing the need for strict rules. Peirce modeled these teaching principles throughout his life. His theme of gentle caring is universally recognized in the reminisces about "Father Peirce." Dozens of journals and testimonials emphasize his love, gentle manner and moral guidance. His gentleness, however, did not exclude holding students to high academic standards, another recurring theme in the journals and reminiscences of his former students.

The timeline stretching from Peirce to the classrooms of today is visible and traceable. Hundreds of teachers left his classroom and had an impact on thousands of students during his lifetime. Many thousands more graduated from normal schools modeled on the Lexington Normal School. Many students of the new progressive teachers themselves became teachers, continuing to practice Peirce's teaching philosophy. It is no exaggeration to claim that Peirce's teacher-descendants number in the hundreds of thousands.

Some of those he taught became famous and influential citizens whose contributions can be cited. The majority, however, did not leave easily-researched records. Nevertheless, these hundreds of dedicated teachers made education significantly better in the United States. Children benefited from teachers trained by normal schools, teachers who cared about their intellectual, physical and mental wellbeing. Classrooms themselves changed as tangible proof that treatment of students mattered. Schools became more comfortable, better lit, better ventilated, and more inviting. Bare walls were no longer acceptable and it was expected that schools keep up with new classroom apparatus, including globes, maps and blackboards.

A few of Peirce's students founded normal schools elsewhere. Anna Gardner opened one of the first normal schools in the segregated South to train black teachers to teach the freedmen after the Civil War. She founded the Jefferson Normal School in Charlottesville, Virginia in 1869, which applied Peirce's philosophy of teaching. Dozens of Gardner's students taught black children during the worst years of Reconstruction and Jim Crow. Ex-slave Isabella Gibbons, who Gardner taught, and then hired, continued to teach in Charlottesville long after the demise of the Freedman's Bureau. Benjamin E. Tonsler, another graduate, served as the principal of a black school in Charlottesville until 1917.[1]

The twenty-five young women who comprised the first graduating class of the Lexington Normal School were fully aware of their historical significance as the first specifically trained teachers in the United States. From the start, Peirce made it clear to them that their success was critical to the success of the entire endeavor. It was a heavy burden for those teenagers to bear.

So cognizant were those graduates of their place in history, they recorded their achievements in a journal kept yearly for over fifty years and eventually published in 1903. In it, Mary Swift Lamson comments, "we had learned at Lexington how to keep a journal, and fortunately, began to practice it then, every line of this large book being valuable as historic material." The class had its first reunion ten years after its graduation, and its last in 1895.[2]

Critics expected the newly minted teachers of the Lexington Normal School would prove unworthy of the public investment that had been made in their educations. Legislators questioned the women several years after their graduation to find out if they had taught at all. And, if they had taught, had they left the state to do so? "Or have you been disloyal and, as we feared, married and left Massachusetts?"[3]

The graduates proved the skeptics wrong. In 1901, Lamson compiled a record of the women for the Biennial Meeting of the Alumnae of the Framingham Normal School, seventy years after her graduation. She listed each graduate and her contribution to education. The majority had taught for several years before marriage prevented them from continuing. Some of those married women, however, were elected to their local school committees. For example, Lydia Stow Adams taught in Dedham and in Fall River until her marriage; she then became the first woman elected to the school committee in Fall River.

Similarly, Susan Burdick taught until she married. She was the principal of several high schools in New Bedford and Lowell, Massachusetts for ten years. After her marriage to inventor Dr. William F. Channing, she remained involved in various projects in the interest of the public good. She returned to Nantucket after her divorce, and was part of a group that helped establish the Nantucket Historical Association.

Two of Horace Mann's nieces were also in that first class in Lexington. Eliza R. Pennell Blake taught for five years, but died young. Her sister, Rebecca Pennell Dean taught for over twenty-five years. She was the first woman appointed as a full professor to the faculty of an American college, and one of the ten founding professors of Antioch College. At Antioch she received equal pay to her male counterparts, another first in American educational history, an achievement that would have pleased Cyrus Peirce as he had fought for equal pay for women throughout his life.

Those who remained single had long careers. The longest was that of Adeline Ireson who taught in the Cambridge public schools for fifty years. Ireson also taught during Reconstruction for the Freedman's Bureau. Louise E. Harris taught for thirty-three years at various schools in Massachusetts, as did Mary A. Davis who managed a boys' school in East Boston for many years. [4]

Three graduates of the school were associated with the Institution for the Blind under Dr. Samuel Gridley Howe. It was Howe's remarkable success with the deaf and blind Laura Bridgman that made him famous. Howe discovered Bridgman in 1837 when she was just seven years old. Laura had contracted scarlet fever when she was a toddler and had lost her vision, her hearing, and most of her sense of taste and smell.

Laura was the child that Howe was seeking, determined to prove that she was educable based on his belief in phrenology and progressive new teaching techniques. Howe rejected the Calvinist notion that the little girl was incapable of being educated, or even worse, possessed by the Devil. He convinced her parents to give him their daughter to raise at the Institution for the Blind in Watertown.

Laura Bridgman

Thus began a famous multi-year experiment on Bridgman. The intelligent youngster made great progress at the Institute for the Blind, eventually becoming a teacher there. Hundreds came to watch her perform her skills, and she became a legend during her lifetime, drawing crowds wherever she went. Among the things she performed in public were reading and writing, as well as exhibiting her skill at embroidery. [5]

Besides Howe himself, Bridgman's first teacher was Lydia Drew. It was Drew who taught Bridgman the names of objects through a system of raised letters, and later taught her finger spelling. When the Lexington Normal School opened its doors in 1839, two years after Drew started to work with Bridgman, Howe enrolled Drew to expose her to the latest teaching techniques. She returned to teaching Bridgman, but left shortly thereafter in order to get married.[6]

Two other graduates of the Lexington Normal School replaced

Drew: Eliza Rogers and Mary Swift. Swift taught Bridgman for five years and wrote a book, *Life and Education of Laura Bridgman*, chronicling their efforts. Helen Keller's famous teacher, Anne Sullivan emulated Swift's insights and techniques in teaching Bridgman. Both Rogers and Swift left the school when they got married. [7]

After her marriage, Lamson was elected to the Worcester school committee, and sat on the board of the Lancaster State Industrial School for nine years. For thirty-six years, she worked for, and promoted, the Boston Young Women's Christian Association.

Other graduating classes of teachers from the Lexington and Newton schools were equally successful, but no other class kept a journal systematically documenting their achievements. Betsey Canedy, from the class of 1842, was among the first teachers to go South during the Civil War to teach freedman. Canedy was teaching in New Bern, North Carolina, as early as 1862, even before the creation of the Freedman's Bureau. Like Anna Gardner, Canedy founded a normal school for black teachers, hers in Richmond. Gardner and Canedy became close friends and visited each other during their stay in the South. They must have been surprised to find they shared Peirce as their mentor.[8]

Charlotte Bacheler helped establish a normal school in Burma. She spent almost twenty years there with her husband, Benjamin C. Thomas, as a Baptist missionary, mostly in remote regions of Burma.[9] (Note)

One of Peirce's nieces, Elizabeth Brown, daughter of his sister Relief, served as principal of the West Newton model school after Allen's resignation. After marrying Frederick Stones, she became a leader in women's rights, forming the School Suffrage Association in Waltham. Brown was the first woman elected to the Waltham school committee.[10]

Electa Lincoln remained active in education and reform movements after her marriage to George Walton. Together, they wrote a successful series of mathematics textbooks based on what became known as the "Walton System." Their books became standards in classrooms across the country throughout the century. Both Waltons were active in politics and the Unitarian church. Electa Lincoln Walton was so admired in the women's movement that Juliet Ward Howe, abolitionist, women's leader, wife of Samuel Gridley Howe, and author of the *Battle Hymn of the Republic,* wrote a poem in her honor in 1903.[11] (Note)

Harriet Peirce also had influence on education long after her death in 1884. With the money her husband left her, she set up a scholarship in her will to "aid indigent girls [of Nantucket] in getting an education." The majority of the scholarship recipients returned the money later, enabling the scholarship to continue for an amazing forty-nine years after her death. Most of the women studied at normal schools and became teachers.[12]

Vera Sickles, the single graduate of Nantucket High School's class of 1905, had a long and illustrious career in the field of speech and language. She attended Bridgewater Normal School with the aid of the Peirce scholarship. After graduating, Sickles went to Columbia University where she earned Bachelor of Science and Masters degrees. She joined the faculty of Smith College in Northampton, Massachusetts, where she taught literature and theater for thirty-nine years. Sickles' textbook on speech training was used as a college text for at least two decades.[13]

Harriet Peirce also left money in her will to "aid indigent girls" not living on Nantucket, administered by Electa Lincoln Walton. Money was given to young women for tuition and board, as well as for textbooks and other necessities. Most of the recipients attended state normal schools, although the scholarship also funded girls to attend Wellesley, Cornell and Boston University. The money in this fund lasted until 1909, over twenty years after Harriet's death.

Note: Charlotte Bacheler returned to the United States in 1868 with her husband who came home to recuperate from ill health. He died shortly thereafter.

Note: Last verse of the poem:

> Friends, we ever shall respect her
> Clubs, we never will reject her,
> Wiseacres, we will not direct her,
> Critics, we will not correct her,
> And if alive
> At ninety-five
> She shall still be our Electa.

Dedicated to Peirce and Mann

Peter John Roberts

Afterword

Over nine years of research went into the writing of this biography of Cyrus Peirce. My original goal was simply to prepare a short presentation for the students of Nantucket who attend the Cyrus Peirce Middle School, but who knew nothing about the man for whom the school was named.

I knew something about the role Peirce had played on the island, including some of his role in the Latimer Petition, from my graduate work at Boston University about the integration of the Nantucket public schools, which eventually became a book as well as a documentary film. (Note)

As the story of Peirce unfolded, I realized that his contribution was far greater than I had at first perceived, having seen Peirce first and foremost as an abolitionist. I soon understood that, while his abolitionist contribution was significant, it paled in comparison to his importance in my chosen field – public education.

The more I learned about Peirce and his struggle to professionalize teaching, the more I was drawn to him. It took years of research before the story about his battle with Matthew Hale Smith was completely revealed because the story of their epic battle has never been fully documented. It was alluded to in several sources, but it took a great deal of digging in primary sources before the full scope of the attack on Pierce was uncovered.

As I read about Peirce, he began to seem like a colleague, especially after my thirty-three years as a public school teacher, most of it in a school named after him. I could easily imagine what his opinions would have been on vouchers, standardized testing, the Common Core

Curriculum, and teacher evaluation.

I found myself agreeing with Peirce on many topics. Like Peirce, I believe that the future of our country lies in the hands of our children, and it is our responsibility to provide them with the best education possible. Like Peirce, I believe a good education should be accessible to every child. Because school funding is based on property taxes, we have abysmal gaps between schools from neighborhood to neighborhood. Rich districts have excellent public schools, while poor districts suffer with substandard buildings and materials and underpaid teachers. I think Peirce would encourage us to abandon the way schools are funded. Because of the underfunding of the public schools, too many parents opt for private schools where the privileged receive excellent education. It was true when Peirce was teaching, and is true today.

Peirce and Mann also worried about private schools. They would be concerned about the charter school and voucher movement, which lures children, parents and teachers away from the public schools. Charter schools drain money, students and teachers away from our public schools and result in a two-tiered system of education at public expense.

The result is that our public schools are left with the most needy students, students too poor for their parents to have alternatives. Their parents are less likely to afford supplemental activities or private lessons. Public schools, facing financial crises, have largely eliminated enriching activities in the arts, barely able to provide basic level education. Most immigrant children attend the public schools, requiring extra language instruction, again at an expense that many public schools cannot afford to do adequately. Special needs students disproportionately attend public schools. State and federal laws rightly mandate that public schools provide for the needs of special needs children. Most private schools, particularly high schools, do not have the motivation or resources to focus on children with special educational needs and do not accept them. These students cost more money to educate than others.

As in Peirce's time, the ability of our teaching corps is questioned. There is doubt that the best and the brightest choose teaching as a profession. People assume that those who choose teaching must have been poor students because they 'resorted' to teaching. Unfortunately, it is also true that the best and the brightest graduates do spurn teaching careers, and, as in Peirce's day, it is increasingly important to attract capable students to become teachers. As in Peirce's day, teachers continue to be paid less than those who choose professions requiring the same amount of education, but that are more lucrative. Just as Peirce was torn between being a preacher or a teacher in a time when ministers were highly regarded, students today who would make excellent teachers, often choose professions with higher status. Like Peirce, I believe that teachers hold the key to good education; as such, they deserve trust and respect, and should be given the resources and academic freedom to individualize instruction as they see fit. Peirce would not have approved of the one-size-fits all mentality that pervades American education.

The religious right continues to attack progressive education. In the 1840s, the religious right attacked Peirce as he tried to reform education. They did not agree with his optimistic view of human nature. The right continues to favor strict discipline and corporal punishment in our public schools as instrumental in character building. Then and now, they support the expulsion of unruly children and the incarceration of juveniles. Principals face daily pressure in administering discipline, from those who believe in 'throwing the book' at disruptive students, to those who question a school's authority to punish their children at all.

Peirce never gave up hope about the future. Subject to periods of depression, he always rallied, certain that an educated America populace would right society's wrongs. Like Peirce, we must put our faith in hard work and adherence to principle. Reform does happen. People like Horace Mann, Dorothea Dix, Frederick Douglass, Nathaniel Allen, Samuel Gridley Howe, Anna Gardner, and Cyrus and Harriet Peirce succeeded in making their world a better place.

Note: The book is *A Line in the Sand* and the film is *Rock of Changes: Race, Faith and Freedom in Nantucket* produced by Harlan Reiniger in 1999.

Endnotes chapter 1

[1] Murray Rothbard, *Conceived in Liberty, Volume 1.* Mises Institute. 1999, mises.org, 174-181.
[2] *Massachusetts Soldiers and Sailors of the Revolutionary War, Vol XII.* Secretary of the Commonwealth. (Boston: Wright and Potter,1904).
[3] Elizabeth Castner, Tercentennial History of the First Parish in Waltham, MA 1696-1996. (Printed by the First Parish in Waltham, 1998,) 25.
[4] Samuel, J. May, *Memoir of Cyrus Peirce, First Principal of the First State Normal School in the United States,* Barnard's *American Journal of Education,* December 1857, 1.
[5] May, 1.
[6] Lynn J. Cadwallader, A Case Study in the Professionalization of Nineteenth Century
Teaching: Nathaniel T Allen, 1823 – 1872, Dissertation at University of Massachusetts, 1983, 14.
[7] Cadwallader, 32.
[8] Cadwallader, 33.
[9] Annual Reports of the Massachusetts Board of Education, 1837-1849. Massachusetts State Archives, 32.
[10] Arthur O. Norton, (ed.) *The First State Normal School in America,* (Cambridge: Harvard Documents in the History of Education. 1926), 247.
[11] Jonathan Levy, "The Dramatic Dialogues of Charles Stearns: An Appreciation,"*Spotlight on the Child: Studies in the History of American Children's Theatre* Bedard, Roger L and Tolch, C. John.(ed), (New York: Greenwood Press, 1989) 6-18.
[12] Castner, 26.

Endnotes chapter 2

[1] Daniel Walker Howe, *The Unitarian Conscience: Harvard Moral Philosophy, 1805- 1861,* (Middletown, Ct: Wesleyan University Press, 1970), 5-7.
[2] David. E. Bumbaugh, *Unitarian Universalism: A Narrative History,* (Chicago: Meadville Lombard Press, 2000), 101.
[3]Bumbaugh, 105.
[4] May, 2.
[5] John Quincy Adams, diary. Massachusetts Historical Society; Samuel Eliot Morison, *Three Centuries of Harvard, 1636-1936.* (Cambridge, MA: Harvard University Press, 1936), 177
[6] Webber Papers at Harvard Pusey Library Archives. Call No. UAI-15.878.
[7] Morison, 107.
[8] http://www.hds.harvard.edu/library/exhibits/online/palfrey/images/ divsch3.jpg.

[9] Morison, 249.

[10] Webber papers.

Endnotes chapter 3

[1] Unitarian Church Records, Nantucket, MA. and Betsy Tyler, *Unitarian Meeting House, Nantucket: A History Commemorating 200 Years1809-2009.* (Nantucket: Nantucket Preservation Trust, 2009).

[2] Morison, 216.

[3] Harvard University: *Quinquennial catalogue, 1636-1930.* (Cambridge: Harvard University, 1930), 1112.

[4] Herbert F.Vetter (ed) *Harvard's Unitarian Presidents.* www.harvardsquarelibrary.org

[5] May, 7-8.

[6] May 11 and Unitarian Church Records, Nantucket.

[7] *Reading North Parish Meeting Records, 1796-1856, Volume 2.* North Reading Library.

[8] Chester W. Easton and Warren E. Eaton (eds), *Proceedings of the 250th Anniversary of the Ancient Town of Redding, (*Reading, MA: Loring and Twombly, 1896) 244.

[9] Robinson,14.

[10] Cyrus Peirce, *Sermon Delivered on Christmas Day, December 25,1824 at Reading,North Parish*, (Andover: Flagg and Gould, 1824).

[11] Dorrian, 38.

[12] *Reading North Parish Meetings Records, 1796-1856, Volume 2.*

Endnotes chapter 4

[1] May, 7.

[2] Eric Jay Dolin, *Leviathan: The History of Whaling in America*, (New York: WW Norton & Company. 2007), 123; Frances Ruley Karttunen, *The Other Islanders: People who pulled Nantucket's Oars*, (New Bedford: Spinner Publications, 2005), 67.

[3] Conrad Wright, (ed), *A Stream of Light: A Short History of American Unitarianism*, (Boston: Skinner House Books, 1975), 24

[4] Carl F.Kaestle, *Pillars of the Republic: Common Schools and American Society, 1780-1860*, (New York: Hill and Wang,1983), 41-42.

[5] Gardner Family Papers, Collection 87, Folders 2-17. Nantucket Historical Association.

[6] Kaestle, 41.

[7] Frederick M Binder, *The Age of the Common School, 1830- 1865,* (New York: John Wiley and Sons, Inc., 1974), 24.

[8] Lawrence, A. Cremin, *American Education: The National Experience, 1783-*

1876, (NewYork: Harper and Row, 1980), 70.

[9] Kaestle, 120-126.

[10] Jonathan Edwards, *Sinners in the Hands of an Angry God.* Christian Classics Ethereal Library. www.ccel.org

[11] Norton, 275.

[12] May, 12.

[13] Sarah Loring Bailey, *Historical Sketches of Andover,* (Boston: Houghton, 1880), 547

[14] May, 12.

[15] May, 12.

Endnotes chapter 5

[1] Johann N Neem, *Creating a Nation of Joiners: Democracy and Civil Society in Early National Massachusetts*, (Cambridge, MA: Harvard University Press, 2008), 2.

[2] *Inquirer,* September 8, 1837.

[3] *Inquirer*, February 15, 1834.

[4] Betsy Tyler, *The Nantucket Atheneum: A History*, (Nantucket: Nantucket Preservation Trust, 2009.) 9.

[5] *Common School Journal*, November 16, 1846.

[6] Barbara A.White, *A Line in the Sand: The Battle to Integrate Nantucket Public Schools, 1825 – 1847.* (New Bedford: Spinner Publications, 2006.)

[7] Margaret Moore Booker, *The Admiral's Academy: Nantucket Island's Historic Coffin School*, (Nantucket MA: Mill Hill Press, 1998), 20-25.

[8] Norton, xxxvi.

[9] Robert L Straker Collection.

[10] Cyrus Peirce, James Edes, Henry F., Mitchell and William Coffin, *Address to the Inhabitants of Nantucket on Education And Free Schools on December 15, 1837,* (Providence: Knowles, Voss & Company,1838).

[11] *Annual Report of the Massachusetts Board of Education, 1837*, Massachusetts State Archives.

[12] *Inquirer* July 29, 1865.

Endnotes Chapter 6

[1] Henry Mayer, *All on Fire: William Lloyd Garrison and the Abolition Of Slavery*, (NY:St. Martin's Press, 1998), 258.

[2] Mayer, 265.

[3] *Record of the Nantucket County Anti Slavery Association*, Blacks on Nantucket, Collection 222, Folder 9, Nantucket Historical Association.

[4] *Inquirer*, October 22, 1843.

[5] *Quaker Book of Objections.* Collection 35, Folder 9. Nantucket Historical Association.

[6] *Inquirer*, July 2, 1834, Kartunnen, 63.

[7] Unitarian Church Records, Nantucket, MA.

[8] Anna Gardner, *Harvest Gleanings in Prose and Verse,* (NY: Fowler and Wells, 1881), 14-15.

[9] Nantucket Town Records.

[10] *Inquirer*, March 23, 1839.

[11] White.

[12] *Record of the Nantucket County Anti Slavery Association.*

[13] Messerli, 322.

[14] Nantucket Town Records

[15] Robert L. Straker Collection.

[16] Letter from Cyrus Peirce to his pupils, August 5, 1839, Winslow/Foye/Elder Collection, Collection 354, Folder 1, Nantucket Historical Association.

Endnotes chapter 7

[1] *Common School Journal,* October 1, 1846.

[2] Robert L. Straker Collection; *Annual Report of the Board of Education, 1838,* Massachusetts State Archives.

[3] Robert L. Straker Collection.

[4] Robert L. Straker Collection.

[5] Peirce, *Journal*, 258; Frederick Clifton Peirce, *Peirce Geneology, Being the Record of the Posterity of John Pers, an early inhabitant of Watertown, in New England, Who came from Norwich, Norfolk County; with Notes on the History of Other Families of Peirce, Pierce, Pearce, etc.* (Worcester: Chas. Hamilton, 1880).

[6] Peirce in Norton, xlvi

[7] Peirce in Norton, 16-17; Adams.

[8] Messerli, 367.

[9] Eben Stearns, "First Historical Sketch," in *Historical Sketches of the Framingham Normal School.* (Published by the Alumnae Association in Commemoration of the 75th Anniversary, July 1 and 2, 1914),14.

[10] Stearns 14

[11] Peirce, 20

[12] Rebecca Viles, *Lexington Normal School*, Papers Relating to the History of the Town, Read by some of the Members, Volume One, Lexington Historical Society, 1889.

[13] Louisa Harris, *Journal, 1839-1905*, MS 89.1, Framingham State University Research Library.

[14] Robert L. Straker Collection.

[15] Robert L. Straker Collection.

[16] Barnard in Norton, xiv.

[17] Mary Swift Lamson, *The First State Normal School in America: Records of the First Class, 1839,* (Boston: 1903); Harris; Julia Ann Smith, *Journal, October*

25, 1840-March 4, 1841. Framingham State University Research Library.
[18] Harris, Viles; Lamson.
[19] Lamson.
[20] Viles.
[21] *Common School Journal*, April 15, 1840.
[22] Viles; *Memorial of the Quarter-Centennial Celebration of the Establishment of Normal Schools in America*, (Boston: C.P. Moody, 1866), 22.
[23] Viles.
[24] Peirce in Norton, lii.
[25] Ann E. Shannon, *Journal, January 18, 1847-April 12, 1847,* Framingham University Research Library.
[26] Robert L. Straker Collection.
[27] Mary Swift, *The First Normal School in America: The Journals of Cyrus Peirce and Mary Swift*, (Boston: 1903).
[28] Norton, xxvii.
[29] Swift.
[30] Mary Stodder, *The Normal Experiment*, Issue 1, March 13, 1841, Publication of the State Normal School, L3321, Lexington Historical Society Archive.
[31] Harris.
[32] Swift.
[33] Stodder; Lamson.
[34] Stodder; Richard P. Kollen, *Lexington, MA: Treasures from Historic Archives*, (Charleston: History Press, 2006), 51.
[35] Lamson.
[36] Messerli, 367.
[37] Robert L. Straker Collection
[38] Messerli, 309.
[39] Lydia Stow Adams, *Journal, 1840*, Framingham State University Research Library.
[40] Walton 18; Peirce *Journal*; Robert L. Straker Collection.
[41] Peirce *Journal*, 78.
[42] Lamson, 147.
[43] Lamson, 148.

Endnotes Chapter 8

[1] Norton, xiii.
[2] Mann in Norton, 264.
[3] Mann in Norton, 264.
[4] Messerli, 322.
[5] Mann in Norton, 264-268.
[6] Mann in Norton, 274-277.
[7] Norton, xvii.
[8] *Annual Reports of the Massachusetts Board of Education, 1837-1849,* Massachusetts State Archives.

[9] Robert L. Straker Collection.
[10] Robert L. Straker Collection.
[11] Peirce, 52.
[12] Harris.

Endnotes chapter 9

[1] Nantucket Town Records.
[2] *Islander*, January 16, 1841, Nantucket Historical Association.
[3] *Inquirer* February 27, 1841.
[4] Nantucket Town Records.
[5] *Inquirer*, March 2, 1842; *Islander*, March 12, 1842; *The Liberator*, March 18, 1842.
[6] White, 55.
[7] White, 54.
[8] White, 54-55.
[9] *Inquirer*, December 5, 1855-February 13, 1886.
[10] *Inquirer,* February 13, 1886.
[11] *The Warder*, February 7, 1846.

Endnotes chapter 10

[1] *Inquirer*, November 26, 1842.
[2] *Inquirer,* December 10, 1842.
[3] *Inquirer*, December 17, 1842.
[4] *Inquirer,* March 4, 1843.
[5] Cyrus Peirce letter to Electa Lincoln, Collection 88, Folder 16, Nantucket Historical Association.
[6] Cyrus Peirce letter to Electa Lincoln.
[7] *Inquirer*, April 5, 1843.
[8] Cyrus Peirce letter to Electa Lincoln.
[9] *Inquirer*, March 4, 1843.
[10] Nantucket Town Records.
[11] Nantucket Town Records.
[12] Nantucket Town Records.
[13] Nantucket Town Records.
[14] *Islander,* March 18, 1843.
[15] Nantucket Town Records.
[16] *Morning (Daily) Telegraph*, March 19, 1844, Nantucket Historical Association.
[17] Nantucket Town Records.
[18] *The Telegraph,* July 22, 1844.
[19] *The Morning Telegraph,* June 29, July 6, 1844.

Endnotes chapter 11

[1] *Annual Report of the Massachusetts Board of Education*, 1844, Massachusetts State Archives.
[2] Messerli, 414-417.
[3] *Common School Journal*, August 1, 1845.
[4] *Common School Journal,* August 1, 1843.
[5] *Memorial of the Quarter-Centennial Celebration.*
[6] Walton, 34 in *Historical Sketches of the Framingham Normal School.*
[7] John Ogden Fisher, *Window Dedicated to Public School Education and to the Teaching Profession,* First Unitarian Church in Newton Files, undated.
[8] *Common School Journal*, September 2, 1844.
[9] *Annual Reports of the Massachusetts Board of Education, 1848,1849,* Massachusetts State Archives.
[10] Eliza Roger Gould, *Journal*, Framingham State University Research Library.
[11] Cadwallader, 17.
[12] Cadwallader, 24.
[13] Mary A. Greene, *Nathaniel Topliff Allen: Teacher, Reformer, Philanthropist*, privately printed, 1906. Newton Historical Association, 28.
[14] Cadwallader, 30.
[15] Cadwallader, 44.
[16] Messerli, 322.
[17] /Cadwallader, 52.
[18] Cadwallader, 56.
[19] Cadwallader 57.
[20] Cadwallader, 24.
[21] Cadwallader, 64.
[22] Cadwallader 76.
[23] Greene, 50.
[24] Cadwallader, 74; Mary F. Peirce.

Endnotes chapter 12

[1] Daniel Walker Howe, 6.
[2] Dorrien, 86-88.
[3] Dean Grodzins, *American Heretic: Theodore Parker and Transcendentalism,* (Chapel Hill: The University of North Carolina Press, 2002), 233.
[4] Wright, xiv, and Robinson, 83.
[5] Sharlene Voogd Cochrane, *Private Lives and Public Learning: Family Academy for the New Middle Class: The West Newton England and Classical*

School, 1850-1910, for Ph.D., Boston College.

[6] Cochrane.

[7] Matthew Hale Smith, *The Bible, the Rod, and Religion, in Common Schools. The Ark of God on a New Cart: A Sermon*, (Boston: Redding & Co, 1847), 7.

[8] William B Fowle, *The Bible, the Rod, and Religion in Common Schools. The Ark of God on a New Cart: A Sermon, by Rev. M. Hale Smith. Review of the Sermon*, (Boston: Redding & Co, 1847), 19.

[9] *Boston Recorder* October 29, 1846, Congregational Christian Historical Society in Boston.

[10] Fowle, 41.

[11] Horace Mann and Matthew Hale Smith, *Correspondence Between Hon. Horace Mann, Secretary of the Board of Education and Rev. Matthew Hale Smith*, (Boston: Redding & Co, 1947), 28

[12] Smith in Smith and Mann, 27.

[13] Shannon.

[14] Smith in Mann and Smith, 27.

[15] Smith in Mann and Smith, 55.

[16] Smith, 11.

[17] Smith in Mann and Smith, 44.

[18] *Christian Register,* March 26, 1847, Andover Harvard Theological Library..

[19] *Boston Recorder*, May 6, 1847.

[20] *Boston Recorder*, May 27, 1847.

[21] *Eleventh Annual Report of the Board of Education*, Massachusetts State Archives.

[22] Peirce, *Journal*, 131.

[23] Walton, 26 and Shannon.

[24] *Christian Register*, June 12, 1847.

Endnotes chapter 13

[1] *Boston Recorder*, May 6, 1847.

[2] Smith and Mann, 9-11.

[3] *Christian Register,* July 28, 1848.

[4] Horace Mann, *Letter to Matthew Hale Smith in Answer to his "reply" or "supplement,* (Boston: William B. Fowle, 1947), 4.

[5] Matthew Hale Smith, *Universalism Not of God, an Examination of the System of Universalism; its Doctrine, Arguments, and Fruits, with the Experience of the Author, During a Ministry of Twelve Years,* (American Tract Society, 1847).

[6] Mann in *Letter to Matthew Hale Smith,* 12-15.

[7] Mann in *Letter to Matthew Hale Smith,* 14.

[8] Mann in *Letter to Matthew Hale Smith,* 16.

[9] Smith in Smith and Mann, 9-10.

[10] *Boston Recorder,* May 6, 1847.

[11] *Boston Recorder* May 6, 1847.

[12] *Boston Recorder*, June 17, 1847.

[13] *Common School Journal*, July 15, 1848.

[14] *Boston Recorder*, February 18, 1848.

[15] *Boston Register*, July 28, 1848; *Christian Register*, July 15, 1848.

[16] *Christian Register*, July 22, 1848.

[17] *Boston Recorder,* July 28, 1848.

[18] *Christian Register*, July 29, 1848.

[19] *Christian Register*, July 8, 1848.

[20] Robert L. Straker Collection.

[21] *Thirteenth Annual Report of the Board of Education*, Massachusetts State Archives.

[22] Robert L. Straker Collection.

[23] *Boston Recorder*, July 28, 1848.

[24] *Christian Register*, August 19, 1848.

[25] *Common School Journal,* July 15, 1849.

Endnotes chapter 14

[1] *The Evils of the Revolutionary War,* (Boston: New England Non-Resistance Society, 1846).

[2] Cyrus Peirce, letter to his former pupils, Collection 88, Folder 16, Nantucket Historical Association.

[3] Sanderson Beck, *Abolitions, Emerson and Thoreau,* www.sanbeck/org/GPJ16-Abolitionists.html.

[4] *Inquirer*, May 7, 1842.

[5] White, *A Line in the Sand.*

[6] Beck.

[7] Cyrus Peirce Passport Application, National Archives and Records Administration.

[8] Elizabeth W. Allen, *Memorial of Joseph and Lucy Clark Allen, 1891 by their children,* Boston Public Library.

[9] Allen.

[10] *Proceedings of the Second General Peace Conference*, (London: Gilpin, 1849), 12.

[11] Allen.

[12] *Proceedings of the Second General Peace Congress*, 17.

[13] *Proceedings of the Second General Peace Congress,* 33.

[14] *Proceedings of the Second General Peace Congress*, 50.

[15] *Proceedings of the Second General Peace Congress*, 57.

[16] *Proceedings of the Second General Peace Congress*, 71

[17] *Proceedings of the Second General Peace Congress*, 77-84.

[18] Allen.

[19] *Proceedings of the Second General Peace Congress*, 87.

[20] Allen.

[21] *Proceedings of the Second General Peace Congress* , 89.
[22] *Proceedings of the Second General Peace Congress*, 92.
[23] *Proceedings of the Second General Peace Congress*, 93.
[24] Allen.
[25] Allen.

Endnotes chapter 15

[1] Julian C. Jaynes, "Unitarianism in Newton," *Mirror of Newton, Past and Present,* (Newton Federation of Women's Clubs, 1907).
[2] Electa Walton, *The Journal of Electa N. Lincoln*, Massachusetts Historical Society.
[3] *Annual Reports of the School Committee of the town of West Newton, Massachusetts, 1854—1893.* Newton History Museum at the Jackson Homestead..
[4] Cadwallader.
[5] Robert L. Straker Collection.
[6] *Census Records of 1850, 1860, 1870*, Machias Court House, Machias, Maine.
[7] Judd Bragg, *A History of Washington Academy,* Undated pamphlet, given to the author by Christine Small, historian in East Machias.
[8] Lamson, 24-25.
[9] Bragg.
[10] Cyrus Peirce, *Crime: Its Cause and Cure: An Essay*, (Boston: Crosby, Nichols & Co., 1854).
[11] Michael B. Katz, *The Irony of Early School Reform: Educational Innovation in Mid-Nineteenth Century Massachusetts*, (New York: Teachers College Press, 2001), 158.
[12] Peirce, *Crime: Its Cause and Cure.*
[13] *Inquirer*, February 17, 1854.
[14] *Annual Reports of the School Committee of the Town of West Newton.*

Endnotes chapter 16

[1] Cochrane.
[2] Cadwallader, 91.
[3] *Nantucket Schools Collection*, Collection 88, Box 12, Book 25B, Nantucket Historical Association.
[4] Greene, 231; Caroline Allen, "Memories of One Home," *The Mirror of West Newton: Past and Present*, (Newton Federation of Women's Clubs, 1907), 145.
[5] *The First Reunion, 1871,* Newton History Museum..
[6] *Historical Sketch of the West Newton England and Classical School with annual Circular, established in West Newton, Massachusetts in 1854, the Centennial Year, 1876,* Newton History Museum, 3.

[7] Greene, 111.

[8] Greene, 116.

[9] Greene, 100.

[10] Cadwallader.

[11] Abbie Pitman Ray, *Memoirs, 1842-1991*, Collection 88, Nantucket Historical Association and Betsy Tyler, *12 Westminster Street*, NAN 728N15, pt No.6, Nantucket Historical Association, 16.

[12] John Ricketson, "Address," *Reunion of 1893*, Newton History Museum.

[13] Greene, 103.

[14] Cadwallader, 95-96.

[15] John Hillison, *The Role of the Agricultural Education Today Yesterday, Today and Tomorrow,* 1997 Distinguished Lecture, American Association for Agricultural Teaching Meeting, 1997.

[16] Greene, 95.

[17] Cadwallader, 95.

[18] Ricketson.

[19] Ricketson.

[20] Greene, 102.

[21] Ricketson.

[22] Robert L. Straker Collection.

[23] Robert L. Straker Collection.

[24] Greene 45, and Robert L. Straker Collection.

[25] Robert L. Straker Collection.

[26] *Annual Report of the American Anti-Slavery Society: by the executive committee, for the year ending May 1, 1860,* Samuel J. May Anti-Slavery Collection, Cornell University Library.

[27] Lamson, 115-121.

Endnotes chapter 17

[1] *Inquirer*, November 5, 1865.

[2] Richard F. Miller and Robert F. Mooney, *The Civil War: The Nantucket Experience*, (Nantucket: Wesco Publishing, 1994)

[3] Barbara White, "Anna Gardner: Teacher of Freedmen," in Robert Johnson, (ed), *Nantucket's People of Color: Essays on History, Politics, and Community*, (University Press of America, 2006.

[4] *Inquirer*, January 30, 1875.

[5] Nantucket Town Records.

[6] "Women in Caucus at Nantucket, *Women's Journal*, September 2, 1876.

[7] *Inquirer*, May 11, 1889.

[8] *Inquirer*, February 1, 1880.

[9] *Inquirer*, February 28, 1880.

[10] *Inquirer*, February 12, 1881.

[11] *Inquirer*, September 22, 1877.

[12] *Inquirer*, October 14, 1876.

[13] *Inquirer*, September 14, 1867.

[14] *Inquirer*, April 6, 1878.

[15] *Inquirer*, October 26, 1878.

[16] *Inquirer*, January 18, 1879.

[17] Gardner Family Papers, Collection 87, Folders 2-17, Nantucket Historical Association.

[18] Sharp Family Papers, Collection 270, Folders 4, 4.5, Nantucket Historical Association.

[19] Nantucket Town Records.

Endnotes chapter 18

[1] Gayle M. Schulman, "The Gibbons Family: Freedmen, *The Magazine of Albemarle County History*, Volume 55, 1997, 60-93 and Liz Sargent and Jacky Taylor, "The Establishment of the Jefferson Graded School," ca 1894, *The Jefferson School Oral History Project*, The Virginia Foundation for the Humanities, 2004, 31-36 and Barbara White, "Ann Gardner: Teacher of Freedmen."

[2] Lamson, 191.

[3] Lamson, 188.

[4] Lamson.

[5] Harold Swartz, *Samuel Gridley Howe: Social Reformer, 1801-1876*, (Cambridge: Harvard University Press, 1956), 1; Elisabeth Gitter, *The Imprisoned Guest: Samuel Howe and Laura Bridgman, the Original Deaf-Blind Girl*, (New York: Picador USA, 2001), 106-107.

[6] Sally Hobart Alexander and Robert Alexander, *She Touched the World: Laura Bridgman, Deaf-Blind Pioneer*, (New York, Clarion Books, 2008)

[7] Mary Swift Lamson, *Life and Education of Laura Dewey Bridgman: The Deaf, Dumb and Blind Girl*, (Boston: Houghton Mifflin and Company, 1890)

[8] Walton, 47.

[9] *The Baptist Missionary Magazine*, The American Baptist Missionary, Volumes 47-38, 1868, 381.

[10] Grace F. Shepard, "Historical Sketch, 1889-1914," *Historical Sketches of the Framingham Normal School*, (Alumnae Association in Commemoration of the 75th Anniversary, July 1, and 2, 1914.

[11] *An Illustrated Biographical Catalogue of the Principals, Teachers, and Students of the West Newton English and Classical School*, 166.

[12] Nantucket Probate Court Records.

[13] "News and Notes," *Quarterly Journal of Speech*, Volume 20, Issue 3, 193

Bibliography

Adams, John Quincy. Diary, 1785, 1786, 1843. Massachusetts Historical Society.

Adams, Lydia Stow. *Journal, 1840.* Framingham State University Research Library.

Alexander, Sally Hobart and Alexander, Robert. *She Touched the World: Laura Bridgman, Deaf-Blind Pioneer.* New York: Clarion Books. 2008.

Allen, Elizabeth W. *Memorial of Joseph and Lucy Clark Allen, 1891 by their children.* Boston Public Library.

Allen Brothers' West Newton English and Classical School. Boston: George H Ellis. 1899. Newton Historical Association.

Allen, Caroline. "Memories of One Home" in *The Mirror of Newton: Past and Present.* The Newton Federation of Women's Clubs, 1907.

An Illustrated Biographical Catalogue of the Principals, Teachers, and Students of the West Newton English and Classical School,West Newton, Massachusetts, 1854-1893. Compiled by "An Early Pupil." Boston: Rand Avery Supply Company. 1895.

Annual Report of the American Anti-Slavery Society: by the executive committee, for the year ending May 1, 1860. Samuel J May Anti-Slavery Collection. Cornell University.

Annual Reports of the School Committee of the town of West Newton, Massachusetts, 1854-1893. Newton History Museum at the Jackson Homestead.

Annual Reports of the Board of Managers of the Massachusetts Anti-Slavery Society. 1835-1851. Samuel J. May Anti-Slavery Collection. Cornell University.

Annual Reports of the Massachusetts Board of Education, 1837-1849. Massachusetts State Archives.

Bailey, Sarah Loring. *Historical Sketches of Andover.* Boston: Houghton. 1880.

The Baptist Missionary Magazine. The American Baptist Missionary.Volumes 47-48. 1868. 381.

Beck, Sanderson. *Abolitionists, Emerson & Thoreau.* www.san.beck.org/GPJ16-Abolitionistss.html)

Bernard, Richard M. and Maris A Vinovskis. "The Female School Teacher in Newton Ante-Bellum Massachusetts," *Journal of Social History.* 2001.

Beegel, Susan F. "The Brotherhood of Thieves Riot of 1842." *Historic Nantucket.* Fall, 1992.

Binder, Frederick M. *The Age of the Common School, 1830- 1865.* New York: John Wiley and Sons, Inc. 1974.

Blacks on Nantucket. Collection 222, Folder 9. Nantucket Historical Association. Contains the *Record of the Nantucket County Anti-Slavery Society.*

Boston Recorder, 1846-1848. Congregational Christian Historical Society.

Boston.

Boston Courier, 1846-49.

Booker, Margaret Moore. *The Admiral's Academy: Nantucket Island's Historic Coffin School.* Nantucket Ma: Mill Hill Press. 1998.

Boyden, Wallace C. "The Educational Life of Newton" in *The Mirror of Newton, Past and Present.* The Newton Federation of Women's Clubs. 1907.

Bragg, Judd. *Washington Academy: An Historical Overview.* 1992. Written when Bragg was a senior at Washington Academy.

Brooks, Charles, *History of the Town of Medford.* Boston: The Franklin Press. 1886.Bumbaugh, David. E. *Unitarian Universalism: A Narrative History.* Chicago: Meadville Lombard Press. 2000.

Cadwallader, Lynn J. *A Case Study in the Professionalization of Nineteenth Century Teaching: Nathaniel T Allen, 1823 – 1872.* Dissertation at University of Massachusetts, 1983.

Capper, Charles and Conrad E Wright (eds.) *Transient and Permanent: The Transcendentalist Movement and its Contexts.* Boston: The Massachusetts Historical Society. 1999.

Carter, James G. *Essays Upon Popular Education, containing a particular examination of the schools of Massachusetts, and an outline of an Institution for the education of teachers.* Boston: Bowles & Dearborn. 1826.

Carter, James G. *Outline of An Institution for the Education of Teachers* in Barnard, Henry. *Normal Schools, and Other Institutions: Agencies, and Means Designed for the Professional Education of Teachers, Part I.* Hartford: Case, Tiffany and Company. 1851.

Castner, Elizabeth. *Tercentennial History of the First Parish in Waltham, MA. 1696-1996.* Printed by the First Parish in Waltham. 1998.

Census Records of 1850, 1860, 1870. Machias Court House, Machias, Maine.

Christian Register 1847 – 1848. Andover Harvard Theological Library.

Circular and Register of the State Normal School, at West Newton, Ma, from Its Commencement at Lexington, July, 1839, to Dec, 1846. For 1849-1871. Framingham State Normal School. Published by the Alumnae. Lexington Historical Archives 3321.

Cochrane, Sharlene Voogd. *Private Lives and Public Learning: Family Academy for the New Middle Class: The W Newton English and Classical School 1850-1910.* For Ph.D. May 1985, Boston College.

Commemorating 200 Years, 1809-2009. Nantucket Historical Association.

Common School Journal. 1839- 1852.

Cooke, George Willis. *Unitarianism in America: A History of its Origin and Development.* Boston: American Unitarian   Association. 1902.

Cremin, Lawrence, A. *American Education: The National Experience, 1783-1876.* New York: Harper and Row. 1980.

Curti, Merle Eugene. *The American Peace Crusade 1815-1860.* New York: Octagon Books. 1973.

Cyrus Peirce Passport Application. National Archives and Records Administration.

Daily Record. New England Freedmen's Aid Society Records 1862-1876. Massachusetts Historical Society. Ms N-101. Boxes 1, 2.

Deese, Helen. "Caroline Healey Dall: Transcendental Activist" in *Ordinary Women: Extraordinary Lives: Women in American History.* Kriste Lindenmeyer (ed). Rowman & Littlefield Publishers. 2000. Pp 59-71.

Dolin, Eric Jay. *Leviathan: The History of Whaling in America.* New York: WW Norton & Company. 2007.

Dorrian, Gary. *The Making of American Liberal Theology: Imagining Progressive Rebellion, 1805-1900.* Louisville: Westminster John Knox Press. 2001.

Drisko, George W. *The Town of Machias: The Old and the New, the Early and the Late.* Archive.org. Undated.

Edwards, Jonathan. *Sinners in the Hands of an Angry God.* Christian Classics Ethereal Library. www.ccel.org.

Emerson, George B. *Reminiscences of an Old Teacher.* Boston Alfred Mudge and Sons. 1878.

Everett, Mary C. *Journal, December 23, 1846-May 13, 1847.* Framingham State University Research Library.

The Evils of the Revolutionary War. Boston: New England Non-Resistance Society. 1846.

First Parish Norwell Church History. www.firstparishnorwell.org/history.

First Reunion, 1871. Newton History Museum.

First Unitarian Society in Newton. Records 1848-1861.

Fisher, John Ogden. *Window Dedicated to Public School Education and to the Teaching Profession.* From files at the First Unitarian Church in Newton. Not dated.

Fowle, William B. *The Bible, the Rod, and Religion, in Common Schools. The ark of God on a New Cart: A Sermon, by Rev. M. Hale Smith Review of the Sermon.* Boston: Redding & Co. 1847.

Funsten, Allegra L. *Nantucket During the War of 1812: Quakers, Whalers, and Political Parties.* Williamstown, Massachusetts: Thesis, April 16, 2007.

Gardner, Anna. *Harvest Gleanings in Prose and Verse.* NY: Fowler and Wells. 1881.

Gardner Family Papers. Collection 87, Folders 2-17. Nantucket Historical Association.

Gitter, Elisabeth. *The Imprisoned Guest: Samuel Howe and Laura Bridgman, The Original Deaf-Blind Girl.* New York: Picador. 2001.

Greene, Mary A. *Nathaniel Topliff Allen: Teacher, Reformer, Philanthropist.* Privately printed. 1906. Newton Historical Association.

Grodzins, Dean. *American Heretic: Theodore Parker and Transcendentalism.* Chapel Hill: The University of North Carolina Press. 2002.

Gould, Eliza Rogers. *Journal, 1841.* Framingham State University Research

Library.

Harper, Charles. A. *A Century of Public Teacher Education: The Story of the State Teachers Colleges as They Evolved from the Normal Schools.* Westport, Connecticut: Greenwood Press. 1939.

Harris, Louisa. *Journal, 1839-1905.* MS 89.1. Framingham State University Research Library.

Harvard Divinity School. http://www.hds.harvard.edu/library/exhibits/online/palfrey/images/divs ch3.jpg

Harvard University: Quinquennial catalogue, 1636-1930. Cambridge: University. 1930.

Herbst, Jurgen. *And Sadly Teach: Teacher Education and Professionalization in American Culture.* Madison: The University of Wisconsin Press. 1989.

Hillison, John. "Cyrus Peirce: First Public School Teacher." *Journal of Teacher Education.* Volume 35, No. 4, 55-56. 1984.

Hillison, John. "The Role of the Agricultural Education Teacher Yesterday, Today and Tomorrow." 1997 Distinguished Lecture, American Association for Agricultural Teaching Meeting 1997.

Historical Sketch of the West Newton English and Classical School, with Annual Circular, established in West Newton, Massachusetts in 1854, Centennial Year. 1876. Newton History Museum..

Howe, Daniel Walker, *The Unitarian Conscience: Harvard Moral Philosophy, 1805-1861.* Middletown, Ct: Wesleyan University Press. 1970.

Inquirer. Nantucket Historical Association. 1821 - 1890, March 2, 1895.

Ireson, Adeline. *Autograph Album.* Framingham State University Research Library.

Islander. Nantucket Historical Association. March 10, 1840 - March 18, 1843.

Jaynes, Julian C. "Unitarianism in Newton," in *The Mirror of Newton, Past and Present. T*he Newton Federation of Women's Clubs. 1907.

Jones, Jacqueline. *Soldiers of Light and Love: Northern Teachers and Georgia Blacks, 1865-1873.* Chapel Hill, U of NC Press 1980.

Journal of Electa N Lincoln (Walton). Massachusetts Historical Society.

Journal of the House of Representatives, 1845. Massachusetts State Archives.

Journal of the Senate, 1845. Massachusetts State Archives.

Kaestle, Carl F. *Pillars of the Republic: Common Schools and American Society, 1780-1860.* New York: Hill and Wang. 1983.

Kantrowitz, Stephen. *More Than Freedom: Fighting for Black Citizenship in a White Republic, 1829-1889.* New York: The Penguin Press. 2012.

Karttunen, Frances Ruley. *The Other Islanders: People who pulled Nantucket's Oars.* New Bedford: Spinner Publications. 2005.

Katz, Michael B. *The Irony of Early School Reform: Educational Innovation in Mid-Nineteenth Century Massachusetts.* New York: Teachers College Press. 2001.

Kollen, Richard P. *Lexington, MA: Treasures from Historic Archives.*

Charleston: History Press. 2006.

Lamson, Mary Swift. *Life and Education of Laura Dewey Bridgman: The Deaf, Dumb and Blind Girl.* Boston: Houghton, Mifflin and Company.1890.

Lamson, Mary Swift. *The First State Normal School in America: Records of the First Class, 1839.* Boston. 1903.

La Plante, Eve. *Marmee and Louisa: The Untold Story of Louisa May Alcott and Her Mother.* New York: Free Press. 2012.

Leach, Robert J. and Peter Gow. *Quaker Nantucket: The Religious Community Behind the Whaling Empire.* Nantucket: Mill Hill Press. 1997.

Levy, Jonathan. "The Dramatic Dialogues of Charles Stearns: An Appreciation," *Spotlight on the Child: Studies in the History of American Children's Theatre.*Bedard, Roger L and Tolch, C. John. (ed) Greenwood Press: New York, 1989. 5-24.

Lowell Mason. cyberhymnal.org & lowellmasonhouse.or

Mann, Horace. "Attack on Normal Schools in the Legislature: 1840," in Norton, Arthur O. (ed) *The First State Normal School in America.* Cambridge: Harvard Documents in the History of Education. 1926.

Mann, Horace. *History, Regulations and Curriculum of the First Normal Schools:Narrative and Documents* in Norton, Arthur O. (ed) *The First State Normal School in America.* Cambridge: Harvard Documents in the History of Education. 1926.

Mann, Horace and Smith, Matthew Hale. *Correspondence Between Hon. Horace Mann, Sec. of the Board of Education and Rev. Matthew Hale Smith.* Boston: Redding & Co. 1847.

Massachusetts Acts of 1845, Chapter 214.

Massachusetts State House Vaults. Seven petitions presented to the House, 1845.

Massachusetts Vital Records, Nantucket, 1662-1900.

Massachusetts Soldiers and Sailors of the Revolutionary War, Vol XII. Secretary of the Commonwealth. Boston: Wright and Potter. 1904.

May, Samuel, J. *Memoir of Cyrus Peirce, First Principal of the First State Normal School in the United States.* Barnard's American Journal of Education, December 1857.

Mayer, Henry. *All on Fire: William Lloyd Garrison and the Abolition of Slavery.* NY: St. Martin's Press. 1998.

Malone, Dumas (ed.) *Dictionary of American Biography, Volume XIV* NY: Charles Scribner's Sons. 1934.

McKissack, Patrica and McKissack Frederick. *Black Hands, White Sails: The Story of African-American Whalers.* New York: Scholastic Press. 1999.

Marshall, Megan. *The Peabody Sisters: Three Women Who Ignited American Romanticism.* New York: Houghton-Mifflin. 2005.

Memorial of Joseph and Lucy Clark Allen, 1891, by their children. Boston Public Library.

Memorial of the Quarter-Centennial Celebration of the Establishment of

Normal Schools in America. Boston: C.P. Moody. 1866.

Messerli, Jonathan. *Horace Mann: A Biography.* New York: Alfred Knopf. 1972.

Miller, Richard F. and Robert F. Mooney. *The Civil War: The Nantucket Experience.* Nantucket: Wesco Publishing. 1994.

Milligan, Frank D. "The Best Nantucketer of Us All: Dr. Benjamin Sharp," *Historic Nantucket.* Volume 52. Number 3. 2003.

Morning Telegraph (Nantucket). April 3, 1844; April 10, 1844; March 21, 1845; April 9, 1845.

Morison, Samuel Eliot. *Three Centuries of Harvard, 1636-1936.* Cambridge, MA: Harvard University Press. 1936.

Nantucket Mirror. Nantucket Historical Association. June 14, 1845 - 1848.

Nantucket Probate Court.

Nantucket Registry of Deeds.

Nantucket Supreme Judicial Court. 1846.

Nantucket Town Records. 1807 - 1852.

Nantucket School Collection. Collection 88, Box 12, Book 25B. Nantucket Historical Association.

Neem, Johann N. *Creating a Nation of Joiners: Democracy and Civil Society in Early National Massachusetts.* Cambridge, MA: Harvard University Press. 2008.

"News and Notes," *Quarterly Journal of Speech,* Volume 20, Issue 3, 1934. *Newton Local Landmarks.* Newton Historical Commission. 1997.

Ogren, Christine. *The American State Normal School: "An Instrument of Great Good."* NY: Palgrave Macmillan. 2005.

Palfrey, John Gorham. *Divinity School of the University of Cambridge.* Cambridge: Cambridge Press, Metcalf, Torrey and Ballou. 1836. www.div.hds.harvard.edu/library/exhibits/online/palfrey/divsch.html.

Peirce, Cyrus and Swift Mary. *The First State Normal School in America: The Journals of Cyrus Peirce and Mary Swift.* Cambridge: Harvard University Press. 1926.

Peirce, Cyrus, James Edes, Henry F., Mitchell, and William Coffin. *Address to The Inhabitants of Nantucket of Education And Free Schools.* December 15, 1837. Providence: Knowles, Voss & Company. 1838.

Peirce, Cyrus. *Crime: Its Cause and Cure: An Essay.* Boston: Crosby, Nichols, & Co. 1854.

Peirce, Cyrus. Letter to Electa Lincoln. Collection 88, Folder 16. Nantucket Historical Association.

Peirce, Cyrus. Letter to his former pupils. Collection 88, Folder 16. Nantucket Historical Association.

Peirce, Cyrus. *Sermon Delivered on Christmas Day, December 25, 1824 at Reading, North Parish.* Andover: Flagg and Gould. 1824.

Peirce, Frederick Clifton. *Peirce Geneology, Being the Record of the Posterity of John Pers, an early inhabitant of Watertown, in New England, Who came from Norwich, Norfolk County England; with Notes on the*

History of Other Families of Peirce, Pierce, Pearce, etc. Worcester: Press of Chas. Hamilton,1880.

Peirce, Mary F. *Journal, 1849-1852.* Framingham State University Research Library.

Proceedings of the 250th Anniversary of the Ancient Town of Redding. Eaton, Chester W.and Eaton, Warren E. (eds) Reading, MA: Loring and Twombly. 1896.

Proceedings of the Second General Peace Congress. London: Charles Gilpin. 1849.

Quaker Book of Objections Collection 35, Folder 9. Nantucket Historical Association.

Ray, Abbie Pitman. *Memoirs 1842-1919.* Collection 88. Nantucket Historical Association.

Reading North Parish Meeting Records, 1796-1856, Volumes 2, 3, 4. North Reading Library.

Record of the Nantucket County Anti-Slavery Society. Blacks on Nantucket. Collection 222, Folder 9. Nantucket Historical Association.

Records of the Old Town of Reading, MA, Vol 3, 1813-1853. North Reading Library.

Remini, Robert V. *John Quincy Adams.* New York: Henry Holt & Company. 2002.

Richards, Laura Elizabeth Howe. *Two Noble Lives: Samuel Gridley Howe, Julia Ward Howe.* Boston: Dana Estes and Company. Undated.

Ricketson, John. "Address," *Reunion of 1893*. Newton History Museum.

Robert L Straker Collection of Horace Mann Papers. Olive Kettering Library. Antioch College.

Robinson, David. *The Unitarians and the Universalists.* Westport, Connecticut: Greenwood Press. 1985.

Rothbard, Murray No. *Conceived in Liberty, Volume 1.* Mises Institute. 1990. 174-181. Mises.org.

Sargent, Liz and Jacky Taylor. "The Establishment of the Jefferson Graded School, ca. 1894. *The Jefferson School Oral History Project.* The Virginia Foundation for the Humanities. 2004: 31-36.

Sanderson, Edmund L. *Waltham as a Precinct of Watertown, and as a Town, 1630-1884.* Waltham Historical Society: Waltham, MA. 1936.

Schulman, Gayle M. "The Gibbons Family: Freedmen," *The Magazine of Albemarle County History.* 55. 1997: 60-93.

Schwartz, Harold. *Samuel Gridley Howe: Social Reformer, 1801-1876.* Cambridge: Harvard University Press. 1956.

Shannon, Ann E. *Journal, January 18, 1847-April 12, 1847.* Framingham State University Research Library.

Sharp Family Papers. Collection 270, Folders 4, 4.5. Nantucket Historical Association.

Sharp, James Roger. *American Politics in the Early Republic: The New Nation in Crisis.* New Haven: Yale University Press. 1993.

Shattuck, Lemuel. "History of Lincoln, Massachusetts," in *The History of Concord, Massachusetts*. 1835.

Shepard, Grace, F. *Historical Sketch 1889-1914.*" In *Historical Sketches of the Framingham State Normal School.* Published by the Alumnae Association in Commemoration of the 75th Anniversary, July 1 and 2, 1914.

Smith, Julia Ann. *Journal, October 25, 1840- March 4, 1841.* Framingham State University Research Library.

Smith, Matthew Hale. *The Bible, the Rod, and Religion, in Common Schools. The ark of God on a New Cart: A Sermon.* Boston: Redding & Co. 1847.

Smith, Matthew Hale. *Universalism Not of God, as Examination of the System of Universalism; its Doctrine, Arguments, and Fruits, with the Experience of the Author, During a Ministry of 12 Years.* The American Tract Society. 1847.

Smith, S.F. *History of Newton, Massachusetts, Town and City from its Earliest Settlement to the Present Time: 1630-1880.* Boston: The American Logotype Co. 1880.

Starbuck, Alexander. *The First Normal School in America.* Proceedings of the Nantucket Historical Association. Fifteenth Annual Meeting. July 21, 1909. 41-57.

Stearns, Eben. S. *First Historical Sketch.* In *Historical Sketches of the Framingham State Normal School.*Published by the Alumnae Association in Commemoration of the 75th Anniversary, July 1 and 2, 1914.

Story, Ronald "Harvard Students, the Boston Elite, and the New England Preparatory System, 1800 – 1876, *History of Education Quarterly*. Volume 15, Issue 3, 1976.

Stodder, Mary. *The Normal Experiment:* Issue 1, March 13, 1841. Publication of the State Normal School. L3321. Lexington Historical Society Archive.

Stout, Kate. "Helping Hands,"*Historic Nantucket.* Volume 50. Number 1.

Thoreau, Henry David. *Reistance to Civil Government.* 1849.

Tiffany, Francis. *Life of Dorothea Lynde Dix.* Boston and New York: Houghton, Mifflin and Company. 1892.

Tomlinson, Stephen. *Head Masters: Phrenology Secular Education, and Nineteenth- Century Social Thought.* University of Alabama Press. Tuscaloosa. 2005.

True Copy of the Church Book of the Pleasant Street Baptist Church of Nantucket, Massachusetts, 1848 -1858.

Tyler, Betsy. *12 Westminster Street.* NAN 728 N15 pt No. 6. Nantucket Historical Association.

Tyler, Betsy. *The Nantucket Atheneum: A History.* Nantucket: Nantucket Preservation Trust. 2009.

Tyler Betsy. *Unitarian Meeting House, Nantucket: A History Commemorating*

200 Years 1809-2009. Nantucket: Nantucket Preservation Trust. 2009.

Unitarian Church Records, Nantucket MA.

Unraveling the "Teacher Shortage" problem: Teacher Retention is the Key. A symposium of The National Commission on Teaching and America's Future and NCTAF State Partners. August 20-22, 2002.

Vetter, Herbert F. (ed.) *Harvard's Unitarian Presidents.* www.harvardsquarelibrary.org.

Viles, Rebecca. *Lexington Normal School.* Papers Relating to the History of the Town, Read by some of the Members, Volume One. Lexington Historical Society. 1889.

Von Frank, Albert J. *The Trials of Anthony Burns: Freedom and Slavery in Emerson's Boston.* Cambridge: Harvard University Press. 1998.

Walker, Albert Perry. "Pages from Newton's History," in *The Mirror of Newton, Past and Present.* Newton Federation of Women's Clubs. 1907.

Walker, Daniel Howe. *The Unitarian Conscience: Harvard Moral Philosophy, 1805-1861.* Middletown, Connecticut: Wesleyan U Press. 1970.

Walton, Electa Lincoln in *Historical Sketches of the Framingham State Normal School.* Published by the Alumnae Association in Commemoration of the 75th   Anniversary, July 1 and 2, 1914.

Walton, Electa Lincoln. "Through the Looking Glass," in *The Mirror of Newton, Past and Present.* The Newton Federation of Women's Clubs. 1907.

The Warder. January 3, 1846-September 19, 1846. Nantucket Historical Association

Washington Academy Yearbook. East Machias, Maine. 1992.

Waterson, Robert C. *Address at the Third Triennial Convention of the West Newton State Normal School, July 26, 1848.* Boston: Leonard C. Bowles.

Watson, Rebecca. "Diary Kept While a Student at West Newton Normal School." Collection 30. Nantucket Historical Association.

The Weekly Mirror. June 14, 1845-January 6, 1848. Nantucket Historical Association

Webber, Samuel. Papers at Pusey Library, Harvard. Call No. UAI-15.878.

White, Barbara A. *A Line in the Sand: The Battle to Integrate Nantucket Public Schools, 1825 – 1847.* New Bedford: Spinner Publications. 2006.

White, Barbara. "Anna Gardner: Teacher of Freedmen," in *Nantucket's People of Color: Essays on History, Politics and Community,* ed. Robert Johnson. University Press of America. 2006.

Whitney, Edson, L. *The American Peace Society: A Centennial History.* Washington, D.C.: The American Peace Society. 1928.

Whittier, Henry Smith. *History of East Machias 1765-1926.* Typewritten copy in possession of Christine Small, former treasurer of East Machias. Undated.

Winslow/Foye/Elder Collection. Letter from Cyrus Peirce to his pupils from

Lexington, August 5, 1839. Collection 354, Folder 1. Nantucket Historical Association.

Woodward, Hobson. "Island Educator Remembered," *Inquirer and Mirror*, August 9, 1990, 1C.

"Women in Caucus at Nantucket," *Women's Journal,* September 2, 1876.

Worthley, Harold. *An Inventory of the Records of the Particular (Congregational) Church of Massachusetts Gathered, 1620-1805.* Cambridge: Harvard University Press. 1970.

Wright, Conrad. (ed) *A Stream of Light: A Short History of American Unitarianism.* Boston: Skinner House Books. 1975.

About the Author

Barbara Ann White is a research fellow at the Nantucket Historical Association. Her previous book, *A Line in the Sand: The Integration of Nantucket Public Schools*, was published in 2009 by Spinner Publications. It documents the important role the island played in the passage of the first law in the country to guarantee access to equal education. The documentary film, *Rock of Changes*, produced by WGHG in Boston, was based on her work on Nantucket's school integration. The film won the Jury Award at the USA Film Festival in 1999.

She taught in the Nantucket Public Schools for thirty-three years, most of it at the Cyrus Peirce Middle School.

Made in the USA
Charleston, SC
17 October 2014